GOD AND ME

Other books by Charles Mills:

Professor Appleby and Maggie B Series

Mysterious Stories From the Bible
Amazing Stories From the Bible
Love Stories From the Bible
Adventure Stories From the Bible
Miracle Stories From the Bible
Heroic Stories From the Bible

Shadow Creek Ranch Series

Mystery in the Attic
Secret of Squaw Rock
Treasure of the Merrilee
Whispers in the Wind
Heart of the Warrior
River of Fear
Danger in the Depths
A Cry at Midnight
Attack of the Angry Legend
Stranger in the Shadows
Planet of Joy

The Truth Trackers

Eyes of the Crocodile
Bible-based Answers to Questions Kids Ask About Love and Sex
Echoing God's Love
My Talents for Jesus/When I Grow Up (Pacific Press)
The Touch of the Master's Hand

To order, call 1-800-765-6955.
Visit us at www.reviewandherald.com for information on other Review and Herald products.

CHARLES MILLS

REVIEW AND HERALD® PUBLISHING ASSOCIATION
HAGERSTOWN, MD 21740

The author assumes full responsibility for the accuracy of all facts and quotations as cited in this book.

This book was
Edited by Andy Nash
Copyedited by Lori Halvorsen and James Cavil
Cover and interior design by Madelyn Ruiz
Cover and interior art by Eileen Mueller Neill
Electronic makeup by Shirley M. Bolivar
Typeset: 12.5/16 Futura Book

PRINTED IN U.S.A.

05 04 03 02 01 5 4 3 2 1

R&H Cataloging Service
Mills, Charles Henning, 1950-
God and me.

1. Children—Religious life. 2. Devotional literature—Juvenile.
3. Devotional calendars—Seventh-day Adventist. I. Title.

242.62

ISBN 0-8280-1560-0

Dedication

To my beautiful wife, Dorinda.
I'm so happy it's God and me and YOU!

Contents

Hello, Boys and Girls!

Are you ready for some adventure and fun? You've come to the right place, because this book is bursting with all kinds of exciting stories and stuff to do.

Every week or so, you're going to meet a different boy or girl who has decided to be as loving and kind as Jesus wants him or her to be, no matter what anyone says or does. Each one is determined to help a neighbor, encourage a friend, or show love to a family member, even if Satan gets in the way and tries to mess things up. When that happens, you can be sure that there's going to be a battle. Now *that's* adventure!

You'll also find some Bible texts to look up, mysteries to solve, and new places to visit. Oh, and have some paper, color markers, and a bottle of glue ready because . . . Well, you'll see.

Turn the page and begin to read. Or, if you'd like, invite someone to read the stories to you. Either way, you're going to learn something amazing about your heavenly Father. He's the God who loves you and is preparing a beautiful home for you and your family far beyond the clouds.

Make yourself comfortable, kick off your shoes, and enjoy reading a new adventure every day for the next year. Sounds like fun to me!

Your friend in Jesus,

–Charles Mills

I'M AN EVANGELIST WHEN I . . .

Make Plans

1 JANUARY

Go and proclaim everywhere the kingdom of God. Luke 9:60, NASB.

Last night Mom read the story of Peter's escape from prison. It was exciting! I especially liked the ending, when the young servant girl, Rhoda, was so glad to hear Peter's voice that she forgot to let Peter into the house when he knocked at the front door. And when she ran and told the others in the house, no one believed her when she said Peter was there!

"What was that big word we learned during worship?" I asked while eating my breakfast cereal.

"You mean *evangelist?"* Mom said. "That's someone who shares the good news about Jesus."

"That's what I'm going to be," I announced. "I like telling others about Jesus."

"Good for you," Mom said with a smile. "An evangelist is always looking for opportunities to talk about God's love."

That's why I'm making a list of all the people I know. Right beside their names I'm putting some ideas of how I can share God's love with them. My friend Tarri likes stories, so I'm learning some new ones from the Bible. Mark enjoys sports, so I'll tell him how God teaches us to be healthy. Uncle Tony lost his job; I think he needs some happy texts. And Mrs. Andrews next door gets lonely; I'm going to stop by and say something cheerful every day.

I think being an evangelist is going to be fun!

–Josh

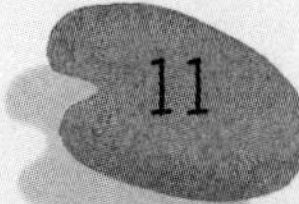

2
JANUARY

The earth is the Lord's, and everything in it, the world, and all who live in it. Psalm 24:1, NIV.

I'M AN EVANGELIST WHEN I . . .

Encourage My Friend

After I decided to be an evangelist, I quickly chose my first assignment. Beth. She worries *a lot*. Just last week I said, "Good afternoon, Beth."

She frowned. "There's nothing *good* about it. Rivers are polluted, the air is dirty, there are millions of people going to bed hungry, and I think I'm catching a cold."

See what I mean? I've got to tell her that Jesus says we shouldn't worry so much, because He's willing to help us with our problems.

The next day, instead of saying "Good afternoon," I just held up a piece of paper. On it I'd written, "God wants us to clean the rivers, stop air pollution, feed the hungry, and heal faster."

"How?" Beth sniffed.

I knew that God had created the world clean and beautiful. So I said, *"We* people messed it up. *We've* got to make it better."

"How?" she sniffed again.

"Let's go ask Mr. Mason, our teacher," I suggested. "He's smart and can give us some ideas."

Now Beth and I recycle our trash, ride together to school, collect canned goods for the hungry, and eat a lot less candy.

Seems being an evangelist is good for your health, and for the earth!

–Sarah

I'M AN EVANGELIST WHEN I . . .

Change From Fearful to Friendly

3
JANUARY

In the same way you judge others, you will be judged. Matthew 7:1, NIV.

"He gives me the creeps," I said quietly, hurrying up the driveway.

"Who?" Dad asked.

"Our neighbor, Mr. Thomas. Every time he sees me, he just stares and doesn't even smile."

"Maybe he doesn't feel well," Dad suggested. Then he paused. "Or maybe he needs a visit from an evangelist."

I sighed. "How can I be an evangelist to a grumpy old man who never smiles?"

"Smile first," Dad encouraged. *"Show* him God's love."

The next day I was in my yard playing with my trucks when old Mr. Thomas walked slowly up his driveway. This time, instead of ignoring him, I smiled a great big smile and waved. "Hi, Mr. Thomas," I called.

The old man stopped in his tracks and stared at me for a long moment. Then he lifted his hand just a little and waved back. It looked like it hurt him.

I ran over to see if he was OK. And guess what? Mr. Thomas couldn't wave, he couldn't smile, and he couldn't talk, because three months ago he had a heart attack and had to go to the hospital. The sickness made parts of his body not work right.

When you're an evangelist, you sometimes learn *why* people do what they do.

–Josh

4
JANUARY

I'M AN EVANGELIST WHEN I . . .

Give

I have hidden your word in my heart. Psalm 119:11, NIV.

My aunt Jessica and cousin Lisa don't go to church. They don't sing songs, listen to sermons, or figure out their tithe. You see, they're not Christians. They don't believe God lives in heaven and loves all the people on the earth.

"Jesus was just a nice man," Aunt Jessica insists. "And that's all."

Since I want to be an evangelist, I had to think of some way to share God's love with my aunt and cousin.

The next time Lisa visited me, I had a plan. I got my Bible and read to her the story of Jonah and the big fish. Then I read about how Jesus healed the centurion's sick daughter. I did a pretty good job because I'd practiced reading the stories before she arrived.

"Wow. That's really cool," Lisa said.

"Doesn't your mom read to you each night?" I asked.

"No." Lisa sighed. "She's too busy."

When my cousin left, she had something in her backpack she'd never had before—a Bible. I gave her mine. Now she can read the stories herself.

Being an evangelist sometimes means having to spend your allowance on a new Bible.

–*Sarah*

I'M AN EVANGELIST WHEN I . . .

Preach to Myself

5
JANUARY

Wednesday night is my favorite television night. There's a program about zoos, one about computers, and just before I go to bed, I watch *Science Today.*

Last week as I was settling down to enjoy my programs I switched to another channel to see what was going on. There was a man with a gun chasing a screaming woman. She looked scared. I thought to myself, *Maybe I'd better watch this program so I can see if that woman gets away OK.*

Then something strange happened. I began to preach to myself! Isn't that weird? I said right out loud, "You know you're not supposed to watch television programs that show people hurting other people. Jesus wouldn't want you to put such ugly pictures in your brain."

Then I said, "Pick up the remote control and change the channel *right now!"*

I pressed the button, and there was my zoo program. It was neat, too. Scientists were taking a family of beavers from one pond to another pond deep in the mountains. Soon I forgot all about the man chasing the screaming woman.

I guess sometimes evangelists have to preach to themselves. After all, Jesus wants everyone to be saved, even the person doing the preaching.

—Josh

Whatever is true, . . . whatever is right, whatever is pure, whatever is lovely, . . . let your mind dwell on these things. Philippians 4:8, NASB.

6 JANUARY

Honor the Lord with your wealth. Proverbs 3:9, NIV.

I'M AN EVANGELIST WHEN I . . .

Put God First

Why don't you buy another one?" my neighbor Chrissy asked me one day as we were playing jungle in my backyard. "Sam looks kinda old and worn-out."

Sam is my favorite stuffed gorilla toy.

"I could buy another one," I said, "but then I wouldn't be a good evangelist."

Chrissy frowned. "Why?"

I picked up Sam and tried to smooth his matted hair. "People in the Bible worked hard for Jesus. They gave money, food, and clothing to help missionaries like Paul, Barnabas, and Silas. They needed help to pay for boat tickets, motels, and stuff like that."

"So?"

"Well," I continued, "a good evangelist is very careful with money. Every penny is important. So after I return my tithe, I spend most of my allowance on helping other people. Each week I give a mission offering at church, and just yesterday I bought a box of animal cookies for my uncle Chuck. He loves animal cookies. I told him it was a gift from God and me. He said he was very thankful to both of us."

My friends may have more toys than I do, but that's OK. I'm an evangelist and have found other ways to spend my money.

–Sarah

I'M AN EVANGELIST WHEN I . . .

Change Sad to Glad

7

JANUARY

He will wipe every tear from their eyes. There will be no more death or mourning or crying or pain. Revelation 21:4, NIV.

I don't like coming here," I said softly.

"Why?" Dad asked.

"This is where they put *dead* people," I reminded him.

Dad nodded. "But don't forget, your grandmother is here, waiting for Jesus to bring her back to life. That's why we bring these pretty flowers to put on her grave—to remind us that Jesus will someday make her alive again."

"But the cemetery makes me feel sad," I said.

Dad looked down at Grandmother's name carved in the big stone. "I know. But someday Jesus will speak Grandma's name, and she'll open her eyes. We'll be able to talk to her again and listen to her sing songs about heaven, just as we used to. Won't that be exciting?"

I thought about my grandmother and all the songs she sang in the evenings when she tucked me into bed. Then something strange happened. Right there in the middle of the cemetery . . . I smiled!

"Dad," I gasped, "you're an evangelist. You just changed my sadness to gladness, just as Jesus did for people in the Bible."

"Hey," Dad said with a grin. "Why don't we tell others about what we've learned by Grandmother's grave? We'll both be evangelists and change sadness to gladness."

–Josh

8 JANUARY

I'M AN EVANGELIST WHEN I . . .

Tell the Truth

Speak truth, each one of you. Ephesians 4:25, NASB.

This morning I made a big mistake.

Mom asked me if I remembered to take out the trash. I was busy talking to my friend on the phone, so I answered "Yes," even though I hadn't. By the time I'd finished talking, I was late for school.

"What's that smell?" Mom asked as we were eating supper. I sniffed and suddenly remembered what I *hadn't* done that morning.

"Oh, it's just the neighbors," I lied again. "They're messy."

Mom shook her head. "That smell is pretty bad. It's like rotten vegetables." She paused and then looked at me with sadness in her eyes. "Did you really remember to put the trash out by the curb this morning?"

I stared at my soup. "I'm sorry, Mom," I said. "I didn't do what you told me to do. Then I lied about it two times. I was too embarrassed to tell you. Will you forgive me?"

Mom nodded. "Lying is a sin, and sin is like that trash bag. The longer you put off taking it away, the more it bothers you. Yes, I'll forgive you, and we'll ask God to forgive you too. Then you'd better do something about the garbage."

Now I know why evangelists should always be honest. Lies stink!

—*Sarah*

9

JANUARY

What is desirable in a man is his kindness. Proverbs 19:22, NASB.

I'M AN EVANGELIST WHEN I . . .

Tell Bible Stories

Last month my friend J.R. had to go to the hospital.

"Now what am I going to do?" I moaned when my dad told me the bad news. "I'm trying to share God's love with J.R., and he's in the hospital."

I thought and thought. *How can I tell Bible stories to a friend without seeing him*? Then I had an idea.

"Dad," I said, "may I borrow your cassette recorder?"

I hurried to the store and bought some tapes with my allowance—long-playing tapes, because when I tell stories my dad says I tend to ramble. Then I set up the machine, slipped in one of the new cassettes, and pressed the record button.

"Hey, J.R.," I said. "How are you feeling? Since I can't come to visit you and since I know you like Bible stories, I thought I'd make some tapes for you."

I told J.R. the story of Samson and Delilah, Moses in the basket, and about when missionary Paul got beat up at the city gates.

J.R.'s mom told me later that when he got the tapes, he listened to them three times in a row! I guess I can be an evangelist, even when I can't even see the people I'm talking to.

–Josh

10
JANUARY

Be kind and compassionate to one another, forgiving each other, just as in Christ God forgave you. Ephesians 4:32, NIV.

I'M AN EVANGELIST WHEN I . . .

Ask Forgiveness

Last Sabbath at church someone came around a corner and walked right into me. *Bang!* Knocked me down on the floor. As I stumbled to my feet I noticed my shirt was torn. Not only was I embarrassed, I was mad!

"Why don't you watch where you're going?" I said a little too loudly. "Couldn't you hear me coming?"

The girl who'd bumped into me started to cry, and then she turned and ran away without saying a word.

"Are you all right?" a woman asked. "Please excuse my daughter. We're visiting for the first time. She didn't hear you coming because . . . she's deaf."

"Deaf?" I gasped.

I felt terrible for getting upset. Then I had an idea. "Please," I said to the woman, "will you teach me something?"

When church was over, I found the two visitors by the back door. Tapping the girl on the shoulder, I smiled and lifted the little finger of my right hand. Then I made a fist and put it over my heart, moving it around and around just like the woman had shown me.

The girl's eyes opened wide when she realized what I was telling her in sign language. Sometimes evangelists must learn new ways to say "I'm sorry."

–Sarah

I'M AN EVANGELIST WHEN I . . .

Teach Forgiveness

11
JANUARY

Though your sins are like scarlet, they shall be as white as snow. Isaiah 1:18, NIV.

"Oh no!" my friend Chad moaned. "Look at my new sweater. I got mud all over it. My mom's going to freak out."

"Don't worry," I said. "We can make it clean again. Follow me."

We hurried into the house and found my mom in the laundry room, right where she usually is every Monday afternoon. "I think Chad's sweater needs a little forgiveness," I told her.

Mom looked at the sweater, then at Chad. "Yup. I'd say it needs a *lot* of forgiveness."

"What are you talking about?" Chad asked as Mom dropped the muddy cloth into the washing machine.

"You'll see," I said with a grin.

After a while we headed back to the laundry room, and I pulled his sweater out of the machine. "All right!" Chad declared with a relieved laugh. "It's clean again." Then he paused. "So why did you tell me that my sweater needed *forgiveness?"*

"I was thinking about something my dad read last night," I told him. "The Bible says that when sin makes our hearts dirty, Jesus can wash them clean again with His forgiveness. Get it?"

"Got it!" Chad chucked. "Now whenever I wear my sweater, I'll think about how Jesus washes hearts clean."

Evangelists can find lots of ways to teach others about Jesus' love.

—Josh

12
JANUARY

I will give you the crown of life. Revelation 2:10, NIV.

I'M AN EVANGELIST WHEN I . . .

Look Forward to Heaven

"What are you making?" my little 4-year-old brother asked.

"What's it look like?" I invited.

"A hat!" Matthew shouted.

"Well, it's sorta like a hat," I laughed. "This is a crown."

"Are you a king?" Matthew gasped.

"No. I'm an evangelist. That's someone who shares God's love with others."

"Do they all wear pretty hats like that?"

"Someday they will," I explained. "Jesus is going to give a crown to anyone who chooses to live with Him in heaven. If you've been a hardworking evangelist, then you'll have many stars in your crown, one star for each person you helped teach about Jesus." I added another red stick-on star to my project. "I going to have lots because I'm telling everyone I know that Jesus loves them and wants to take them home to heaven."

Matthew studied my handiwork for a long moment, then he frowned. "I wish I had a pretty crown like that," he said.

"If you'd like, I'll make you one," I offered. Matthew jumped up and down for joy.

–Sarah

I'M AN EVANGELIST WHEN I . . .

Enjoy Heaven's Beauty

13
JANUARY

He has done everything well. Mark 7:37, NIV.

"Those are pretty," I said when my mom put a vase of colorful flowers on the counter.

"Makes the whole house happy, don't you think?" she stated with a satisfied smile.

I frowned. "But, Mom, why buy flowers? They just die, and you throw them in the trash."

Mom looked up in surprise. "That doesn't sound like something an evangelist would say. Someone who's looking forward to heaven enjoys God's nature, even though it's filled with death and pain. When a flower blooms or a bird sings or the wind whispers softly in the trees, God is giving us a little hint of heaven. This lovely bouquet can remind us of the never-dying flowers waiting for us in the new earth."

I reached out and touched one of the soft petals. The blossoms smelled sweet, and the colors were so bright and happy. "I see what you mean," I said. "Jesus made them for us to enjoy, even if it's for a little while."

"That's right," Mom nodded. "Evangelists remind people of the wonderful world to come, where there'll be no death or pain. Only joy. When I look at nature, that's what I think about."

I hope Jesus comes soon. When He does, I'll pick some never-dying flowers just for Him.

–Josh

14
JANUARY

I'M AN EVANGELIST WHEN I . . .

Talk About Angels

He will give His angels charge concerning you, to guard you in all your ways. Psalm 91:11, NASB.

We have a baby in our family. Her name is Zoe, and she's 3 weeks old.

Mom lets me watch over Zoe during her naps. She takes *lots* of naps. "You do a great job taking care of the baby," Mom told me. "I'm proud of you."

"No problem," I said. "I'm just doing what the angels do. Remember when the preacher talked about how angels are with us all the time, helping us keep out of danger by putting safe thoughts in our minds?"

"Yes."

"Well, as soon as Zoe can understand words, I'm going to tell her about hot things and sharp things and stuff she shouldn't put in her mouth."

Mom nodded. "Good idea. Then Zoe will have *two* angels."

"And," I continued, "when she's old enough to sing, I'm going to teach her the song that says, 'All night, all day, angels watching over me.' Then when she gets scared or worried, she can sing it too, just like me."

Mom bent and kissed my cheek. "Thanks for reminding me about how much my angel cares for me. You're a good evangelist when you talk about angels."

"But," I whispered, "we gotta be quiet now. Zoe is going to sleep!"

–Sarah

THE BIBLE TEACHES ME ABOUT . . .

Love

15 JANUARY

Dear children, let us not love with words or tongue but with actions and in truth.
1 John 3:18, NIV.

What would you think if someone said, "I love you," then hit you with a stick?

Look in today's text to find a verse that tells you how to love the way God loves.

If we love someone we do more than say "I love you." We love them with our actions!

Think about your mom or dad. They not only *say* they love you; they also take care of you—give you food, toys, and a home.

If trouble comes, they protect you. That's love *with action.*

When you hang out with your friends, God wants you to be kind to them. He wants you to share, let others be first, and try to make them happy.

Loving with action means helping others, listening instead of talking, wearing a big smile instead of a frown.

When you love with your actions, you're loving the same way God loves you.

Today, put love in your hands and feet, in your eyes and voice, and especially in your heart. Let others see Jesus in you!

–Uncle Charles

16
JANUARY

True worshipers will worship the Father in spirit and truth, for they are the kind of worshipers the Father seeks. John 4:23, NIV.

THE BIBLE TEACHES ME ABOUT . . .

Worship

Every Sabbath a wonderful thing happens. Millions of people—some with brown skin, some with white; some wearing brightly colored clothes, and others dressed in simple shirts and pants—go to church and Sabbath school.

Why? To *worship*.

Some worshipers sing songs; some preach and tell stories; others read their Bibles and pray. Primary boys and girls worship too, doing fun activities in Sabbath school class and singing action songs.

Worshiping God in "spirit and truth" means you worship Him because you want to. Do you *want* to go to Sabbath school each week? Great! And when the Bible tells you to be loving and kind, do you want to do that, too? Terrific! That means you're worshiping your heavenly Father.

But what if you can't go to church? What if you're sick or your mom and dad say no? Relax. Just go to your room, close the door, and have your own church. Sing a favorite song and look at a nature book. That's worship too. And God loves every minute of it!

–Uncle Charles

THE BIBLE TEACHES ME ABOUT . . .

Prayer

17 JANUARY

Our Father which art in heaven, Hallowed be thy name. Matthew 6:9.

Have you ever wanted to say something but couldn't find the right words?

Some primary-age boys and girls (and adults) have the same problem when they talk to God. They don't know what to say.

Don't worry. Even if you don't say anything, God understands the problem you're facing or the fears hidden in your heart.

Once Jesus told His disciples what words to use when they weren't sure what to pray. You might want to try some of His ideas for your own prayer time. Here's what He suggested:

"Father in heaven, we pray to You because You're holy. Let Your Spirit live in our hearts so we can share Your love with others.

"Give us a daily portion of Your power so we can fight evil. And forgive our sins the same way we forgive the sins of others.

"Help keep our thoughts focused on good instead of evil, and when Satan attacks, please deliver us! You deserve our love and praise forever. Amen" (Matthew 6:9-13, paraphrased).

The next time you kneel down and don't know what to say, remember Jesus' suggestions, open your mouth, and talk to God. He's always listening!

–Uncle Charles

18
JANUARY

Peace I leave with you; my peace I give you. . . . Do not let your hearts be troubled and do not be afraid. John 14:27, NIV.

THE BIBLE TEACHES ME ABOUT . . .

Fear

This world can be scary sometimes. Barking dogs, strangers, and violent television programs—what's a kid to do?

The word *fear* means "to be afraid of something or someone." Not all fear is bad. When you hear a train coming, you jump off the tracks. That's fear keeping you safe. But Satan wants you to have another kind of fear. He wants you to think that you're so bad that God doesn't love you anymore. It makes you feel like you're in a strange place and suddenly you can't find your parents. *Help!*

How did Jesus say we should feel when Satan tries to make us afraid? Read today's text.

When the devil tries to make us afraid, Jesus is waiting to give us peace! He says, "Tasha, Perry, Zack, Megan, don't be afraid. I still love you, and together we'll figure out how to ease your fear." When you run to Jesus, Satan can't follow. With peace in your hearts, there's no room for fear.

Bow your head right now and thank God for the peace He offers you today.

–Uncle Charles

THE BIBLE TEACHES ME ABOUT . . .

Forgiveness

19
JANUARY

Jesus answered, "I tell you, you must forgive him more than 7 times. You must forgive him even if he does wrong to you 77 times." Matthew 18:22, ICB.

One day a friend of Jesus asked Him an important question. He said, "How many times should I forgive someone who does a mean thing to me?"

Have you ever had a friend who did something unkind to you, such as break a favorite pencil or pull your hair? Makes you a little upset, right?

What if that friend broke your pencil or pulled your hair seven times? Now you're getting steamed!

Wait. What if your so-called friend broke your pencil or pulled your hair 77 times? Now you can't write a letter, and you're almost bald! What should you do?

Read today's text and find out what Jesus said.

Amazing! If you forgave someone that many times, you'd be forgiving all day long. Well, that's the point. When someone does something bad, hurtful, or mean to you, Jesus wants you to forgive him or her all day long. Why? Because that's how much Jesus forgives you.

Oh, you might want to hide your pencils and wear a football helmet whenever your "friend" happens by. Just a suggestion.

–Uncle Charles

20
JANUARY

You must love each other as I loved you. John 13:34, ICB. Do for other people the same things you want them to do for you. Matthew 7:12, ICB.

THE BIBLE TEACHES ME ABOUT . . .

Friendship

Your Bible is like a wonderful school in which Jesus is the teacher and you're the student sitting on the front row right next to the water fountain.

Read today's texts. We're suppose to love others as Jesus loves us? Well, Jesus forgives you. He cares about you. He listens to your problems and defends you against the greatest evil power in the universe.

Can you *ever* be that good a friend to someone? Sure!

A classmate hurts your feelings. Instead of getting even, you say, "Hey, that's OK."

Someone is having trouble in math. You offer to help him or her learn the multiplication tables.

A shy neighbor kid looks sad. You find out that his mom is sick, so you invite him to eat supper at your house.

A bunch of fourth graders are making life miserable for the new student, and you tell the troublemakers to back off—politely, of course.

What would this world be like if everyone decided to be the kind of friend Jesus said we should be?

–Uncle Charles

THE BIBLE TEACHES ME ABOUT . . .

Knowing God

21
JANUARY

Anyone who has seen me has seen the Father. John 14:9, NIV.

Have you ever looked up into the night sky and seen all the stars shining brightly? God created every star.

Have you ever smelled a fragrant flower or listened to a bird singing deep in a forest of pine trees? God created those, too.

Have you ever felt lonely, and then your mom or dad held you in their arms and said they loved you? Made you feel better, didn't it? God created love.

The God we worship is powerful enough to build a universe, yet tender enough to notice when a tiny sparrow falls. He also knows when you're sad or hurting and need help. Why? Because God created *you*.

Some people once asked Jesus, "Please show us the Father. We want to know what He's like. We want to understand God so that when we look up at the stars or smell a flower or hear a bird sing, we can say to ourselves, 'Oh, yes, God made those things, and I know about God.'"

Look in today's text to see what Jesus said to them.

If you've ever wondered what God is like, think about Jesus. Imagine Him healing the sick, loving little children, crying over sinners. Then you'll know.

—Uncle Charles

22
JANUARY

The person who obeys God's commands lives in God. And God lives in him.
1 John 3:24, ICB.

THE BIBLE TEACHES ME ABOUT . . .

Obeying God

Read today's text to discover what happens when you obey God.

"I don't want to!" Ever heard someone say that?

What if *God* told you to do something you didn't want to do, such as take good care of your body by eating fruit instead of candy or get enough rest instead of staying up all night? What if God wanted you to keep His Sabbath holy by spending time worshiping Him, but you'd rather play soccer with your friends?

The Bible is full of things God wants you to do, such as care for others, be honest, and work hard. With God living in your heart, doing those things is a lot easier.

Satan hates it when we do what our heavenly Father tells us to do. When we refuse, he jumps for joy! "Now I've got him!" he says gleefully. "If he doesn't want to obey God, there's only one other power on earth to obey. And that's *me!* Now *I* can live in his heart."

You can have God in your heart making you a kind, loving person, or you can have Satan living there. It's your choice.

Choose God. Dump Satan.

—Uncle Charles

THE BIBLE TEACHES ME ABOUT . . .

Salvation

23 JANUARY

**Therefore, if anyone is in Christ, he is a new creation; the old has gone, the new has come!
2 Corinthians 5:17, NIV.**

S*plash!* You just fell into the deep end of the community swimming pool. You thrash around because you can't swim. You're going to die. Then you feel the strong arms of the lifeguard lifting you to safety.

Whew! That was close!

You've just been saved. You couldn't help yourself. You needed help. And it arrived just in time.

So do you go back to the deep end of the pool and jump in again? *No!* You keep far away until you've learned how to swim.

God wants to save you, not from deep water, but from deep trouble caused by the devil. He wants to forgive you when you don't let a friend play with your new computer game or when you laugh at a classmate at school who doesn't know the answer. You're drowning in the devil's ocean.

When you allow Jesus in your heart, something happens. Read today's text to find out what.

That's the way salvation works: God saves; you change. No more being selfish, no more laughing at other people's hurt, no more deep water.

No more *splash!*

–Uncle Charles

24 JANUARY

THE BIBLE TEACHES ME ABOUT . . .

Faith

Faith means being sure of the things we hope for. And faith means knowing that something is real even if we do not see it. Hebrews 11:1, ICB.

When you went to sleep last night, you knew that the sun would come up the next morning, didn't you? You couldn't see the sun when you went to bed. It was dark outside. But you knew that after a few hours had passed and you'd finished that dream about the brown-and-white pony you've always wanted, the sun would peek through your curtains. That's faith.

Jesus wants you to have faith in what He said in the Bible. For instance, He promised that He'd come back to earth to take us to heaven. True, you've never seen Jesus. And this old world is a kind of dark and scary place. But He is coming back because He said He would. You have to have faith.

One day like the bright sun coming up, Jesus will appear. And because your faith kept you looking for Him, you'll say, "Whew, it's about time. I've been waiting so long for You."

And He'll say, "Come on. Let's go to heaven as quickly as we can. I've got a brown-and-white pony waiting just for you!"

—Uncle Charles

THE BIBLE TEACHES ME ABOUT . . .

Hearing God's Voice

25
JANUARY

Have you ever been in a big room where lots of people were talking? Noisy, huh?

Now, if your mother or father or brother and sister were in the same room and they were talking, guess whom you would hear the clearest. Yup. You'd know the sound of your family's voices right away.

God has a voice. It's a sweet, gentle voice that can be heard even in a crowded room *if* you've come to know the One who is speaking.

Read today's Bible verse. The door represents your life. Jesus is knocking because He wants to be part of it. He wants you to share with Him what's going on. Then He wants to fill your mind with good thoughts, happy plans, and important suggestions. And when you listen to preachers preach and teachers teach and when your parents guide you, that's God speaking to you through them, telling you what's best for your life.

If you hear Jesus knocking today, if you hear Him softly saying, "I'd like to be a part of your life," why not open the door and let Him in?

—Uncle Charles

Here I am! I stand at the door and knock. If anyone hears my voice and opens the door, I will come in. Revelation 3:20, ICB.

26
JANUARY

THE BIBLE TEACHES ME ABOUT . . .

Being a Missionary

Jesus said to the followers, "Go everywhere in the world. Tell the Good News to everyone." Mark 16:15, ICB.

Would you like to be a missionary? Great! Here's what you need:

1. A big smile on your face.
2. Hands willing to work hard.
3. Feet ready to run to help others.
4. A heart full of love for Jesus.
5. A mouth ready to speak words of comfort and hope.

"Hey," you say, "I have all of those things!" Then you can be a missionary.

"But I'm in school. I can't leave my friends, home, and family!" Who said you have to?

"You mean I can be a missionary where I am right now?"

Check out today's Bible verse and read what Jesus said. Yes, it says "everywhere," and that means in your school, your town, and your home. Wherever people don't know how much God loves them, you can be a bona fide, certified, registered, where's-my-Bible missionary.

"This is great! I'll start with my best friend. She needs to know that Jesus loves her. And my uncle—he's totally messed up. My cousin's in jail. That's gotta be embarrassing. I'd better ask Jesus to power up my hands, feet, mind, and smile right way."

Go get 'em, missionary!

–Uncle Charles

THE BIBLE TEACHES ME ABOUT . . .

Heaven

27
JANUARY

[God] will wipe away every tear from their eyes. There will be no more death, sadness, crying, or pain. All the old ways are gone. Revelation 21:4, ICB.

Read today's verse.

Wow! Imagine a world without crying or death, where people don't even grow old. No wars, bombs, or bullets. No anger and hate. Everyone—white people, brown people, black people, tan people, purple, green, and orange people live together in peace.

But that's not the best thing about heaven. Carefully read this beautiful verse:

"The throne of God and of the Lamb will be there. . . . They will see his face" (Revelation 22:3, 4, ICB).

Someday you'll walk streets of gold. Every animal will be glad to see you. Every group of children will invite you to join whatever game they're playing. Every sound will be kind and gentle. Every food will be healthy and taste *wonderful.*

But the very best thing about being in heaven is that Jesus (the Lamb) and God the Father will walk, talk, play, and sit down to eat supper with you. You'll see their smiles and listen as they tell stories about how they helped you fight Satan and finally brought you to your new home.

Seeing the face of Jesus. That's heaven!

—Uncle Charles

28
JANUARY

Children are a gift from the Lord. Psalm 127:3, ICB.

THE BIBLE TEACHES ME ABOUT . . .

Me

According to today's text, you're a gift . . . from God!

It's Christmas morning. You've been watching the sun climb over the horizon just waiting for your mom and dad to call. When they do, you're out the door in a flash, ready to attack the pile of gifts under the Christmas tree.

You tear into your presents. And while you like all of them, there are a couple gifts that really get your heart racing.

Let me ask you: What makes some gifts more special than others?

"Hey, I really *wanted* this red truck with the racing stripe," one kid says.

"My new coat is a perfect match for my yellow boots," another explains.

"Are you serious?" yet another gasps. "This gift will be so much fun to play with."

In other words, a gift is special when you really want it and it makes your life happier or more fun.

Guess what? Since you're a gift, that's your job, too—to make other people's lives happier or more fun. How do you do that? By being kind, considerate, forgiving, and fun to be with.

–Uncle Charles

MY SPECIAL WORSHIP . . .

Studying My Sabbath School Lesson

29
JANUARY

Study to shew thyself approved unto God.
2 Timothy 2:15.

I've discovered there are many ways to worship God. Going to church each week is one of the best, but I like worshiping God a little bit every day! I call it my "special worship."

Each evening my dad and I sit down and study my Sabbath school lesson together. We find the texts in my Bible, read the stories, and look at the pictures. Then on Sabbath I enjoy taking part in the lesson study because I already know the memory verse and most of the answers to the questions the teacher asks.

A couple times each week Dad and I do something extra cool. He asks me to teach him the lesson!

So I show him the pictures, tell him the stories, and have him read the texts to me. If he can't remember something, I tell him the answer and suggest that he study a little harder. He says he'll try.

We're learning about people who loved and obeyed God no matter what anyone said or did to them. My dad and I ask Jesus to help us be strong Christians too and do what we should, even if people laugh at us.

Dad makes a great teacher, and a very smart student—when he remembers to study!

–David

30
JANUARY

I meditate on your precepts and consider your ways.
Psalm 119:15, NIV.

MY SPECIAL WORSHIP . . .

Reading Books About God

Going to church is important. But I worship God during the week, too.

I choose a couple of my favorite books and my *Primary Treasure* for my special worship. I read stories about how God came to earth to help people, and about boys and girls just like me who love and obey their heavenly Father no matter what happens to them.

One book I especially like has pictures of animals in it. I read about camels and tigers, groundhogs and elephants, and even a little chipmunk. The book tells me that God made all these creatures.

Now when I see an animal, it makes me think of the Creator and how powerful He is.

I have a Bible with lots of pictures in it. I enjoy reading the stories about Daniel and how he was thrown into a lions' den, but the lions didn't eat him. Then there's Jonah and the big fish, David standing against Goliath, and the little man sitting in the big tree waiting to see Jesus.

If you'd like to have a special worship time each day, just grab some books that talk about God, find a place where no one will bother you, and spend a few minutes reading. Why not start today? Have fun!

–Jason

MY SPECIAL WORSHIP . . .

Singing

31
JANUARY

Sing to the Lord . . . praise his holy name. Psalm 30:4, NIV.

A couple weeks ago I learned a new song in Sabbath school. It goes like this: "Jesus, Jesus, Jesus; there's just something about that name."

I *love* that song! It makes me feel good every time I sing it.

When I sing a song about God, it's like I'm worshiping Him with music. He must like that because the Bible says angels sing a *lot.*

I made a music book to use during my special worship each day. It has the names of the songs I like, some of the words I can't remember, and pictures that show what's mentioned in each song.

When I learned "Give Me Oil in My Lamp," I drew a picture of a lamp in my music book. Now whenever I turn on the light in my room at night, it reminds me of the song, so I sing it.

Another favorite is "I Will Make You Fishers of Men." I drew a boat and some fish.

Sometimes when I'm sitting in the living room, I'll start singing one of my special worship songs. My mom will begin humming along. Then my sister Lucille will join in, and that always makes my dog Buster howl. I think our goldfish is singing too, but I can't tell.

If you want to worship Jesus, just sing a simple song to Him!

–Trisha

1
FEBRUARY

Remember your Creator while you are young. Ecclesiastes 12:1, ICB.

MY SPECIAL WORSHIP . . .

Remembering

Singing songs and listening to stories in Sabbath school and church is fun. But during the week, when I have my special worship times, I do something you might think is a little strange. I find a quiet place, sit down, rest my head against a pillow or tree trunk, and just remember.

What do I remember? Well, if the Sabbath school teacher told an interesting story last Sabbath, I'll pretend like he's telling it to me again. If someone did something nice for me, I'll smile and remember how kind that person was. And if God has helped me with a big problem, I'll remember to thank Him for being my friend.

Remembering things about God is a great way to worship Him. My mother showed me some verses in the Bible that say "Remember the Sabbath day" (Exodus 20:8, NIV) and "Remember the Creator while you are young" (Ecclesiastes 12:1, ICB). As a matter of fact, she told me that the word *remember* is in the Bible more than 140 times. That's a *lot* of remembering!

So if you see me sitting quietly someplace, don't worry—I'm not sad or lonely. I'm just having my special worship time. I'm busy remembering something about God, like how much He loves me. The more I remember Him, the less I forget Him.

–Tara

MY SPECIAL WORSHIP . . .

Praying

2 FEBRUARY

Pray for one another. James 5:16, NASB.

A long time ago, when I was in first grade, my teacher said something interesting. She said praying was the same as *talking* to God.

I began thinking. Talking to God is a good way to worship Him. So I came up with a plan. Since I like to worship during the week and not just on Sabbath, I decided that one of my special worships would be a talk with God. Here's what I do.

First, I make a list of everything I want to talk about. Last week my list included thanking God for the beautiful flowers growing in the field behind our house, asking Him to help the doctor make my friend Jerry feel better so he could come back to school, and a question about what I should do with my sister. She's always telling Mother I did something bad when I wasn't even around!

My prayer list also helps me remember when God answers my prayers. I put a star sticker beside each one, such as when Jerry got better and came back to school and when I learned to be patient with my sister.

My special prayer worship helps me remember that I don't have to do everything all by myself. God wants to help. You should see all the stars on my list!

–Jon

3 FEBRUARY

You will be my witnesses . . . to the ends of the earth. Acts 1:8, NIV.

MY SPECIAL WORSHIP . . .

Sharing

Yesterday, right after school, I worshiped God. And I wasn't even at church! I walked up to my sister, and my aunt, and my best friend and said, "Did you know that Jesus made a big fish swallow a little man?"

They looked surprised. Then I told them the story of Jonah.

It's called "sharing," and it's a great way to worship God.

Two weeks ago I told the clerk at the grocery store about how Jesus fed a big group of people with just a few loaves of bread and some fish. She was amazed.

Last Monday I asked the paperboy if he'd ever heard about a man who walked on top of water. He said that would really be news.

Every time I hear an exciting Bible story at church or in school, I share it with someone during the week. Then I tell people that I love Jesus and that I'm glad He's my friend.

Tomorrow we're going to visit my grandmother. She's in the hospital. I'm going to tell her about when Jesus healed the man who couldn't walk. Then we'll thank God for doctors and nurses who have that healing touch too. I hope she likes my sharing.

–Andrew

MY SPECIAL WORSHIP . . .

Enjoying Nature

4
FEBRUARY

When I worship God, two things happen. First *I* do something; then *God* does something.

I talk; He listens. I sing; He enjoys my music. I study the Bible; He helps me understand what I'm reading.

One of my favorite special worship times during the week is my dad and I going for a walk in the park. And just like any other worship, two things happen.

First I see many wonderful things: squirrels gathering nuts, birds building nests, mother ducks swimming across the pond with baby ducks close behind.

Then I think about a loving God who provides food for animals, and people, too. I remember my house and my room with the pictures on the wall and how much my mother loves me.

When I enjoy nature, I think God is reminding me of something. He's making me realize just how much He cares for me every day. He shows me how He watches out for His creatures. Then I know He's watching out for me, too.

So I pretend that each colorful flower is a picture postcard from God, telling me how much He loves me. I pretend each bird's song is a happy hello from heaven. Then I say, "Thank You, Jesus, for showing me Your beautiful nature. Thank You for loving me."

–Natalie

Don't be afraid; you are worth more than many sparrows. Matthew 10:31, NIV.

5
FEBRUARY

Come near to God and he will come near to you. James 4:8, NIV.

MY SPECIAL WORSHIP . . .

Family Worship

We have family worship every day of the year, even on Christmas. It's just like Sabbath school and church, except fewer people show up.

Each evening after the news Dad calls us to the living room. He says he likes to have worship after the news, because then he's got a lot more stuff to pray about.

We sing songs, my brother Chad and sister Heather recite a Bible verse, Mom reads a story from the devotional book, and I tell two things I'm happy for.

Last night I said I was happy that my friend Terry didn't get hurt when he fell down the stairs at school, and that I got a B in addition. We also tell anything we're worried about.

Then we pray.

The next night we do the same things, except different people do them. I recite a Bible verse, Dad reads from the devotional book, and Chad and Heather tell two things they're happy about.

Then we pray.

I look forward to family worship because it's something we all do together. You can have a special worship time every day, too, even if you do it all by yourself. But remember, whenever you worship, you're not really alone. God is there.

–Hunter

FINDING GOD IN NATURE . . .

Mountains Like Jesus' Shoulders

6
FEBRUARY

His foundation is in the holy mountain. Psalm 87:1.

When you were younger, did your mom or dad ever put you up on their shoulders? You could see a lot more up there than when you were standing on the ground, right?

You can see more of this earth when you're standing on a mountaintop, too. Valleys and fields, maybe a big city—everything looks smaller from up there.

When you climb to the top of a tall mountain, it's as though Jesus were lifting you onto His broad shoulders. You look down at the earth and see things you've *never* seen before.

You discover that we all live together in one big, beautiful world. You realize that everything we do affects someone else. If a city pollutes the air with its factories and cars, the wind blows the problem to another community and makes their air dirty too.

From a mountaintop you can also see how people can help each other. If one valley doesn't have much food to eat, you can see where a road needs to be built so another valley can send over trucks filled with fruits and vegetables. We all need each other in order to live happily and healthfully. That's what you see from a mountaintop.

–Uncle Charles

7

FEBRUARY

Let heaven and earth praise him, the seas and all that move in them. Psalm 69:34, NIV.

FINDING GOD IN NATURE . . .

Oceans and Jesus' Feet

Waves race onto the shore, tossing foam across shimmering sands and chasing long-legged shorebirds into the air.

The ocean spreads its waters all around the world. By His Holy Spirit, Jesus does what the ocean does. He goes everywhere, looking for people who will share His love.

Beneath the ocean's surface millions of sea creatures live their lives. Brightly colored fish swim among tall, green grasses and bushes. Lumbering whales and swift dolphins move through the waves, looking for plants and other good things to eat.

The ocean shares its water with the sky. Warm air lifts sea mists up, up, up, forming billowy clouds. Then the mists fall back to earth in the form of rain. This falling water has been cleaned by sunshine and refreshed by the air. It's like the ocean is taking a shower!

Wherever Jesus' feet took Him, He helped people. He washed away their tears and made them smile again. Jesus brought love to everyone who invited Him into their hearts.

What waits beyond the oceans? Maybe, after you've grown, you'll go and find out. Maybe you'll discover boys and girls who need to hear about Jesus.

Listen. Do you hear them calling you from the far side of the oceans?

–Uncle Charles

FINDING GOD IN NATURE . . .

Flowers Make Me Think of Jesus' Smile

Have you ever seen a field filled with flowers—red ones, yellow ones, pink ones, blue ones? What a beautiful sight!

Most flowers smell nice, too. Sometimes, especially in spring, the air seems full of nature's sweet perfume.

Jesus created flowers to remind us of His love. They're like His smile. They make us happy.

Flowers nod sleepily in the sunshine. Bees buzz about, gathering nectar for honey. Bugs scurry among the colorful petals, searching for food and places to live. Wonderful things happen where flowers grow.

But if you were to pick one of those beautiful creations and put it in your bedroom, something sad would happen. In a few days the leaves would turn brown, the petals would drop off one by one, and the lovely, sweet-smelling flower would die.

Sin causes death. Satan doesn't want us to enjoy the wonderful things Jesus created, so he destroys them.

Someday Jesus will make another world for us. Satan will be gone forever. The flowers in this new, wonderful place will never, *ever* die. We'll be able to see two very beautiful things in our home—perfect flowers and Jesus' smile. Won't that be great?

–Uncle Charles

8
FEBRUARY

Then I saw a new heaven and a new earth. Revelation 21:1, NIV.

9
FEBRUARY

All the rivers flow into the sea, yet the sea is not full. Ecclesiastes 1:7, NASB.

FINDING GOD IN NATURE . . .

Rivers Like Jesus' Voice

Many rivers begin high in the mountains. Snows melt, sending millions of drops of water down winding streams. Streams join together to form rivers that tumble into valleys.

A river can be many things all at the same time. A beaver creates ponds in which to raise a family. A boat captain uses the river as a watery highway, taking people and products many miles from where they started.

Fish live in the swirling waters as birds skim the waves looking for bugs to take back to chirping babies.

The sun lifts water vapor from rivers and makes clouds that eventually rain over farmers' fields, helping crops grow.

If you listen closely to the sound of a river, you can pretend that you hear Jesus speaking. Sometimes the voice is gentle, musical, soft—the way Jesus speaks when He says, "I love you and will take care of you if you want Me to." Sometimes the currents rush over stones or tumble over cliffs. The river rumbles with a strong, deep, powerful voice, as when Jesus tells Satan to stop bothering you!

Think about Jesus the next time you stroll by a river. Listen to the sound and allow His voice to speak to you.

–Uncle Charles

FINDING GOD IN NATURE . . .

Trees Like Jesus' Arms

10 FEBRUARY

On each side of the river stood the tree of life, bearing twelve crops of fruit. Revelation 22:2, NIV.

Jesus lives in heaven and is busy building beautiful homes for us to enjoy. But even though He's working hard, He's always ready to listen to our prayers and help us when we're afraid.

Jesus used to live here on earth. He kept busy here, too, making sick people well, sad people happy, and fighting people peaceful. Jesus wants us to know that He loves us, even though He's not living on this earth anymore. So, long ago He made something special to remind us of His love.

Trees have strong branches that reach out in every direction. They cool the earth, providing shade from the hot sun. And sometimes they seem to whisper when the wind blows through their green leaves. During those moments it's easy to pretend that it's Jesus talking to us!

When a bad storm comes and the rain pours down, trees stand straight and tall. Many little animals find shelter in their rugged limbs and thick, sturdy trunks.

So the next time you see a tall, strong tree, think of the arms of Jesus—how they protect, shelter, and long to hold us close.

In heaven you can sit under a tree with Jesus and hear Him speak words of love. Won't that be wonderful?

–Uncle Charles

11
FEBRUARY

FINDING GOD IN NATURE . . .

Soil and Jesus' Hands

Others, like seed sown on good soil, hear the word, accept it, and produce a crop. Mark 4:20, NIV.

S*oil* is the ground under your feet and the dirt you use to make mud pies.

Farmers plant seeds in the soil. Soon, with the help of the rain and sunshine, green plants appear. In a few weeks yellow squashes, green cucumbers, red tomatoes, sweet blueberries, and many other wonderful things grow from the ground. *Mmmmm!*

Soil is like a giant factory. It mixes rain and sunshine to make food for plants so they can grow and feed us . . . so *we* can grow.

But soil can be hurt. If the farmer harvests too many crops and doesn't let the soil have time to replace the good things that growing plants need, it becomes weak and useless.

We need to protect soil by being very careful about how we use it. That way it can stay healthy and keep growing food.

When Jesus was here on earth, He helped many people. He placed His hands on them and healed their diseases, took away their pain, calmed their fears.

Jesus' hands were like the soil, bringing life to so many.

And Jesus' hands were hurt, too. Satan made people drive nails through them. Then they hung Him on a cross where He died. But He rose again!

Now, like the soil, He gives us power every day to keep on growing.

–Uncle Charles

HOW I HONOR MY PARENTS . . .

I Obey Them

My Sabbath school teacher told us that God wants us to be happy, so He made some rules for us to follow.

One rule says we should honor our moms and dads. I wasn't sure what the word *honor* meant, so I asked Dad. He said, "To honor someone means that you think about that person first." I said I'd try.

Last week my mom told me to come inside when I was right in the middle of making an airport in the backyard. I didn't want to stop, but I knew I should honor my mom. So I went inside even though my runway was *way* too short.

Yesterday my dad told me to clean up my room (which kinda looked like a toy store exploded in it). But I'd just started reading a book about fighter jets.

Then I had an idea. I asked my dad if he'd look at the book with me when I finished straightening up my room. He said, "Sure."

So after I'd picked up all my stuff and put away my clothes, I got to learn about jets with my dad.

Sometimes obeying your parents isn't fun in the beginning, but later it works out just fine. Maybe that's what Jesus had in mind when He made the honor rule.

–David

Honor your father and your mother, so that you may live long in the land the Lord your God is giving you. Exodus 20:12, NIV.

13
FEBRUARY

My son, pay attention to what I say; listen closely to my words. Proverbs 4:20, NIV.

HOW I HONOR MY PARENTS . . .

I Take Care of Them

The other day my dad came home from work and sat down on the couch. He looked very tired.

Even though I wanted him to play a game with me, I tiptoed out to the kitchen and got him a big glass of orange juice. He smiled and said, "Thank you."

Then I brought him a pillow so he could take a nap on the couch. Soon he was sleeping, and I made sure our cat didn't jump up on his legs.

When he woke up, I told him the story about a man who got swallowed by a whale. He said that reminded him that he'd better start supper. He didn't seem so tired anymore. As a matter of fact, he sang while he worked in the kitchen.

Most of the time my dad does what I want to do. We play catch or read storybooks. But sometimes moms and dads need us to take care of them, such as when they're tired or sad or sick. This is a wonderful way to honor them.

Jesus wants us to help everyone in the world. Being loving and kind to our parents teaches us how to do that. Then when we're older and someone needs our help, we're ready!

–Jason

HOW I HONOR MY PARENTS . . .

I Help Them

14

FEBRUARY

A wise son heeds his father's instruction. Proverbs 13:1, NIV.

My dad can do anything. He can fix the car, paint a swing, mow the lawn, wash the dishes, and vacuum the floor all in one afternoon. I get tired just watching him.

Sometimes I help.

The other day my dad said, "Let's fix that squeaky door on the porch."

"OK," I said. "What do you want me to do?"

He handed me a can with a funny-looking snout on it. "Put a little of this oil on the hinge."

I carefully put a couple drops of oil where he showed me. By mistake, I also put a couple drops on the floor, too. Dad said, "Now the floor won't squeak either."

Then we raked the yard. After Dad gathered up the leaves, I put them into a basket and carried them to a spot by the fence. Soon we'd made a great big pile. Then we jumped into it.

Whenever I see my dad doing something, I ask if I can help. Sometimes he lets me. Sometimes he says I'm too little. But he appreciates my asking.

Helping isn't always fun. Sometimes you'd rather be doing something else. But when you see the smiles on your mom's or dad's face, you know Jesus is smiling too because you're honoring your parents!

–Jon

15
FEBRUARY

HOW I HONOR MY PARENTS . . .

I'm Happy

May your father and mother be glad. Proverbs 23:25, NIV.

Moms and dads really like it when their children are happy. That's why Jesus wants us to honor them with happiness.

Last week my mom came into the kitchen and sat down at the table. She looked sad.

I thought, *What can I do to make her feel better*? Then I remembered something funny that had happened to me earlier. "Hey, Mom," I called. "Do you know what Douglas did?" (Douglas is my dog.)

"What?" Mom asked.

I began to giggle. "Well, this morning, out in the backyard"—I giggled some more—"I threw a stick for him to fetch"—I giggled harder and harder—"and just as he got to where the stick had landed"— by now my mom was giggling too—"he slipped on the grass and fell right into my swimming pool." I laughed so hard my stomach hurt.

"Then," I continued, "Douglas went and shook water all over Dad's tomato plants. Dad said he'd never seen a *dog* sprinkler before."

Mom laughed and laughed at my story. She wasn't sad anymore because a big smile spread across her face. I like it when Mom smiles.

Being happy is a great way to honor your parents. You feel good. They feel good. And God giggles along with you.

–Trisha

HOW I HONOR MY PARENTS . . .

I'm Loving to Them

16 FEBRUARY

A happy heart makes the face cheerful. Proverbs 15:13, NIV.

Have you ever had a day that made you mad? I had one last week.

First, I fell down and hurt my ear. Then I lost my dump truck. Next the cat scratched my leg. Mom put a bandage on it. The cat looked sorry, but I'm not sure.

Then my favorite television program didn't come on because of some basketball game.

But Mom fixed me a delicious supper and read to me before bedtime just as she always does. I'd had a bad day, but she loved me anyway.

Sometimes my mom has a bad day. I can tell. She mumbles. That's when I remember how nicely she cared for me when I was mad. So I do nice things for her.

I put my arms around her and give her a hug. I tell her how much I liked my spaghetti. At bedtime I don't moan and groan about going to my room. I just brush my teeth and hop right into bed.

Being loving is easy when everyone's happy. It gets a little harder when a cat scratches your leg or you can't find your dump truck.

Moms and dads have bad days too. If we want to honor them as Jesus says we should, we'll be loving . . . even when they mumble.

–Tara

17
FEBRUARY

Children, obey your parents in the Lord, for this is right. Ephesians 6:1, NIV.

HOW I HONOR MY PARENTS . . .

I Respect Them

The other day my friend Jerry said he didn't love his mom anymore. "Why?" I asked.

"Because she won't let me go swimming."

"Does your mom always keep you from doing stuff you want to do?" I gasped.

"Well, not always," Jerry admitted.

I got to thinking. My Sabbath school teacher said children should respect their parents. It's a great way to honor them. Respect means you remember how important someone is to you.

Well, moms and dads are very important to kids. They feed them, tuck them in at night, take them to museums or the zoo. Without parents, kids would be lonely . . . and very hungry!

"Does your mom *ever* do nice things?" I asked.

Jerry began to smile. "Yesterday she showed me how to make oatmeal cookies. And last week she let me send an e-mail to my cousin." Jerry smiled more and more. "Tomorrow we're going to the store to buy new shoes!"

"Hey," I chuckled, "I thought you didn't love your mom anymore."

Jerry blushed. "Well, maybe I do love her . . . even when I don't feel like it."

When we remember all the good things parents do for us, we won't get so mad when they don't let us do what we want to do. Hey, that's respect!

—Andrew

HOW I HONOR MY PARENTS . . .

We Have Fun Together

18

FEBRUARY

Happy . . . is the people . . . whose God is the Lord! Psalm 144:15, Amplified.

Yesterday my dad came home from work and said, "Let's have a picnic!" I *love* picnics, especially if baked beans are involved.

We packed a lunch and headed for the park.

Dad pushed me super-high on the swing, showed me a caterpillar, watched me climb a tree, let me paddle a boat, told me about woodpeckers, and listened to a story I made up in my own head.

Then we ate baked beans.

After we finished eating, we lay on the blanket and looked up at the sky. I started counting the clouds, but there were just too many. That's probably why it began to rain.

Dad and I quickly gathered up the food basket and blanket and ran to the car.

I love being with my dad. We have tons of fun together. Yes, sometimes it rains on our picnic or the ants try to eat our food, but we still enjoy ourselves.

Having fun with your mom or dad is a wonderful way to honor them. They can be great friends when you're happy or even when you're sad.

When we have fun together, it reminds me of what heaven will be like. Only we won't have to worry about rainstorms or hungry ants.

Have fun with your parents today!

—Natalie

19
FEBRUARY

Cast all your anxiety on him because he cares for you. 1 Peter 5:7, NIV.

HOW I HONOR MY PARENTS . . .

I Share Secret Thoughts

Last Tuesday I had a secret thought day. I sat on my favorite rock and wondered how I'd feel when my brother Terry left to go to college. He'd be gone for a long time. I knew I'd be lonely without him. But was it OK to feel like that? Maybe I should act happy even when I'm sad inside. I didn't know what to do.

When my mom came home from work, she asked me why I was looking sad. I told her about Terry.

When I finished, she told me one of her secret thoughts. Guess what? She'd been wondering the same thing herself! Isn't that amazing?

We talked about it and decided that when I felt sad, I should come and ask her to help me. And when she felt sad, she would ask me to help her. Then together we would ask Jesus to help us know what to do. I felt much better knowing we were in this thing together.

Sometimes, thoughts and feelings can be a little scary. That's a good time for kids like us to honor our moms and dads by telling them what we're thinking. Then, with Jesus' help, we can find answers to our problems.

Try it on your next secret thought day. It works!

–Hunter

BIBLE ZOO . . .

The Awesome Eagle

20
FEBRUARY

He was like an eagle building its nest. It flutters over its young. It spreads its wings to catch them. It carries them on its feathers. The Lord alone led them. Deuteronomy 32:11, 12, ICB.

The eagle is one of nature's most beautiful creatures. Maybe you've seen this strong, proud bird flying high among the clouds.

Eagles have powerful wings that carry them long distances over mountains and valleys, over raging rivers and hot desert sands.

The Bible says God takes care of us the same way a mother eagle takes care of her babies. When trouble comes, the eagle defends her young using her powerful wings and sharp talons. If the sun gets too hot or if rain clouds gather overhead, this mighty bird will spread her wings over the nest and protect the little baby birds from the storm.

When spiritual trouble comes to God's children here on earth, when Satan tries to attack with evil thoughts and hurtful temptations, God offers protection. When we're afraid, we can remember that God wants to help us keep sin out of our lives. Just like the eagle taking care of its young, our heavenly Father wants to make sure we're safe from Satan's power.

I'm glad He takes such good care of us. Aren't you?

—Uncle Charles

21
FEBRUARY

"I will call for my people like a lion calling for its young. My children will come and follow me." Hosea 11:10, ICB.

BIBLE ZOO . . .

The Roaring Lion

There's an animal in the Bible Zoo that's kind of scary. Some people call it the king of beasts.

The lion looks mean, with sharp teeth, fluffy mane, and shining eyes. When a lion roars, you *know* this is a powerful animal.

God loves us and wants to keep evil things away from each one of us. When Satan tries to hurt us or make us do something evil, God tells him, "Leave that kid alone. He belongs to *Me!"* To our ears, God's voice is gentle and kind. But Satan hears words that sound like a lion's roar. The devil turns and runs!

Lions are interesting animals. They tenderly care for their cubs. They play with them, bring them food to eat, and make sure they have a safe place to sleep at night. But if some other animal or a hunter tries to hurt those babies, lions become fierce and fight hard until the danger passes.

God has promised to care for us and help us fight Satan. To us, God is a loving Father. To Satan, He has the voice of a roaring lion!

—Uncle Charles

BIBLE ZOO . . .

The Fluffy Lamb

In one corner of our pretend Bible Zoo is a beautiful green pasture. Here we find soft, cuddly lambs grazing under the afternoon sun.

Some lambs are white; some black. They all look so peaceful and friendly.

Lambs grow up to be beautiful sheep covered with thick coats of wool. Shepherds carefully cut off this soft covering each year—kind of like a sheep haircut! Then people weave warm jackets and cozy blankets from the sheep's wool.

Lambs depend on their shepherd. Without the kind guardian watching over the flock, lambs could get lost or hurt. Whenever danger comes near, lambs run to the shepherd for protection. This kind man or woman enjoys caring for the lambs and knows each one by name.

John the Baptist said Jesus was the "Lamb of God." When Jesus was here on earth, He always depended on His Father to help Him when trouble came. Today Jesus wants every boy and girl to live in peace, just like lambs. He wants us to think of God as our loving shepherd—a guardian who offers protection from sin all day, every day.

Like lambs, we can trust our heavenly Shepherd.

—Uncle Charles

John saw Jesus coming toward him. John said, "Look, the Lamb of God. He takes away the sins of the world!" John 1:29, ICB.

23
FEBRUARY

The Lord led the people through the deep waters. Like a horse walking through a desert, the people did not stumble. Isaiah 63:13, ICB.

BIBLE ZOO . . .

The Strong Horse

There's a big, powerful animal in our Bible Zoo today. This beautiful creature is a work animal, especially in countries where there are few cars and trucks.

The horse works hard no matter what the job. When pulling a wagon, taking someone for a ride, or helping move a heavy load, the horse uses its thick muscles and strong back to make the job easier for others.

The Bible tells many stories about horses. They've made it possible for armies to win battles. They've carried messengers between cities, dragged loads of wood and stone for new buildings and temples, and carried families to visit relatives in faraway towns. Whenever horses are mentioned, they're busy doing some important task.

Jesus works hard for His children just like the horse works hard for its master. God's Son uses His mighty power to help kids win battles against Satan. And when we want to tell others about the love of God, Jesus is right with us, ready to help.

Workers with Jesus can do anything—build a church in a faraway country or help people right next door. What a wonderful work partner!

–Uncle Charles

BIBLE ZOO . . .

The Active Ant

24

FEBRUARY

Go watch the ants, you lazy person. Watch what they do and be wise. Proverbs 6:6, ICB.

Have you ever seen someone who refuses to help when everyone else is working? This person just sits around and does nothing. If you say anything, they yawn. "No, I don't want to work today. It'll make me tired. I'd rather sit and rest." Now *that's* a lazy person.

Of course, some people are sick or hurt and can't work. We need to help *them,* don't we?

In our Bible Zoo we find the ant doing what ants do best—working hard.

Maybe you've seen an ant near your house. One thing's for sure. If the critter you saw was alive and breathing, it was busy doing something!

Ants carry twigs, leaves, and even stones that are much bigger and heavier than they are. They never say "I can't do that" or "I'm not going to help my friends." They square their tiny shoulders, lift their little chins, and *get busy.*

Jesus fed, healed, and talked to anyone who needed Him. He was like the ant—always working.

With Jesus' help, Christian boys and girls never act like lazy people. They're constantly busy making the world a better place for someone.

So what are you going to do today?

–Uncle Charles

25 FEBRUARY

Jesus was baptized and came up out of the water. Heaven opened, and he saw God's Spirit coming down on him like a dove. And a voice spoke from heaven. The voice said, "This is my Son and I love him. I am very pleased with him." Matthew 3:16, 17, ICB.

BIBLE ZOO . . .

The Gentle Dove

One of the most beautiful animals in our Bible Zoo is the dove. This lovely bird brightens the forest with its gently curved wings and soft, sweet call.

When Noah wanted to find out if there was any dry land after the rain stopped, what did he send? A little dove. He knew that bird would fly far and wide looking for a place to rest.

When Jesus was baptized, God the Father sent a dove too. When Jesus saw it, He knew it was a special message from heaven, a message that said, "I love You, Son."

Today when we think of doves, we think of peace, happiness, and joy—the very gifts Jesus offered everyone when He walked the dusty roads of this earth.

Jesus wants us to be like humble doves, ready to bring peace and beauty into the lives of others. From now on, whenever you see this beautiful creature flying through the sky, ask Jesus to help you be as pure and gentle as a dove.

–Uncle Charles

BIBLE ZOO . . .

The Daring Deer

He makes me like a deer, which does not stumble. He helps me stand on the steep mountains. Psalm 18:33, ICB.

If you've ever traveled to mountain country, you may have seen a thin-legged creature moving calmly from ledge to ledge high on a rocky cliff, where winds blow and clouds swirl.

You probably gasped and said, "If that animal slips, it will fall to its death!" But it doesn't fall. It walks, jumps, hops, and runs as if it was on flat land.

That's a deer. Even shepherd boy David was amazed at its ability to walk along the sides of cliffs without tumbling down. Then he said God can make *us* like a deer!

Living in a sinful world can be like walking on a high cliff. The devil makes us afraid. We look down at the rocks far below and tremble with fear. But, like the deer, God has made it possible for us to walk without falling. No, He didn't give us little hooves and narrow legs. He gave us minds to fight Satan's temptations and feet to hurry us away from sin.

Today, if you see something you know is wrong or think a thought that might get you into trouble, use your feet and mind. Remember the deer high on the mountain, and run away to safety.

–Uncle Charles

27
FEBRUARY

Your promises are so sweet to me. They are like honey to my mouth! Psalm 119:103, ICB.

BIBLE ZOO . . .

The Busy Bee

I *love* honey. My wife often uses it to make special treats for us to enjoy.

The animal that makes honey is one of the smallest members of our Bible Zoo. Like the tiny ant, bees are busy creatures, buzzing about, taking care of their hive, guarding against predators, and making life miserable for anyone who tries to hurt their young.

The bee does two quite incredible things. First, it takes pollen from flower to flower, making it possible for them to grow strong and healthy. Second, it creates honey. Not bad for an animal the size of your big toe!

I think when God looks down and sees His bees hard at work in the fields and meadows, He sighs a happy sigh. Bees don't attack; they protect. Bees don't steal food; they *make* food. Bees don't kill flowers; they help them grow.

Shepherd boy David said God's promises are as sweet as honey. That meant they made his life more enjoyable and fun, like honey on the tongue. So today if you hear the *buzz, buzz, buzz* of a bee, take a moment and think of the many ways you can make someone's life sweeter. Then get busy and do it!

–Uncle Charles

BIBLE ZOO . . .

The Strange Oyster

28 FEBRUARY

Our pretend Bible Zoo is home to a creature that's usually found deep in the salty waters of the ocean. It's not exactly what you'd consider beautiful. As a matter of fact, it kinda looks like a bumpy rock!

Oysters live very simple lives. They sit around and eat tiny animals that float by in the ocean. Nothing to get excited about.

But there's more. When an oyster opens its shell to collect a bit of food, sometimes a tiny grain of sand gets sucked in too. Have you ever gotten a rock in your shoe? Same idea.

Instead of tossing out the stone, this creature does something amazing. It begins to surround this intruder with the same material it uses to build its shell. Little by little, the coating grows thicker and thicker. Soon, that grain of sand is completely covered by . . . a pearl! Yup. A beautiful, round pearl—all because the oyster didn't like that sand in its body.

The next time you start to get upset about something that irritates you, pretend that God is saying to you, "Wait. I can take this problem and use it to teach you something beautiful." Hey, it works for the oyster!

—Uncle Charles

The 12 gates [of heaven] were 12 pearls. Each gate was made from a single pearl. Revelation 21:21, ICB.

1

MARCH

Come, all you who are thirsty, come to the waters. Isaiah 55:1, NIV.

HOW I STAY HEALTHY . . .

I Drink Water

God wants all of us to live a happy and *healthy* life. Being healthy means that your body works hard to fight disease. If you get sick, healthy bodies get well faster.

When I'm playing with my dog Gruffy and we get thirsty, we don't run to the refrigerator for a soda. No way! We head straight to the garden hose and drink lots of cool water. It tastes great! Even Gruffy thinks so.

Every day I take a bath so my body will stay clean. I scrub every inch of me, getting all the dirt and sweat off. Water does a terrific job of cleaning me on the outside.

Sometimes I give Gruffy a bath, except he isn't all that interested in getting scrubbed. He runs around and gets soap *everywhere*. By the time that dog is clean, so am I.

Water cleans me on the inside, too. It keeps my blood, heart, and lungs working hard by washing away anything that would make them sick. Not even fruit juice can do that!

So if you want to stay healthy, don't forget to drink tons of water everyday. One more thing—never wash a dog in the living room.

–Trisha

HOW I STAY HEALTHY . . .

I Breathe Fresh Air

2
MARCH

Listen to the wind blow. *Wheewww.* Feels great on your face, doesn't it? Sometimes it roars like a lion. Sometimes it whispers like a friend telling you a secret.

I like the wind. It sounds soothing in the leaves and makes the grasses sway back and forth. *Wheewww.*

God made the wind for an important reason. People need to breathe.

Fresh air helps me stay healthy. Without a constant supply of good, clear air, I'd die!

At night, when I go to bed, I open the windows in my room. Then the fresh air can come in and help me sleep soundly.

Several times during the day I stop and take a couple long, deep breaths. I fill my lungs with sweet-smelling air; then I blow it out again.

Even while I play baseball, air is helping me stay healthy by bringing oxygen to my blood. Dad told me that fresh air can even make me *think* better. Amazing!

If God made fresh air, it must be important. Join me and breathe lots of it today.

–David

Then the Lord God took dust from the ground and formed man from it. The Lord breathed the breath of life into the man's nose. And the man became a living person. Genesis 2:7, ICB.

3 MARCH

Light is sweet, and it pleases the eyes to see the sun [shining]. However many years a man [or woman] may live, let [them] enjoy them all. Ecclesiastes 11:7, 8, NIV.

HOW I STAY HEALTHY . . .

I Enjoy Sunshine

Every morning when I wake up, I look out my window. Guess what I see? Yup. There's the sun shining brightly over the neighborhood. Even if it's cloudy, I know the sun is up there in the sky doing its thing.

God made sunshine for a reason. Its bright rays help our bodies kill germs. Many germs that would make us sick die when the sun shines on them. Cool!

Sunshine brings us warmth in the winter and makes the trees and grasses grow in the summer. Every plant and animal in nature needs sunshine to stay healthy. So do we.

My dad once took me down into a deep, dark cave. I didn't find very many plants or animals living there. Why? No sun.

I like to feel sunshine on my face while I fly my kite in the field behind our house. It makes me glad knowing God made that shining sun to help me stay healthy and strong. He must love me very much. He loves you, too. The next time you feel sunshine on your face, remember God's love.

–Jason

HOW I STAY HEALTHY . . .

I Exercise

4

MARCH

He gives strength to the weary and increases the power of the weak. Isaiah 40:29, NIV.

My friend Chris has a problem. I tried to tell him about it, but he just said, "You don't know what you're talking about." But I do!

I'm learning to stay healthy by taking care of my body. I drink lots of water, breathe fresh air every day, and enjoy sunshine whenever it's not raining.

Exercise helps my body stay healthy too. It makes the muscles in my arms and legs strong, especially when I play on the monkey bars.

And exercise makes me take deep breaths of God's fresh air. Then I get thirsty, so I drink cool, sweet water.

But Chris doesn't exercise much. That's the problem. He sits and watches television hour after hour. When I ask him to come play basketball with me, he says he'd rather play a game that doesn't include running or jumping. *Bor-ing!*

I asked Chris's mother if he was sick. She said no. That's when I told Chris that he needs to exercise. And that's when he told me I didn't know what I was talking about. But I do!

We all should exercise every day. It helps us stay healthy and strong. Television can't do that!

–Jon

5
MARCH

HOW I STAY HEALTHY . . .

I Eat Good Food

God said, "Look, I have given you all the plants that have grain for seeds. And I have given you all the trees whose fruits have seeds in them. They will be food for you." Genesis 1:29, ICB.

The other day while I was eating supper I said to my mom, "This food tastes great!"

"Thank you," she said with a smile. "That food is *good* for you, too."

"Is *all* food good for me?" I wanted to know.

"No," she said sadly. "Some food can make your body weak. You may even get sick. If you were to eat candy all the time, your body would not be able to stay healthy. So instead, I give you apples and oranges, spinach and green beans, brown breads and nuts. Then your body can stay healthy."

"Is that why Dad grows a garden every summer?" I asked. "So we can have healthy foods?"

"That's right," Mom said.

I looked at all the good stuff on my plate and smiled. I decided that from now on I'm going to be happy when Mom gives me an apple instead of a candy bar, and a nice *big* helping of green beans and just a *little* piece of cake. I want my body to stay healthy for a long, long time.

–Tara

HOW I STAY HEALTHY . . .

I Rest

6
MARCH

My sister Charity and I do something every day that helps us stay healthy. Here's a hint. It involves snoring.

Each afternoon at 2:00 Dad says, "Time to hit the hay!" That's his strange way of saying, "Time for your nap."

Some of our friends don't like taking naps. But we do. We run to our rooms, jump onto our beds, and snooze! Why? We want to stay healthy, and resting is a great way to do that.

When we sleep, we're giving our bodies a short vacation from working and playing hard. When we wake up, we feel terrific!

God wants everyone to be healthy—including grown-ups. That's why He made the Sabbath. On that day we're supposed to stop our work and play and give our bodies and our minds a vacation. We think about Jesus and listen to stories from the Bible. Then when Sabbath is over, we're ready for the other six days of the week.

There are many ways to rest. It can be sleeping, taking a nature walk, or sitting in the shade of a tree.

Do you want to be healthy? Then stop what you're doing, and *rest!*

–Andrew

Come to me, all of you who are tired and have heavy burdens. I will give you rest. Matthew 11:28, ICB.

7
MARCH

**To your goodness, add knowledge; and to your knowledge, add self-control.
2 Peter 1:5, 6, ICB.**

HOW I STAY HEALTHY . . .

I'm Careful

The other day Mom asked me if I wanted a glass of orange juice. I replied, "Will it help me stay healthy?"

"It's *very* good for you," she answered.

"Great. Then give me 10 glasses of orange juice," I told her. "I want to stay healthy forever."

Mom laughed out loud. Then she kissed me on the cheek and told me how happy she was that I wanted to stay healthy. "But," she added, "you have to be careful."

"What do you mean?"

"Your body needs good things, but in the *right amounts.* One glass of orange juice will help you. Drinking 10 glasses of orange juice might make you sick. Your body doesn't need so much all at once. The Bible calls this way of being careful *self-control.* Remember last summer when we went to the beach? You stayed out in the sun too long and got a sunburn. You see, sunshine is good for you. Too *much* sunshine at one time isn't."

"Oh," I said. "I have to be careful not to eat, drink, exercise, or rest *too much,* right?"

"Right," Mom said. "So how many glasses of orange juice do you want?"

"Just one." I laughed. "I'm being careful."

–Natalie

HOW I STAY HEALTHY . . .

I Trust in God

8
MARCH

And the Lord shall help them . . . and save them, because they trust in him. Psalm 37:40.

"You look worried," Mom said when she came into my room.

I nodded. "Peter told me his mom and dad don't live together anymore. Are you and Dad going to do that too?"

Mom smiled. "Daddy and I love each other very much. We love our family, we love the dog, and we love the goldfish. You don't have to worry."

"I don't like worrying," I sighed.

"Neither do I," Mom agreed. "Worrying can make you sick."

"Really?"

"Sure. Some people get so worried that they don't take care of themselves. They think only of their problems and forget that Jesus wants to help them. They forget to *trust* in Him."

I scratched my head. "How do you trust in Jesus?"

Mom sat down beside me. "First you believe He'll listen to whatever problem you have. Then no matter where you are or what you're doing, you ask Him to help you find the answer."

"I'm glad Jesus wants to help me when I'm worried," I said. "I feel better already."

"Good," Mom said, hugging me tightly. "Trusting in Jesus is a great way to chase away your worries and stay healthy."

–Hunter

9
MARCH

We love him, because he first loved us. 1 John 4:19.

I LOVE GOD AND GOD LOVES ME . . .

Showing My Love

I'm writing a book. Yes, me! I've always wanted to be an author.

My book is called *I Love God and God Loves Me.* Catchy, huh? It's about how Jesus watches over me and helps when I have problems.

My first chapter is called "Showing My Love." Before I started, I got to thinking, *How can I show Jesus how much I love Him?* Then it hit me. Write Him a poem!

So I sat down in my favorite chair, got a clean piece of paper, cleared my throat (that's what I do before I write), and carefully printed these words: *You made the mountains and the seas; You made the valleys and the trees. You spoke a word, and suddenly there was light for all to see. Each blade of grass, each bird and flower, was given life by Your power. I'm here to tell You, happily, "Thank You, Lord, for making me."*

Do you like it? I hope Jesus will want to read my book too.

Hey, I've got an idea. Why don't you write a book this month too? We'll do it together. Just get some paper and each day write something to God. I'll show you what I wrote to give you some ideas. It'll be fun!

–Sarah

Giving to God

"Ninety-eight, ninety-nine, one dollar."

"What're you doing?" Dad asked.

"I'm counting my tithe and offering money," I said. "When that offering plate comes by at church, I'm going to be ready."

"Good," Dad nodded. "What else are you going to give God this week?"

"What do you mean?"

Dad sat down beside me. "Returning tithes and giving offerings to our heavenly Father is very important. That money is used all around the world to tell other people about Jesus. But God wants us to use some of our *time* and our *talents* to help people right here in our own neighborhood."

"H'mm," I said. "I see what you mean. Mr. Adams always needs someone to help him clean his porch. And Mrs. Kuwalski told me just yesterday that she wishes someone would come and visit her. I could sweep leaves for Mr. Adams on Sunday and visit Mrs. Kuwalski on Tuesday. I could read her pages from my book."

"Good," Dad said. "Now you're sharing *all* you have."

That night I made a new page in my *I Love God and God Loves Me* book. It says, *I can give God some of my time and talent, too. After all, He gave Himself to me when He died on the cross.*

–Sarah

It is more blessed to give than to receive. Acts 20:35.

11
MARCH

There will be no more death or mourning or crying or pain, for the old order of things has passed away. Revelation 21:4, NIV.

I LOVE GOD AND GOD LOVES ME . . .

Good News

"Oh dear!" Mom said, adjusting her newspaper. "Why can't people live in peace with each other? This is filled with stories of wars and hatred. I wish Jesus would come back soon."

"I know," I sighed as I looked up from my homework. "This morning they showed pictures of a storm in Florida and a flood in China. People lost their houses. It was sad."

Mom shook her head. "There's so much bad news in this world. We need a little good news to cheer us up."

"I've got an idea," I said, jumping to my feet. "Let's write down some reasons that Jesus' coming back is good news."

As soon as I returned with my *I Love God and God Loves Me* book, Mom was ready. "When Jesus comes," she said, "there'll be no more wars. People will live together in peace."

"Good," I agreed as I wrote, *"NO WARS!"* "And rivers won't flood, and houses won't blow away. We'll all live in beautiful homes and be safe."

"And," Mom added, "we won't have to be sad anymore, because no one will get hurt or scared." She paused. "Wow. That *is* good news!"

At the bottom of the page I wrote, *Hurry and come back, Jesus. We're waiting for You.*

–Sarah

Saved by My Angel

I was scared. My sitter told me there had been a car accident and that my mom and dad had been hurt.

The next day I went to the hospital. Mom smiled and told me not to worry. Dad said his arm hurt. Soon they came home. I was so glad, I cried.

"Would you like to see the car?" Dad asked. "It will teach you something about Jesus."

We went to the place our car was being stored. The door was bent in, and the front was all smashed, just like a pop can when you stomp on it. "If we hadn't been wearing our seat belts, Mom and I would have been hurt much worse," Dad explained.

I looked at the bent and crushed car and thought about how sad I would be if that had happened.

"Jesus sent His angels to protect us," Dad said. "They helped us remember to put on our seat belts. I think we need to thank God every day for angels who are always nearby to remind us how to be safe."

That night I wrote in my book: *I will remember how angels protected my mom and dad.* Then I closed my eyes and thanked God for caring angels.

–Sarah

The angel of the Lord encamps around those who fear Him, and rescues them. Psalm 34:7, NASB.

13
MARCH

The Son of Man is going to come in his Father's glory with his angels. Matthew 16:27, NIV.

I LOVE GOD AND GOD LOVES ME . . .

Getting Ready for Jesus

Last Monday my grandmother came to visit me. I was so excited!

The day before, Mom asked, "Would you like to help me get the house all ready before your grandmother comes?"

"Sure," I said. "I want everything to be perfect for her."

Mom and I vacuumed the rug, dusted the furniture, cleaned the windows, and put clean sheets on her bed. I went out and picked some flowers to put in a vase on the dresser. Soon everything was ready.

When Grandmother arrived, she gave me a big hug. "Look at my beautiful room!" she said with a smile. "I especially like those pretty flowers. Thank you."

I grinned so hard my cheeks hurt. I love my grandmother. When I make her happy, it makes me happy too.

That night in my *I Love God and God Loves Me* book I wrote about my grandmother's visit and how hard we had worked to get her room ready. Then I remembered that Jesus is coming soon to take us all to heaven.

Mom says we have to get ready for Him, too, by keeping our bodies strong and healthy and our minds filled with good thoughts. So I wrote, *I'm going to be ready when Jesus comes back.* That will be the happiest day ever!

–Sarah

Being Kind to Jesus

"I don't like her," I said. "She makes fun of me and tells everyone I look like a weasel."

"A weasel?" Dad gasped. "You don't look like a weasel. A hound dog, maybe—"

"Dad!" I giggled, then tried to look serious. "She tries to get me into trouble with my teacher, and last week she hit me with a pickle."

He frowned. "Sweet or dill?"

"Dad!" I groaned, trying not to smile. "I don't want to invite Martha to my party. She hates me, and I don't like her, either."

"But don't you want Jesus to enjoy your birthday too?" Dad asked. "The Bible says that when we're kind to others, even people we don't like, we're being kind to Jesus. We're all God's family. He wants us to love and care for each other."

I wanted to be kind to Jesus, because He died for me on the cross. If that meant inviting Martha to my party . . . well, I guess that's what I needed to do.

"OK." I sighed. "Martha can come. But I'm not going to give her any pickles!"

That night I wrote in my book, *When I'm kind to Martha, I'm kind to Jesus.* Then I asked God to help me remember that during my party.

–Sarah

Love your enemies and pray for those who persecute you. Matthew 5:44, NIV.

15 MARCH

Whenever you eat this bread and drink this cup, you proclaim the Lord's death until he comes. 1 Corinthians 11:26, NIV.

I LOVE GOD AND GOD LOVES ME . . .

Jesus' Body

Is that real blood?" I whispered to my uncle Sid.

"Where?" he gasped. "Did someone get hurt?"

"No. There, in your glass. The preacher said that the grape juice was Jesus' blood and that the bread was His body."

"Oh," Uncle Sid said. Then he leaned down and whispered in my ear, "It's not real blood. It's supposed to remind us that Jesus died on the cross. He bled and died so we could live forever with Him in heaven."

"So," I said thoughtfully, "when they pass out those little glasses of juice and pieces of bread, we're supposed to remember what happened?"

"That's right. The preacher said Jesus had a last meal with His disciples. They drank juice and ate bread. Today we have this very small meal to remind us of that night long ago."

I looked at the bread and juice. Then I remembered the story of the Lord's Supper. How sad Jesus must have been to know that this was the last meal He would enjoy with His friends.

That night I made another page in my *I Love God and God Loves Me* book. In careful letters I wrote, *Jesus loves me so much that He died for me. The juice and the bread help me to remember that.*

–Sarah

Prayer Power

16
MARCH

I can do everything through him who gives me strength. Philippians 4:13, NIV.

"You're killing the grass!" I looked down. My right foot *was* stepping on the green grass of my neighbor's yard, but only a little.

"You children should watch where you're going," old Mr. Peterson shouted from his porch. "Next thing I know, you'll be breaking my windows and stomping my roses into the ground. So, *go away!*"

My friend Alicia and I turned and ran as fast as we could.

"Sounds like he needs a little love," Dad said that night when I told him what had happened. "Why don't you take him a nice gift—some peaches from our tree, maybe?"

"But he's mean," I moaned.

"Just ask Jesus to give you the power to do something nice, even though it's not easy."

Dad was right. Jesus helped people who weren't exactly friendly to Him. So I asked God for *lots* of power to make me willing to visit my grumpy neighbor.

The next day Mom and I took Mr. Peterson a basket of peaches. You should have seen his face. He smiled and smiled.

I wrote in my book, *Prayer gives me the power to live as Jesus wants me to live.* Now when I walk by Mr. Peterson's house, he doesn't yell. He waves. It's amazing what a little "power" can do.

–Sarah

17
MARCH

Each of you must put off falsehood and speak truthfully to [his or her] neighbor. Ephesians 4:25, NIV.

I LOVE GOD AND GOD LOVES ME . . .

Forgiveness

Last week I did something dumb. I told a lie.

My cousin asked me if I'd ever climbed a really tall tree. I didn't want him to think I was scared, so I said, "Sure. Lots of times."

"Did you make it all the way to the top?" he wanted to know.

"Of course," I lied again.

He looked at me for a moment. "I guess you're OK."

Great. My cousin thought I was OK because I did something that I really didn't do.

When we went to the park that afternoon, he pointed at a big oak by the swings. "Climb that one," he said.

"Oh . . . I *could,*" I lied for the third time, "but . . . I don't want to get my clothes dirty."

That night I couldn't sleep. Jesus wouldn't ever tell a lie, and I had told three in one day! So I got up and wrote my cousin a letter. I said I was sorry for not telling the truth. The tallest thing I'd ever climbed was a stepladder, and Dad had to help me down from that.

Then I asked God to forgive me. After that, I slept all night.

The newest chapter in my book says, *Jesus is always happy to forgive me.* And that's the truth!

–Sarah

I LOVE GOD AND GOD LOVES ME . . .

Making the Right Choice

18
MARCH

Let us walk honestly. Romans 13:13.

"That will be $2.86," the salesperson said.

I counted out the money with a big smile on my face. That cool red-and-black umbrella I'd always wanted was mine!

That night Dad admired my purchase. "Nice," he said, glancing at the price on the box. "Not bad for $4."

"What? I paid only $2.86."

"Was it on sale?"

"No." I ran to the recycling bin to find the store receipt. "See? It says $2.86."

Dad studied the paper. "The salesperson made a mistake," he said. "This receipt is for a pen-and-pencil set, not an umbrella. She must have typed in the wrong numbers." He glanced at me. "Looks like you have a choice to make."

The store's staff didn't know they'd made a mistake. It was *their* fault. They sold me a $4 umbrella for $2.86. But then I thought, *What would Jesus do? The store will lose money if I don't make it right.* "I'll go see the salesperson tomorrow and pay what I owe," I said. "That's what Jesus would do."

That night I wrote in my book, *I choose Jesus'* way. Tomorrow, after I get back from the store, I hope it rains and rains!

—Sarah

19 MARCH

For God so loved the world that he gave his one and only Son. John 3:16, NIV.

I LOVE GOD AND GOD LOVES ME . . .

Nails in Jesus' Hands

The other day I watched Dad make a new deck chair. He sawed, hammered, sanded, and painted. Then we stood back and looked at his work.

"What do you think?" he asked.

"Mom's going to love it," I encouraged.

Dad smiled. "Will you help me put my tools away?"

We hung up his hammer and screwdriver, put the cut pieces of wood in the woodbin, and swept the workshop clean.

Then I picked up a handful of nails and was about to return them to the plastic box on the shelf when I stopped. I looked at the long, sharp nails and suddenly thought of Jesus.

Once, angry people hammered nails like these, not into a new deck chair, but into Jesus' hands and feet. It made me sad to think about how much pain Jesus felt when He died to save me. If He were here, I'd do what my mom does when I get hurt. I'd kiss His hands and feet so they could get well again.

In my book, I wrote a new chapter called "Nails." I told Jesus how sorry I am that He was hurt. Then I wrote, *Jesus loves me so much He died to save me.* When I see the nails in my dad's workshop, I remember.

–Sarah

I LOVE GOD AND GOD LOVES ME . . .

In the Dark Cave

20
MARCH

The angel said . . . "He is not here; he has risen, just as he said." Matthew 28:5, 6, NIV.

Hello?" I called.

"Hello . . . hello . . . hello," came the distant reply.

"Did you hear that?" I asked my friend Dusty.

"Yeah. It sounds like there are a bunch of you hiding in this cave."

We walked around looking at the stone walls with the drip . . . drip . . . dripping waterfalls. It was fun exploring the cave with our parents. The guide said this particular underground room was bigger than a football field. Who'd want to play football in a deep, wet cave?

Then our guide turned the lights off. Wow! It was *totally* dark. I couldn't see Dusty, my parents, or even my own hand in front of my face. I began to get a little scared.

Then my dad said, "Sorta reminds me of a tomb."

Oh, that helped a lot! But he continued, "When Jesus died, they put Him in a dark tomb and rolled a stone in front of it. Then He rose again, and the darkness went away."

I'm glad the angels pushed away the stone. I'm glad Jesus is going to come again and take us to heaven, because in heaven there will be lots and lots of light. No one will ever have to be put in a tomb again.

In my book I wrote, *Jesus took the darkness away.* Then I added, *Thank You.*

–Sarah

21
MARCH

I will never break my covenant with you. Judges 2:1.

I LOVE GOD AND GOD LOVES ME . . .

Keeping Promises

"What are you doing?" I asked sleepily.

Dad was sitting at the dining-room table with papers spread all around. The cuckoo clock on the wall announced it was midnight.

He looked over at me and smiled. "I'm working on some important papers for my boss," he said with a yawn. "I promised I'd have them ready by morning."

"Can't you get them done later?" I said, stumbling to the sink for a glass of water.

"No. When you make a promise, you keep it even if you have to lose a little sleep. Jesus made a promise to save us from sin. He had to die to keep His word. That's how important a promise is."

I sat on the steps for a while watching my dad work. Before I went back to bed, I wrote the last chapter in my book. Carefully I printed: *Jesus keeps His promises. And so will I.*

Tomorrow I'm going to put all the pages together and color the cover so it's pretty. Then, any time I feel that Jesus has forgotten about me and my problems, the stories will remind me that He is always close, ready to help me. What a wonderful Friend!

I hope your book will remind you, too.

–Sarah

By Making Sabbath Special

22
MARCH

The seventh day is the sabbath of the Lord thy God. Exodus 20:10.

"It doesn't matter what day you go to church," my friend said, "as long as you remember to worship God once a week."

That didn't sound quite right to me. Then I remembered what I had learned in Sabbath school recently.

"Do you have a calendar?" I asked.

My friend hurried away and soon returned with a pretty calendar from the wall. I cleared my throat and smiled, just as Mrs. Williams does in my primary class. "When the children of Israel were in the desert, God sent them manna for six days so they would have something to eat." I pointed at the numbers on the calendar. "The Bible says manna fell on Sunday through Friday. On Friday twice as much covered the ground."

"Why?" my friend asked.

"Because the next day was the Sabbath, and God didn't want everyone out roaming around looking for food. He wanted them to pray, sing, and do other worship stuff. Sabbath was supposed to be special, and it was supposed to be the *seventh day.*"

My friend looked at the calendar for a long moment. Then she pointed. "Now I understand. *That* day is the Sabbath, right?"

Do you know which day she was pointing at?

–David

23
MARCH

Each helps the other.
Isaiah 41:6, NIV.

I SHARE GOD'S LOVE . . .

By Educating My Brother

"Let me do it. Let me do it," my little brother Andrew called.

"Wait," I said. "You don't know how."

"Yes, I do," he insisted. "You put the glass on the plate and then stick the spoon over there."

I giggled. If I let Andrew set the table, Mom wouldn't have room for the food!

Since I want to share God's love, I figured I'd be helpful and educate my little brother at the same time. "Look, Andrew," I said. "Put the plate down first. Then put the silverware on each side and the glass right here, like this. See?"

Andrew nodded slowly. "How about the napkin?" he asked.

"That goes above the plate."

My brother sniffed a few times, then smiled. "Let me try."

Andrew followed my suggestions and put the rest of the plates, silverware, glasses, and napkins in the right spots, sorta.

"Not bad," I encouraged, making a few adjustments. "Now Mom has lots of room for the food. You did great!"

Andrew grinned, showing all his missing teeth. "Thanks," he said. "I like learning how to do it right. You're a good teacher." Then he ran off to play in his room.

His room! What do you think I should teach Andrew next?

—Trisha

I SHARE GOD'S LOVE . . .

By Keeping Lies From Escaping

24 MARCH

Keep thee far from a false matter. Exodus 23:7.

"Just tell Miss Arlana you lost your homework or that your dog ate it."

"I don't have a dog."

"Then tell her your sister flushed it down the toilet by mistake."

I rolled my eyes. "What were my math papers doing in the bathroom?"

Lora giggled. "How am I supposed to know? It was your homework, not mine!"

The truth was, I simply forgot to do the assignment. Miss Arlana had told us to complete problems 10 through 30 on page 88, and I had watched the basketball game instead. My favorite team lost by two points. That was depressing enough.

Suddenly I put my hands over my mouth. "What are you doing?" Lora asked.

I loosened my fingers. "I'm obeying one of God's rules."

"He wants you to put your hands over your mouth?"

"No. He wants me to always tell the truth. I'm keeping lies from escaping. See?"

Just then Miss Arlana walked by. She looked at me and smiled. I smiled back from behind my hands.

I'm going to tell the teacher the truth about my homework. Lying would just make me feel worse. And after that basketball game, I don't need any more grief. But what should I tell Lora?

–Jason

25
MARCH

You shall have no other gods before me. Exodus 20:3, NIV.

I SHARE GOD'S LOVE . . .

By Putting Him First

"Our wood box is getting empty," Mom called just as I was heading out the front door.

"I'm going to Shelley's house," I said. "She's got a new video game."

"Remember, Dad's sick with the flu and can't help," Mom continued. "And I've got to send some e-mail messages. But," she paused, "it's your choice. Just keep in mind what we studied in our Sabbath school lesson."

Each evening we had been reading about how Moses chose to follow and obey God even though others didn't. He put God first. I want to share God's love with others by being helpful and doing my duties gladly. I want to put Him first over everything else too.

"OK," I sighed, walking slowly to the closet for my work coat and gloves. "I'll get the wood."

Then I heard Dad cough. It sounded like it hurt.

Suddenly I forgot all about Shelley's new video game. I forgot how cold it was and how heavy those wood pieces were. I was going to help my dad, even though I'd rather play spaceships with Shelley. I was putting God's work first.

I got the wheelbarrow and began loading in the logs.

How do you think my choice made Dad feel?

–Jon

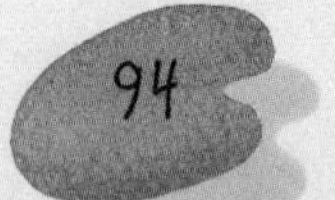

I SHARE GOD'S LOVE . . .

By Showing Respect for His House

26
MARCH

Every skilled person to whom the Lord has given skill and ability to know how to carry out all the work of constructing the sanctuary are to do the work. Exodus 36:1, NIV.

"Hammer and nails?" *Check.*

"Wood glue?" *Check.*

"Saw, drill, and screwdriver?" *Check, check, check.*

"OK," Dad said. "Let's go to church!"

What's going on? Well, it began when Mr. MacKenzie kicked the Communion table. He didn't mean to. He's like 900 years old and can't see very well. *Crack!* The leg fell off—the table, not Mr. MacKenzie. Lucky for us, the only other thing that broke was the pot holding the big green plant. The table tipped right over on top of it. Then Mr. MacKenzie kicked the broken pot. It was an accident.

So now it's Monday night, and we're heading to church to fix the damage. After all, this is God's house, and we don't want our Communion table leaning over to one side.

"Fixing up the church shows our heavenly Father how much we respect His house of worship," Dad announced as we drove through town. "Just as the children of Israel kept their desert sanctuary in top-notch condition, we're going to care for *our* beautiful church."

Guess who showed up to help fix the table? That's right. Old Mr. MacKenzie. He was a big help, too. He knows a lot about carpentry and taught Dad and me some things.

How did it make him feel to help fix the table?

—Andrew

27
MARCH

Tell . . . how much the Lord has done for you. Mark 5:19, NIV.

I SHARE GOD'S LOVE . . .

By Telling a Friend

"Wow," Marcela gasped. "That must have been exciting."

"It was," I nodded. "Especially the part when he went under the water. But he wasn't afraid."

I was telling Marcela about when my older brother was baptized. She doesn't go to our church, and her minister doesn't use a big pool of water when he baptizes people.

"Why do they do that?" she asked.

"Because it reminds us about when Jesus was baptized. Our pastor said John the Baptist lowered Jesus into the Jordan River, and when He came out of the water, a beautiful white dove flew down and fluttered right above His head, and a voice said, 'This is My Son. He pleases Me.' "

"Wow!" Marcela said again. "Whenever someone is baptized in your church, you think about that story?"

"Every time."

I told Marcela that many things at church remind me of Jesus. The singing, praying, preaching, and even shaking hands with the visitors show me how much Jesus enjoyed attending His own church and how He likes it when we worship Him each Sabbath.

"I'm going to start looking for ways to remember Jesus at my church," Marcela said.

What can I do so my friend will think of Jesus when we're *not* at church?

—Tara

I SHARE GOD'S LOVE . . .

By Encouraging My Pastor

28
MARCH

Encourage one another daily. Hebrews 3:13, NIV.

Dear Pastor Beryl. I like the story you told about the boy who got lost in Yellowstone Park and had to sleep under a bush. At the end, when you said that boy was you, I was surprised.

I'm writing a letter to my pastor.

I got lost once too. We weren't in Yellowstone. We were at Kmart.

My pastor likes to get letters from his church members.

Did you see my friend sitting beside me? His name is Chander. That means "moon" in India, where he's from. He liked your story too. Chander says he wants to come back next Sabbath.

Pastor Beryl said a happy note from one of his members is like getting a Christmas present.

Your story made me think about how sometimes I feel afraid. Then I remember God is watching over me, and I shouldn't be scared unless the house is on fire (then I should call 911).

Last month Pastor Beryl had a baby. Well, his wife had a baby, and he almost fainted.

How's your new son? When are you going to bring him to Sabbath school? He can sit with me. Well, I've got to stop now because I can't think of anything else to say.

Do you think Pastor Beryl will like my letter?

–Natalie

29
MARCH

The Lord is my helper; I will not be afraid. Hebrews 13:6, NIV.

I SHARE GOD'S LOVE . . .

By Being Courageous

"Why?"

"Because . . . I'm scared."

Dad lifted his hands. "You've been in the shed before. There's nothing scary out there."

"What if a big dog is hiding behind the lawn tractor," I said, "or hornets begin chasing me, or a snake bites me on the toe, or an escaped prisoner jumps out at me?"

Dad thought for a moment. "Didn't you say you wanted to be like Caleb and Joshua in the Bible?"

"Yes."

"Well, they were told to go to a strange land. But they were smart. They trusted God and kept out of trouble by being careful. That's courage, you know. Besides," Dad continued, "I keep the shed locked and check it often to make sure no critters live in it. And there have been no reports of escaped bad guys on the news lately. Remember, knowledge, combined with God's guidance, can keep you from danger. So how about getting me that can of oil?"

I went to the shed. Sure enough, nothing barked, chased, struck, or grabbed me. I learned that even when Dad isn't there, a shed's just a place where tools and oilcans live. With knowledge like that and God's promises on my mind, I'll always be careful, but I won't be afraid anymore.

Do you have a shed in your yard?

—Hunter

I SHARE GOD'S LOVE . . .

By Helping My Pastor

30
MARCH

Whatever you do, work at it with all your heart. Colossians 3:23, NIV.

Our pastor works hard. He's always visiting sick people in the hospital, giving Bible studies, figuring out his next sermon, attending meetings, or mowing the church lawn. I get tired just thinking about it. So I decided to help.

"You want to visit sick people at the hospital?" Mom asked.

"No. I'm too young."

"You want to preach or give Bible studies?"

"Hardly!" I giggled. "You know how scared I get talking to grown-ups."

"We *are* a frightening bunch," Mom admitted.

"I want to help our pastor by decorating the lobby of the church," I announced.

"What do you have in mind?"

I whispered my idea in her ear, because it was going to be a surprise. "That's great," Mom said with a smile.

If you ever visit my town and attend my church, you'll notice something unusual in the lobby. Each week when you get your bulletin from the lady by the door, you'll see a big poster with a picture painted on it. Below the picture you'll find that week's memory verse written in big black letters. I made the poster. The pastor said I'm a regular Rembrandt.

What can you do to help your hardworking pastor?

–Trisha

31
MARCH

I have hidden your word in my heart. Psalm 119:11, NIV.

I SHARE GOD'S LOVE . . .

By Reciting Bible Verses

We've been very busy sharing God's love with others. But there's one more way to share that anyone can do anytime, anyplace.

If you ever see someone who looks sad or lonely or afraid, recite a Bible verse for them—one that tells how much Jesus loves them. Why not learn one or two beautiful verses so you'll be ready? Here are a few of our favorites:

- *"God is our protection and our strength. He always helps in times of trouble" (Psalm 46:1, ICB).*
- *"Be strong and brave and wait for the Lord's help" (Psalm 27:14, ICB).*
- *"He who believes has eternal life" (John 6:47, ICB).*
- *"The Lord himself will come down from heaven. . . . And those who have died and were in Christ will rise first. . . . And we will be with the Lord forever" (1 Thessalonians 4:16, 17, ICB).*
- *"They will call to me, and I will answer them" (Psalm 91:15, ICB).*
- *"If any of you needs wisdom, you should ask God for it. God is generous" (James 1:5, ICB).*

Now you're ready to share! Keep your eyes open for those who need to know Jesus better. It may be a brother or sister, or maybe a neighbor or friend. Just say, "Here's a Bible verse that may make you feel better." Have fun!

–Uncle Charles

WHEN I GROW UP . . .

Flower Shop

1 APRIL

My sister and I have a secret. Want to know what it is? When we grow up, we're going to have our very own flower shop. We both *love* flowers. In the park near our apartment we find red flowers, pink flowers, yellow and blue flowers, even purple flowers. Each is beautiful and smells sweet. We're glad when Dad takes us to see them.

Even though we're sisters, we aren't the same. One of us likes red flowers the best while the other prefers yellow. But we still love each other even though we're different.

In our flower shop we'll each do different things, too. One of us will *grow* the plants. That's hard work. Flowers need special care. They have to be watered, protected from bad bugs, and kept warm.

The other one will pick the blossoms and arrange them in a pretty vase. Then she'll show them to lots of people. When they see how beautiful they are and how sweet they smell, they'll buy them for sure.

We'll tell our customers that God made all the flowers in our shop. And the reason He made them was so we'd know He loves us. I think those who come to our flower shop will be happy to learn how much God loves them, don't you?

–Tara

How great is the love the Father has lavished on us, that we should be called children of God!
1 John 3:1, NIV.

2
APRIL

WHEN I GROW UP . . .

Parents

Parents are the pride of their children. Proverbs 17:6, NIV.

The other day my friend Ricky and I were playing with my favorite doll Elizabeth.

She was crying, so I held her close and rocked her back and forth in my arms.

"Don't cry, Elizabeth," I said. "I'll take good care of you."

We know Elizabeth isn't a *real* baby, but we like to pretend she is. Ricky makes sure she has food to eat. I put a warm sweater on her when it's cold and always kiss her good night.

Sometimes Elizabeth doesn't feel good, so I stop whatever I'm doing and hold her close. I think this makes her feel better.

Someday Ricky is going to get married, and so am I. I'm going to have a real baby of my own to care for. Ricky says he is going to have three! We'll make sure our children live in happy homes.

We'll help them understand how to be kind and forgiving. And we'll tell them every day that Jesus loves them. That's what parents do.

Parents have an important job. They have to work hard to make sure their children are safe and happy. Boys and girls depend on them for *everything*.

If I have a daughter, I think I'll name her Elizabeth. Why do you think I want to do that?

–*Natalie*

WHEN I GROW UP . . .

Cook

3

APRIL

Jacob gave Esau some bread and some lentil stew. Genesis 25:34, NIV.

Yesterday my friend came to visit me. At suppertime I said, "Would you like to see a surprise?"

We went to the refrigerator, and I took out the milk, lettuce, mayonnaise, and a plate of sliced tomatoes and avocados. Then I got a loaf of whole-wheat bread from the bread box.

"What are you doing?" my friend asked.

"My mom's busy, so I'm fixing us supper," I said.

I put four pieces of bread on a plate and spread a smooth, thin layer of mayonnaise over them. Next I put on tomato and avocado slices, tore off some fresh lettuce, and put another piece of bread on the top.

"You made sandwiches!" my friend gasped. "And you didn't make a big mess at the same time."

I slowly poured milk into two tall glasses. "A cook is very careful and tries to make food look and taste good," I told him. "It's got to be healthy, too, because Jesus wants us to take good care of our bodies. See, I'm using whole-wheat bread and fresh milk. No candy or sodas in *my* kitchen."

My friend nodded. "I'll eat with you anytime!"

Being a careful, thoughtful cook helps people enjoy eating and stay healthy. That's why I want to be a cook when I grow up.

–David

4

APRIL

Keep your spiritual fervor, serving the Lord. Romans 12:11, NIV.

WHEN I GROW UP . . .

Computer Programmer

The other day I visited my mom's office. She showed me her desk, her plants, and her pencil sharpener. Then she showed me her new computer. I was amazed!

She said a computer can help people do all kinds of things like write letters, find information, figure out how much money it costs to do something, and even send an instant message to a friend in a faraway country. Cool!

I asked Mom how the computer knows what to do when you type on it. She said men and women called computer programmers make rules for the computer to follow. Without those rules, it would just sit there and do nothing.

I began to think. Maybe I could learn to make computers help people do their business better. Maybe I could program a computer to help a writer write an exciting story or show a teacher how to explain interesting facts about animals. Or maybe I could even help the preacher at my church study the Bible for his sermons.

"Mom," I said, "I'm going to be a computer programmer when I grow up so I can help people work better."

"Great idea," she said with a smile. "God wants us to be helpful in everything we do."

–Trisha

WHEN I GROW UP . . .

Farmer

5
APRIL

May the Lord bless his land . . . with the best gifts of the earth and its fullness. Deuteronomy 33:13-16, NIV.

Hi. We're brother and sister, and live on a large farm in Maryland. Our dad has worked this land all his life. Grandpa grew up here too.

Living on a farm is hard work. Each day you have to milk the cows, weed the vegetable garden, make sure there are no broken wires in the fences, keep the barnyard clean, feed the chickens, cut the grass, water the flowers, and do a bunch of little jobs around the house.

Some kids might not like living on a farm, but we love it! We get up even before the sun rises to help Dad in the barn. By the end of the day we're very tired and ready to flop onto our comfy beds.

Dad says the best thing about living on a farm is being close to God's nature. It's true. We watch the crops grow tall in the sunshine and listen to the birds singing in the branches high above our heads. At night the stars shine brightly in the sky. It's just like God lives on the farm with us!

When we grow up, we're going to be farmers, just like Dad and Grandpa.

But right now we have to go. It's time to milk the cows.

–Kevin and Pam

6
APRIL

If anyone serves, [he or she] should do it with the strength God provides, so that in all things God may be praised through Jesus Christ.
1 Peter 4:11, NIV.

WHEN I GROW UP . . .

Mechanic

Cla-tick, cla-tick, shi-pop, shi-pop, thump, thump thump, psssssssss, clank!

When my mom's car made sounds like that, she had to call a tow truck to come get us.

At the garage a man dressed in dirty clothes looked at the engine. He twisted this, tapped that, and pulled on something else. Then he put a shiny round thing over on one side of the engine and a rubber tube on the other. He also poured green stuff down a pipe.

When he finished, he asked my mom to start the car. All the clanking, thumping, and shi-popping was gone! The engine went *"Rorrrrr, rorrrrr."* Mom smiled. The man in the dirty clothes smiled. And I smiled too, because I'd decided something.

When I grow up I want to be an auto mechanic—you know, someone who works on engines. Then I can help people when their car makes funny noises. I can help them get home safe and sound. People need their cars to get them to work, have fun on vacations, or go to the grocery store. I know Jesus would be happy for me to fix engines, because He likes it when we help people. Besides, where else can you get real dirty and still make your mom smile?

–Sarah

WHEN I GROW UP . . .

Truck Driver

7

APRIL

Whenever I go on a trip, I like to watch the big trucks driving down the highway. Sometimes they honk their horns for me. *Honk, honk.* Sometimes the drivers just wave. It's fun!

Those big rigs carry tons of stuff from city to city like shoes, apples, computers, groceries, clothes, toys, and even toothpicks. I've seen trucks carrying cars! They must be very strong to handle such heavy weights.

When a truck goes up a steep hill, it makes a roaring sound. *Rhumm, rhumm!* I love to listen to the truck's engine when it's working hard. *Rhumm, rhumm!*

As I go from place to place with my mom and dad, I look out the window and watch the farms and forests pass by. I see cows and tractors, tall buildings, and blue lakes. There's always something to see as we travel down the road.

When I grow up, I'm going to be a truck driver and drive a big, strong rig from city to city. When I meet other truck drivers, I'll tell them about Jesus and how He's coming back again soon. Then they can think about heaven as they drive down the road. If I see a little boy like me, I'll be sure to honk my horn.

Hooooonk!

–Jason

**Each one should use whatever gift he has received to serve others.
1 Peter 4:10, NIV.**

8
APRIL

The gospel must first be published among all nations. Mark 13:10.

WHEN I GROW UP . . .

Printer

I'm learning how to read, and it's fun! My teacher has us stand up in class and read from our textbook. When I find a hard word, I stop and sound it out one letter at a time. Then when I see it again, I'm ready!

Some of my books have neat pictures in them. I like to look at the pictures and then read what they mean.

Some of the books and magazines at school have stories about animals, interesting kids, and mysterious places to visit.

My favorite book is about beavers. When I read that story, I pretend I'm watching the beaver family swim around on their pond, cut down trees, and escape wolves.

For family worship Mom and Dad let me read from the Bible. We're learning about Jesus and how He helped people who were hungry or sick. Exciting stuff!

When I grow up, I'm going to be a printer. That's someone who runs the big presses that print words and pictures in books. I'll make sure the ink is flowing smoothly and that there is just the right amount of red, green, and blue on each page. I'll make books that teach others about Jesus' love. Maybe you'll read one of the books I've printed!

–Jon

WHEN I GROW UP . . .

Photographer

9
APRIL

I think a camera is an amazing thing. It helps me remember how something looked even when it's gone.

My mom takes dozens of pictures with her camera every day. She works for a newspaper and has to take photographs of everything that happens in our city.

Last week she snapped a picture of my friend Carl and me playing soccer in the park. Now when I want to remember the fun we had, I just look at the picture. There we are, laughing and running. I enjoy remembering when I look at pictures.

Mom says God made a whole world of things to photograph . . . like flowers. I want to have a bunch of flower pictures hanging on the wall behind my bed. When I look at them, I'll remember how much Jesus loves me.

Mom let me take some pictures with her camera. I got a great shot of my cat, the tree outside my window, my foot, our next-door neighbor's garage, an old oilcan, and Mom. She was brushing her teeth!

When I grow up I'm going to be a photographer and snap lots of pictures so others can enjoy the beautiful things Jesus has made.

–Natalie

When I consider your heavens, the work of your fingers, the moon and the stars, . . . what is man that you are mindful of him?
Psalm 8:3, 4, NIV.

10
APRIL

WHEN I GROW UP . . .

Veterinarian

God created the great creatures of the sea and every living and moving thing. Genesis 1:21, NIV.

I *love* animals. Big ones, little ones, fat ones, skinny ones—it doesn't matter. I especially love animals that make lots of noise.

I enjoy taking care of animals too. I make sure my dog Sosa has plenty of food to eat and fresh water to drink. When he doesn't feel good and can't play with me in the backyard, I sit and pet him gently, telling him to get well soon. Then I let him sleep.

I think God is happy when we love the animals He created.

When I find an animal that needs special attention, I bring it home and do my best to make it feel better. I've helped a bird with a hurt wing, a cat with a cut on its tail, a goldfish, a squirrel that fell out of a tree, and a brown dog that was cold and hungry.

The bird got well and flew away, the cat sat in my lap and purred, the goldfish swam around and around in the fish tank, the squirrel nibbled a hole in my wall, and the big dog licked me right on the face.

When I grow up, I'm going to be a veterinarian so that I can take care of God's wonderful creatures and make them well and happy again.

–Samantha

WHEN I GROW UP . . .

Preacher

I like to help people. Whenever I see somebody who is sad, I try to figure out how to help him or her be happy.

The pastor at my church says I'm a very good assistant. I always make sure the hymnals are in their racks and there is no paper on the floor.

I enjoy hearing stories from the Bible. Sometimes after school I tell my little sister a story so she'll be quiet. She listens to me and smiles. Then she goes to sleep.

When I pray, I pray for *everybody*. I pray for my sitter Teresa, Mr. Roberts at the grocery store, my friend Barry, my mom, my dad, my sister, Uncle Mike, my grandmother, even our dog Elka. My dad says the whole world gets blessed when I pray.

I don't like it when people get mad at each other. God says we're supposed to love everyone. If people would love instead of hate, the world would be a better and much safer place. I want to tell everyone that.

When I grow up I'm going to be a preacher. Then I'll tell my friends and neighbors that God loves them and that He can help them with whatever problem they have. Oh yes, I'll pray for them too!

–Andrew

I am ready to preach the gospel to you. Romans 1:15.

12
APRIL

Praise the Lord, . . . who forgives all your sins and heals all your diseases. Psalm 103:2, 3, NIV.

WHEN I GROW UP . . .

Doctor or Nurse

Last year, when I was little, I went to the hospital. The doctor looked at my eyes and ears, listened to my heart, and thumped my knee with a soft hammer. While she was working, there were people helping her. They wrote information on a piece of paper and got tools for the doctor to use. They're called nurses.

Now I like to pretend that I'm helping someone get well. I make believe that my doll is sick. I listen to her heartbeat, take her temperature with a thermometer, then write things down on a piece of paper.

My mom pretends that she's a doctor, and we try to figure out how to make my doll well. What we did must have worked. A week ago my doll had a bad cold. She's much better now.

Yesterday my little brother hurt his toe. I sent him right to bed and put two bandages on his foot. He said they didn't help, but I know they did.

I think God wants me to take care of people when they're sick. He helped a lot of people get well when He was here on earth!

That's the reason I'm going to be a doctor or a nurse when I grow up.

–Latisha

WHEN I GROW UP . . .

Musician

13 APRIL

**I will sing and make music to the Lord.
Psalm 27:6, NIV.**

I *love* music. At church we have a huge organ with rows and rows of pipes high overhead. I like to listen to it while we're singing songs and taking up the offering! I especially enjoy it when the organist plays *loud*. It sounds like many, many instruments making music all at the same time.

My older brother can play the trumpet and my cousin, who lives in Miami, knows how to make beautiful music with a violin.

Not long ago we went to a band concert. Wow! There were tons of instruments there—flutes, trombones, bassoons, drums, big shiny cymbals, and a whole bunch of trumpets. They played fast songs, slow songs, and songs that made you want to jump up and march around the room. Totally cool!

But my *favorite* music is when people sing or play songs about God. I think He enjoys hearing them too. It makes me feel like I'm talking to God when I sing a song about Him.

Next year I'm going to start taking piano lessons. I can hardly wait, because when I grow up, I'm going to be a musician. Come listen. I'll be playing *loud!*

–Melissa

14
APRIL

Do you see a man skilled in his work? He will stand before kings. Proverbs 22:29, NASB.

WHEN I GROW UP . . .

Businessperson

I live in a large, busy city. Each day I see thousands of people working hard, making and selling things like clothes, cars, food, and even toys. Some talk on the phone and help customers figure out how to do something while others drive trucks from place to place, delivering what their company made.

These people work in tall buildings, big noisy factories, or even their homes. This is called *business,* and I love it.

Sometimes businesspeople work at computers, typing in letters and numbers, making their company run better.

Others travel to distant cities, finding places to make or sell their products. They ride on airplanes or drive their cars many, many miles.

Last summer I started a business. Yup. I became president of my own company. Whenever I earned money raking leaves or walking dogs, I carefully counted every penny. First my dad helped me figure out how much to return to God as tithe, because God is my business partner. Then I bought a new wheelbarrow, and the rest of my hard-earned money I put in the bank. At the end of the season I had earned enough to buy a really cool skateboard!

Now I want to learn how to run a bigger company, because when I grow up, I'm going to be a businessperson!

–Hunter

WHEN I GROW UP . . .

Construction Worker

15
APRIL

Each one should be careful how he builds.
1 Corinthians 3:10, NIV.

I like to build things, which is good, because my little brother Matthew likes to knock things down.

One of my favorite toys is my box of wooden blocks. I pretend that I'm making a tall office building or a new shopping mall right in my bedroom.

When I build something, I have to think about how to make it strong so it won't fall down. Not only do I want my pretend shoppers to feel safe in my new shopping mall, I want to know that I've done the very best I can.

It's important for me to build buildings I can be proud of. That's why I take my time and do it right, even if I have to build it again.

Sometimes my dad looks at what I'm building and says, "Hey, I'd like to live in that house. I can see you're being careful, making sure it's strong and safe." My teacher says Jesus wants us to do our very best in everything we do.

When I grow up, I'm going to be a construction worker and build lots of buildings, maybe even a house for my dad. If I build a house for Matthew, I'll make it *extra* strong.

–Bethany

16
APRIL

There is the sea, vast and spacious, teeming with creatures beyond number—living things both large and small. Psalm 104:25, NIV.

WHEN I GROW UP . . .

Biologist

I love to learn about animals and flowers. When I go for a walk with my mom, she tells me about nature and about God. She says He created everything in the whole world. I think He did a pretty good job.

Sometimes I wonder what makes it rain and how birds can fly so high. Yesterday I sat and watched a bug climb a blade of grass. Yes, I think even bugs are beautiful.

In my room I have a lot of books about nature. Before I go to sleep at night, I look at them, enjoying the pictures of colorful rocks, mountain lakes, strange creatures from faraway countries, and tiny animals that you have to look at under a microscope. I want to learn their names and try to figure out why God made them.

Did you know that little monarch butterflies travel thousands of miles each year and end up in the very same tree? Have you ever wondered how whales swim from ocean to ocean without getting lost? All they see is water. And how can desert creatures survive under the hot, hot sun each day without any water in sight?

I guess all my questions will be answered someday, because when I grow up, I'm going to be a biologist.

–Becka

WHEN I GROW UP . . .

Firefighter

Near my home is a fire station. Every time we drive by, I wave. The people who work there wave back. They know I want to be a firefighter someday.

Firefighters know how to do many things. If a fire starts to burn in someone's house, they jump into their big yellow truck and rush through town with sirens blaring and lights flashing.

After they get to the house, they make sure everyone is safe. If someone is hurt, they immediately help them. Then they turn on the hoses and spray water on the fire. If it's not too big, they can stop it and save the house from burning down. They also make sure the flames don't spread to other houses nearby. It's hard work.

Firefighters also teach people how to be safe in their homes. They don't want anyone to have a problem with fire. I like that. It reminds me of what Jesus does for us. He wants us all to be safe and happy. But if there's a problem, He quickly comes to help us.

When I become a firefighter, I'll do like Jesus does. I'll teach people how to be safe and happy. But if something happens, I'm there!

–Matt

When you walk through the fire, you will not be burned.
Isaiah 43:2, NIV.

18
APRIL

Out of Zebulun [came] they that handle the pen of the writer. Judges 5:14.

WHEN I GROW UP . . .

Writer

Last night I went to Africa. I saw hardworking farmers digging in the ground and children playing with a monkey. I even saw a lion sitting in a tree.

This may surprise you, but I went to Africa in my pajamas!

Before I went to bed, Mom read me a story about Africa. I learned how beautiful the country is, how friendly the people are. I closed my eyes and pretended to go to places the story talked about.

When I grow up, I'm going to be a writer. A writer puts exciting stories about people and places in books. Then others can enjoy reading about what the writer saw.

A writer can also tell people how to do things like paint a house, sew a dress, cook a nutritious meal, or figure out a personal problem. Most important of all, a writer can tell people about Jesus.

The Bible has many writers. They tell stories—some happy, some sad. But each writes about God and how much He loves us.

I'm going to write books that make people happy. When they read my words, they can close their eyes and see things they've never seen before. If I work hard and write my very best, maybe I can even help someone see Jesus.

–Alicia

WHEN I GROW UP . . .

X-ray Technician

19

APRIL

I fell off my bike and hurt my arm. The doctor said I'd have to have an X-ray.

An X-ray is a picture of what's inside your body taken by a special camera. It can see right through your skin and look at your bones. Amazing!

The doctor studied the picture and said my arm was broken. Well, I could have told him that. It hurt!

I got to thinking. That camera is an awesome machine. It showed my doctor something he needed to know to help me.

The person who takes the pictures is called an X-ray technician. That's what I want to be when I grow up.

When a boy or girl gets hurt and comes to the hospital, I'll take pictures of their bones to see what's the matter. The doctor will look at the pictures and then fix the bone. I'll be helping the doctor make that person feel better.

Sometimes hurt people are scared. They don't know what's going to happen. The X-ray technician explains about the special camera and how it will help the doctor find out what the problem is. It makes patients feel better when they know what's going on.

Hey, that's just like Jesus. He doesn't want anyone to be afraid. And when you're not afraid, you heal faster!

–Brian

Since the creation of the world God's invisible qualities—his eternal power and divine nature—have been clearly seen.
Romans 1:20, NIV.

20
APRIL

The Lord announced the word, and great was the company of those who proclaimed it.
Psalm 68:11, NIV.

WHEN I GROW UP . . .

Radio Announcer

I love to talk. My dad says I talk more than anyone in the world. That must be a lot because my uncle Ray talks in his sleep!

I always try to say something important. The other day Mom asked me if it was raining outside. I told her, "It isn't raining just now, but because there are clouds in the sky and the wind is blowing harder and harder and since it rained yesterday and the day before, it probably will rain again today, perhaps soon."

She said, "Thank you."

My dad once took me to a radio station. He said someday I'll probably own one. I listened to the announcers talk and talk. They told about the latest news, mentioned which baseball teams had won, said which singer was going to sing a song, and invited everyone to buy food at Martin's Fine Food Store.

That's when I decided I want to be a radio announcer when I grow up. Imagine. People pay you money to talk! I could tell my audience to be kind to each other. I could tell them to remember to feed their pets. I could tell them that Jesus loves them. With just a few words, I could make thousands of people happy.

The thought leaves me speechless . . . almost.

–Ricky

WHEN I GROW UP . . .

Pilot

21 APRIL

There are . . . things that are too amazing for me . . . : the way of an eagle in the sky. Proverbs 30:18, 19, NIV.

I love to visit airports where airplanes land and take off. They look so beautiful with their broad wings and tall tails. Someday I'm going to be a pilot.

Being a good pilot isn't easy. You have to learn about clouds, rain, and wind. You have to know how to fly your airplane to distant airports without getting lost. And you have to know what to do if something goes wrong.

That's why good pilots are careful people. They check everything *twice!* You can't stop and fix your airplane when you're flying above the clouds. You must make sure everything is OK *before* you take off.

Businesspeople need pilots to fly them from city to city for meetings. Airplanes can carry packages and gifts, too. Some pilots fly over jungles and mountains in faraway countries, taking doctors and preachers to help people learn about Jesus.

I'm learning how to be a good pilot now, even though I'm just a kid. I take care of my toys and am always careful not to hurt anyone when playing with my friends.

Being careful and safe helps pilots get where they want to go. Being careful and safe *now* will help me become a good pilot someday.

–Jacob

22
APRIL

Go into all the world and preach the good news to all creation. Mark 16:15, NIV.

WHEN I GROW UP . . .

Missionary

It makes me very happy to know that Jesus loves me. But there are many boys and girls—and moms and dads—who don't know that Jesus loves them too.

Jesus says we should go and tell the whole world about His love. That's what I'm going to do when I grow up. I'm going to be a missionary!

Being a missionary is more than telling people about Jesus. It's helping them find enough food to eat and clothes to wear. It's giving them medicines to make them well.

Some don't even have houses to live in, so missionaries get busy and help them build one. If there's not enough food for everybody, missionaries help hungry people plant gardens.

When they find people who don't have enough clothes to wear, missionaries ask friends and neighbors to bring shirts, pants, and shoes to church. Then a boat takes these gifts to the places they're needed most. Missionaries work very hard helping others.

Jesus was the best missionary ever. He traveled from His home in heaven, fed the hungry, healed the sick, and shared His love. He helped many, many people feel happy again.

Feeding, healing, and sharing are what missionaries do best!

–Colin

WHEN I GROW UP . . .

Day-care Operator

23
APRIL

When you hear a baby crying, what do you want to do? Cover your ears? Run away?

When I hear a baby crying, I want to go quickly and see what the problem is. Maybe it's hungry. Maybe it needs changing. To me, a baby's cry is just like talking, only louder!

Babies and little children need special care. They need someone to watch over them, protect them, and love them. That's what moms and dads do.

But sometimes both parents have to work long hours so they can buy food and clothes for their kids. When this happens, they search for kind people to help take care of their little boy or girl while they're earning money at work. These people are called day-care operators. That's what I want to be when I grow up.

Day-care operators make sure boys and girls are safe and happy. They give them healthy food to eat and keep them warm and protected. They talk to the children and read stories from books. This keeps the boys and girls happy while their parents work.

Jesus loves children very much. I want to be the kind of day-care operator Jesus would be. What would *He* do if He heard a baby crying?

–Jenny

Pharaoh's daughter said to [Moses' mother], "Take this baby and nurse him for me, and I will pay you." Exodus 2:9, NIV.

24 APRIL

The contentions of a wife are as a continual dropping [of water through a chink in the roof]. Proverbs 19:13, Amplified.

WHEN I GROW UP . . .

Plumber

Drip, drip, drip. That's the noise water makes when it's leaking out of a pipe.

Drip, drip, drip. Something needs to be done right away!

Don't worry. Here comes the plumber! When water is leaking, the plumber knows just what to do.

He or she moves the pipes around, puts a new connection here and one over there, and tightens everything with a big wrench.

Now listen. . . . No more *drip, drip, drip.* The leak is fixed!

Water can make floors and ceilings buckle and crack. It can make metal rust and break. A little water leak can do a lot of damage if it's not fixed quickly. Plumbers help people save tons of money by keeping water leaks from damaging expensive parts of their houses.

Plumbers know that little leaks now can cause big problems later. I think Jesus understood that because He said little sins in our lives can cause big sadness later. Plumbers fix small problems before they can cause big problems. Good idea, don't you think?

When I grow up I'm going to be a plumber so I can fix little leaks. And today I'm going to work on my little sins, too. I'm going to ask Jesus to help me be kind and loving to everyone I meet. I don't want to *drip, drip, drip.*

–Yolanda

I WANT TO BE A MEMBER BECAUSE . . .

I Love Jesus

25
APRIL

Since God so loved us, we also ought to love one another. 1 John 4:11, NIV.

I want to be a member of the Seventh-day Adventist Church because I love Jesus.

When I come to church and sing songs and pray, I'm telling Jesus how much I love Him. I'm also telling everyone around me that Jesus is important to me.

At church I learn about heaven and God. The stories I hear during Sabbath school and the sermons preached during church service teach me important things I need to know about my heavenly Father. Each Sabbath I get to know Him better.

Last week when I was coming home from school, our car was almost hit by another car. It scared me so much that I cried, even though I'm 8 years old. But then I remembered what the preacher said just a few days before. He told us, "Jesus is with you, even when you're afraid. He longs to help you feel happy again."

Well, when I remembered that, I stopped crying and felt much better. After all, if Jesus is with me, help is always just a prayer away!

Jesus loves everyone. That's why you'll find me sitting on the front row at church each week showing everyone how much I love *Him*.

–David

26
APRIL

I WANT TO BE A MEMBER BECAUSE . . .

I Learn the Truth

You will know the truth, and the truth will set you free. John 8:32, NIV.

I want to be a member of the Seventh-day Adventist Church because my Sabbath school teacher and my preacher tell me what Jesus said.

Satan tries to make me believe stuff that isn't true. He says bad people will burn forever in hell fires and that Jesus isn't coming back to earth.

But at church I learn the truth! I learn that Jesus loves everyone—good people and bad people—and someday those who love Him will live in a new earth. Sin will be gone forever. No ever-burning fires or never-ending suffering. Gone. Period!

And Jesus promised that He'd come back to take us to heaven if we choose to go. If Jesus said it, that's what's going to happen!

When I hear about a lie Satan has said, I think, *I'd better check that out for myself.* So I head straight to my Sabbath school teacher or the preacher. I tell them what I heard, and they sit down with me and show me what the Bible says.

Someone told me that smoking and drinking are fun. Then my preacher showed me a verse in the Bible that says that our bodies are God's temple. Imagine filling God's temple with smoke and beer. Ridiculous!

Go to church. Learn the truth!

–Jason

I WANT TO BE A MEMBER BECAUSE . . .

I Want to be Happy and Healthy Now

27
APRIL

I pray that you may enjoy good health. 3 John 2, NIV.

I want to be a member of the Seventh-day Adventist Church because I can learn how to live a happy, healthy life on earth right now!

In church I learn about nature and how God created many things to make me glad, like flowers and puppies. Just watching a puppy play with a rubber ball makes you happy, right? That was *God's* idea.

In church I learn how to take care of my body so that I can be as healthy as possible. My mom goes to classes to learn how to cook good nutritious food. My uncle went to a stop-smoking clinic and . . . well . . . stopped smoking. It works!

In church the preacher tells me how to keep my mind strong, too. When I hear about how much Jesus loves me and how He's building a home for me in heaven, I'm never afraid of the future.

Sometimes I hear people saying, "You need to do this or buy that or go here to be happy." Well, I just say, "I'm going to do what Jesus tells me to do *first,* because He knows what I need better than anyone."

And where do I learn all this? Yup. In church!

What have you learned at your church lately?

—Trisha

28
APRIL

No eye has seen, no ear has heard, no mind has conceived what God has prepared for those who love him.
1 Corinthians 2:9, NIV.

I WANT TO BE A MEMBER BECAUSE . . .

I'm Getting Ready for Heaven

I want to be a member of the Seventh-day Adventist Church because I'm getting ready to live in heaven with Jesus.

Each week in Sabbath school and church I hear about heaven and how wonderful it is. In heaven people won't hurt each other. Everyone will be kind and loving. So I'm trying to be like that now.

Sometimes I make mistakes and say or do unkind things. Today at school I didn't share my apple with my friend. Hey, I was hungry. But my friend's family is poor, and they can't afford big, shiny apples. After I ate it, I felt sad. Then I remembered what the preacher had said about heaven—how everyone will share everything they have. So I gave her half of my sandwich instead. I felt better. And my friend felt full.

Getting ready to live in heaven makes living on this earth much more fun. After all, heaven is just like earth but without sin, anger, disease, and sadness. So why wait for all that happiness?

Would you like to learn more? Then head straight to church this Sabbath and listen carefully. Trust me. You'll enjoy getting ready for heaven too!

–Tara

I WANT TO BE A MEMBER BECAUSE . . .

My Church Needs Me

29
APRIL

Here am I.
Send me!
Isaiah 6:8, NIV.

I want to be a member of the Seventh-day Adventist Church because my church needs me.

My pastor told me that there is no one in the whole world like me. He said God gave me special talents to help my church. So I make sure that I use my talents each week. Here's how.

I enjoy helping my Sabbath school leader. She lets me straighten the chairs, set up the Picture Roll for the stories, run the overhead projector during song service, and pass out papers for class. It's great fun, and I'm happy to do it. As a matter of fact, she said I have a talent for helping. That made me feel great!

But I do more. When I see someone at church that I've never seen before, I smile at them. They always smile back. The pastor says that's another talent God has given me.

Every church needs boys and girls like you and me. We need to help make our church a happy place to visit by always being friendly and reverent.

I'm glad I'm a part of my church family. I'm glad I'm needed.

So how are you going to put your talents to work for Jesus this week at your church?

–Jon

30
APRIL

If we walk in the light, as he is in the light, we have fellowship with one another.
1 John 1:7, NIV.

I WANT TO BE A MEMBER BECAUSE . . .

I Enjoy My Friends

I want to be a member of the Seventh-day Adventist Church because I like to have lots of friends who love Jesus.

When I'm with my friends at church, we have fun doing things together. We sing songs as loud as we can, hear exciting stories, and play games that make us laugh. The best part is that we're learning about Jesus at the same time!

Some of the boys and girls at school or near my house don't like to sing songs about Jesus. The music they listen to doesn't remind me of how much Jesus loves me. And they want to play the kinds of games we won't be playing in heaven—pretend games where other people get hurt or mad.

But at church things are different. All of my buddies enjoy playing happy games and singing fun songs. We have a great time and don't pretend to hurt anyone.

Would you like to be with other people who enjoy the same things you enjoy? Well, put on your cleanest clothes, grab your Bible, and head for church this week. There's a whole bunch of happy kids waiting for you! And to make it even more fun, bring along a neighbor or classmate from school. See you there!

–Andrew

IN OUR FAMILY WORSHIP . . .

We Learn About the Creator

1
MAY

In the beginning God created the heaven and the earth. Genesis 1:1.

"Come on, everyone. Time for family worship." My dad says these same words each evening at 7:00 sharp.

Last night I hurried to the living room with my mom, and we all flopped down on the couch. This week we're learning about how God made the world by just speaking. "When God talks, we'd better listen!" Dad insisted.

"During the first four days of Creation, what did God make?" Mom asked.

"Light, air, water, land, plants, the sun, moon, and some stars," I answered.

"Is there anything in this house that needs most of those to grow?"

"How about the plant on the bookcase? It needs clean soil and cool water for its roots and fresh air and warm sunshine for its leaves. Without those, it would dry up and fall over."

"You're right," Mom said with a smile. "And *you* need them too! The Creator made sure His new world included all the important ingredients that growing plants, animals, and people must have to be healthy. He was very wise, don't you think?"

We looked at the plant and tried to imagine what it was like when God made the world. Dad said, "Let's pray and thank the Creator for taking such good care of us."

And that's exactly what we did.

–Josh

2
MAY

God said, "Let us make [man and woman] . . . and let them rule over the fish of the sea and the birds of the air, over the livestock, . . . and over all the creatures that move along the ground." Genesis 1:26, NIV.

IN OUR FAMILY WORSHIP . . .

We Learn to Care for Pets

"Don't eat so fast," I said. "You'll get a tummyache."

Most of my friends have pet dogs, cats, or hamsters. I have ducks. We got them when they were like little balls of feathers and peep-peep-peeped all the time. Now they quack-quack-quack. Yesterday in family worship we studied about the fifth day of Creation when God made fish and birds. It must have been really fun to see all those beautiful creatures flying through the blue skies or swimming under the waves.

Mom looked at me and smiled. "Did you know that you're doing the same kind of work as Adam?"

"I am?" I gasped.

"Sure. God showed Adam how to care for the animals. He even let him name them. That's how ducks became ducks and horses became horses."

Mom pointed out the window in the direction of the duck pen. "You take good care of your pets and have given each a name. That's what God taught Adam to do."

"Wow," I said. "I guess taking care of animals must be an important job." Outside I could hear my ducks quacking. "Right after worship I'm going to go and care for my animals, just as Adam cared for his." And that's exactly what I did.

–Josh

IN OUR FAMILY WORSHIP . . .

We Learn to Make Sabbath Special

3 MAY

What're you doing?" Mom asked.

"I'm making Sabbath special," I said.

"How?"

"By reading my Sabbath book."

Mom scratched her head. "That's just an ordinary book about nature. You have lots of them, with pictures of lions and horses and elephants. You even have one about skunks. What makes that one a Sabbath book?"

"Don't you remember?" I asked. "Last week at family worship, we read how Adam and Eve did special activities during the Sabbath. Maybe they went to a quiet place by the river or played a fun Sabbath game or talked to Jesus under the shade of a favorite tree."

"Yes," Mom said.

"Well, I decided to read this book only on Sabbath. I've got several others picked out, too. I made a list. Then when it's Sabbath, like today, I look at my list and choose a special book. It's fun."

Mom smiled. "You're making Sabbath special by making it *different* from all the other days of the week." She thought for a moment. "I think I'll call my friend, Mrs. Potter. She's kind of lonely. And if I call her every week at this same time, I'll be making Sabbath special too, just like Adam and Eve." And that's exactly what she did.

–Josh

If you call the Sabbath a delight . . . then you will find your joy in the Lord. Isaiah 58:13, 14, NIV.

4
MAY

God so loved the world that he gave his one and only Son, that whoever believes in him shall not perish but have eternal life. John 3:16, NIV.

IN OUR FAMILY WORSHIP . . .

We Learn That Jesus Loves Us

"What's that?" my friend Robert asked, staring at the drawing hanging on my wall.

"What's it look like?" I said.

"Well, it looks like a heart with two lines in it. And there're some words written on it too. Is it a secret message?"

"Sort of."

"What do you mean?"

I sat down at the end of my bed. "Last Monday during family worship Dad read about how God promised Adam and Eve He would someday save them from sin."

"And did He?" Robert asked.

"Yes. But it was terrible. You see, God's Son Jesus had to hang on a cross and die."

"Those lines," Robert said, pointing at the drawing. "They make a cross, don't they?"

"I put them inside the big heart to show how much God loves us." I stood and walked to the wall. "Listen. I'll read the words. They say, *'God so loved the world that he gave his one and only Son, that whoever believes in him shall not perish but have eternal life'* [John 3:16, NIV]."

Robert turned to me and said, "Will you make me a drawing like that so I can remember how much God loves me?" And that's exactly what I did.

–Josh

IN OUR FAMILY WORSHIP . . .

We Learn About Faith

5
MAY

We must obey God rather than men! Acts 5:29, NIV.

"Then what happened?" I asked.

Dad smiled. "We told the man that obeying Jesus was more important than my job."

We'd been talking about faith in family worship, and I'd asked my mom and dad if they had ever had to use any. Then Dad told me a story about when his boss wanted him to do something that wasn't honest. But Jesus wants us to always tell the truth, even at work.

Dad said he wouldn't lie. His boss got mad and told him he had better change his mind or else!

"Were you afraid?" I wanted to know.

"A little," Dad said. "You were just a baby, and we needed the money. That's the reason your mother and I prayed, asking God for strength to do the right thing."

"I thought you said you used faith."

"Yes," Dad continued. "Faith is strength from God to do what's right, even when you're afraid. Noah, Enoch, and Abraham all had faith, and it gave them the power to obey."

"Did you lose your job?"

"Nope. The boss said I was a good worker, even if I insisted on telling the truth. He even invited us to his home so we could tell him about Jesus. And that's exactly what we did."

–Josh

6
MAY

Love your enemies and pray for those who persecute you. Matthew 5:44, NIV.

IN OUR FAMILY WORSHIP . . .

We Learn How to Witness

And Noah and his family were saved in the ark." I looked at my mom and smiled.

"That's a silly story," she chuckled, "and I don't believe one word of it."

"But that's what the Bible says."

Mom laughed. "You should spend your time learning more important things, like making money or becoming famous."

"There's nothing more important than learning about Jesus," I said with a cheerful smile.

Mom frowned. "Go tell your silly stories someplace else. I don't want to hear them."

"OK," I said. "But remember, Jesus loves you. He wants you to be happy too."

I walked to the door, then stopped. "How'd I do?" I asked.

Mom nodded. "Very well."

"What's going on?" Dad asked as he came into the room.

"Our son is learning to do what Noah did—witness to people who make fun."

"Ouch." Dad cringed. "That's not easy."

"No," I said. "But I want to learn how to be as strong and brave as Noah."

"Would you like to practice witnessing to me?" Dad asked. "I'll listen to you politely, like most people will."

And that's exactly what he did.

–Josh

IN OUR FAMILY WORSHIP . . .

We Learn to Pretend

7
MAY

They had with them every wild animal . . . , all livestock . . . , every creature that moves along the ground . . . , everything with wings.
Genesis 7:14, NIV.

"Come on," I called. "The water will be just right."

"OK," Dad said, grabbing his book. "Let me tell your mother where we're going."

Near our house is a little pond with a wooden dock sticking out over the water. From there I love to sail my tugboat. The wind moves my little ship smoothly across the ripples.

While my dad sits under the shade of an oak tree, I play.

Since we'd been studying about Noah in family worship, I pretended I was sailing the ark filled with animals and food. If I listened carefully, I could almost hear the cows mooing and the tigers roaring.

"Keep those critters in their cages!" I shouted. "And make sure the horses have oats to eat." My tug bobbed in the waves. "Gettin' kinda stinky in here. Better clean the pigeon boxes and put fresh straw in the goat stalls."

"Hey, Noah," Dad called when the sun was setting low behind the trees. "Time to head for Ararat. Supper is ready."

I pulled in my ark . . . I mean tugboat. Caring for a load of animals was tiring, and I figured even sea captains needed to stop working and head for the galley (boat's kitchen) once in a while.

And that's exactly what I did.

–Josh

8
MAY

How great is the love the Father has lavished on us, that we should be called children of God! 1 John 3:1, NIV.

IN OUR FAMILY WORSHIP . . .

We Learn How God Shows His Love

Your turn," Mom said.

I cleared my throat. This was going to be easy!

All week long in family worship we'd been studying how God shows us His love. Mom and Dad had talked about it for a few minutes. Now it was my turn.

"Well," I began, "first, I know God loves me because He gave me a tongue to taste peppermint ice cream and big red apples, the kind that go *crack* when you eat them."

Mom and Dad nodded.

"Second, He helped the doctors make Grandma well when she fell and broke her coffee table."

Mom and Dad nodded again.

"And third"—I rubbed my chin— "because He died on the cross to save me from the devil."

"Good!" Dad said. "Those are wonderful ways to remember God's love. Whenever we eat a meal, watch our bodies heal, or sing a song about Jesus on the cross, we can feel happy, knowing Jesus loves us."

Mom walked to the piano. "Why don't we sing 'Jesus Loves Me' to close our family worship?" And that's exactly what we did.

–Josh

IN OUR FAMILY WORSHIP . . .

We Learn to Be Polite

9 MAY

Honor one another above yourselves. Romans 12:10, NIV.

Family worship is my favorite time of the day. Tuesday evening is my second favorite. That's when we watch videos.

Last night Dad pulled open the video drawer. "Which one?" he asked. "Your choice."

Last week was Mom's time to choose. The week before that, Dad selected his favorite.

During family worship we read about a man named Abraham. He let his nephew, Lot, choose *first* which land he wanted for his flocks and herds. We all agreed that that was a very unselfish thing to do and decided we should try to be like Abraham.

I held up two videos. Did I want to watch a movie about the wild horse called Misty or look at animals who lived in Yellowstone National Park? "I think I'll go with the animals, even though I like seeing the horse run across the seashore," I announced.

Mom headed for the kitchen to pop some corn. Dad settled into his favorite chair and fell asleep (like he usually does) while I loaded the tape into the machine.

Letting others choose first works great. Everyone gets a turn. I've learned that being polite is more fun than being first. Abraham thought so too.

And that's exactly how I always want to be.

–Josh

10
MAY

God loves a cheerful giver. 2 Corinthians 9:7, NIV.

IN OUR FAMILY WORSHIP . . .

We Learn How to Return Tithe

"Do I have to?" I moaned. "I worked hard for my $10. Those dogs were always jumping up on me."

Mom shook her head. "No, you don't have to return your tithe to God."

"*He* didn't give me this money. Mr. Pierson did, for walking his dogs."

"Let's talk about that," Mom said. "Who made the world and then put people in it?"

"God," I said.

"And what are we supposed to do with everything God made?"

"Take care of it."

"So if God made the world and everything in it and we're supposed to take care of it for Him, who really owns everything?"

I opened my mouth to answer, then paused. "Well, I guess God does. That means God owns Mr. Pierson's dogs and our house and even my $10."

"And Jesus expects us to use His money wisely," Mom continued. "That includes returning a tithe or *tenth* of His money back to Him so His church leaders can pay the salaries of ministers around the world."

"Now I understand," I said. "Jesus wants me to keep most of His dollars because He saw how hard I worked. But I'll return this one because it belongs to Him."

And that's exactly what I did.

–Josh

IN OUR FAMILY WORSHIP . . .

We Learn to Share

11

MAY

Whatever you did for one of the least of these brothers of mine, you did for me. Matthew 25:40, NIV.

"Look at that boy," I said, pointing in the direction of a new family sitting near the back of our church. "His shirt is too small, and his shoes look worn out."

"That's Mickey Peters," Mom whispered. "His dad lost his job last winter, and they just moved to our town. Someone in the church found them a place to live and brought them some groceries." She sighed. "Now all we can do is hope that Mr. Peters finds a job soon."

I couldn't stop thinking about Mickey and his too-little shirt. Then an idea popped into my head.

As soon as we got home, I rushed to my closet. I had lots of shirts—blue ones, green ones, and a yellow one with a white stripe. "Mom," I called, "remember that family at church?"

"Yes?"

"I want to give Mickey my new orange shirt. I've got others, see? And these shoes are almost good as new. I can wear my old ones a little longer. Is it OK?"

Mom hugged me tightly. "I'm proud of you," she whispered. "Jesus said we will always have poor people around who need our help. By sharing what we have, we're helping God love them."

And that's exactly what we did.

–Josh

12
MAY

He is a shield to those who take refuge in him. Proverbs 30:5, NIV.

IN OUR FAMILY WORSHIP . . .

We Learn How to Be Safe

Boom! Boom! Crash! Thunder echoed across the dark sky while lightning bolts blinked overhead.

"I'm scared," I cried. Just then the lights went out.

"Don't worry," Dad called, stumbling toward the kitchen and returning with a big flashlight. "We'll head for the basement and wait for the storm to pass."

We have a lot of thunder and lightning this time of year. Two weeks ago a tornado touched down just five miles from our street!

Mom, Dad, and I hurried down the stairs. *Boom! Boom! Crash!* The little windows near the ceiling shone brightly, like someone was taking flash pictures of our house.

As we sat in Dad's workshop Mom said, "Why don't we have family worship?"

"Good idea," Dad agreed. "We've already talked about how God saved Lot. Now let's talk about the story of the Flood and how God saved Noah and his family from the waters."

"God showed him how to build an ark," I stated. "Without it, Noah and his family would have drowned."

"The Creator always wants us to be safe," Mom added. "We used our God-given minds to figure out that we'd be safer down here than upstairs or out on the street. Noah followed God's directions. That's exactly what we *all* should do."

–Josh

MY TALENTS FOR JESUS . . .

I Smile

When Jesus created me, He gave me a talent. Just in case you don't know what that is, a *talent* is something you can do that's kinda special.

Some people can stand up and sing songs in church. They don't look scared or anything! That's a talent. Some people can paint beautiful pictures of mountains or animals. That's another talent.

My mom has a talent. She helps people get well. You see, she's a doctor and enjoys using her talent every day at the hospital.

My talent is on my face! When my mother is tired or sad, I smile and say, "Hey, Mom, I love you." She says it makes her day.

I smile at other people, too. Sometimes when my neighbor drives by our house, I smile at him. He waves back or honks his horn. *Beep.*

When my baby brother, Triston, starts to cry, I look right at him and smile. Sometimes he stops crying and laughs. Sometimes he throws his rattle at me. Smiling doesn't work for everybody.

Yup. Jesus gave me a special talent, one I'm going to use every day.

Hey, maybe you have a smile talent too. Why don't you find out today?

–Natalie

A happy heart makes the face cheerful. Proverbs 15:13, NIV.

14
MAY

Serve one another in love.
Galatians 5:13, NIV.

MY TALENTS FOR JESUS . . .

Helpful Hands

I think Jesus gave me a very important talent. It's my helpful hands. Whenever my dad asks me to take out the trash, I drop whatever I'm doing and get busy!

When my mom tells me to clean my room, my helpful hands grab my racing cars, socks, swimsuit, *Mysteries of the Forest* picture book, hairbrush, football, rock collection, tennis shoes, crayons, and dinosaur and put them away *fast!* Dad always comes to my bedroom door when I'm finished and says, "Hey, who lives here?"

My helpful hands do other stuff, too. They feed our dog, dry the dishes, find lost doll dresses under the couch for my sister, and make sure my toys aren't where someone can trip over them and break a leg. Yeah, my helpful hands stay busy all day long.

Mom says my talent is very important because Jesus had helpful hands too. She says He was always busy making sure people were safe and happy. If there was a job to do, He did it without complaining.

Do you like helping people? Will you tackle any job without moaning and groaning? Then maybe you've got helpful hands too. Check it out the next time your mom or dad asks you to do something. And, hey, if you need any help, let me know.

–Hunter

MY TALENTS FOR JESUS . . .

Making Music

15
MAY

Make music to the Lord with the harp, . . . with trumpets and the blast of the ram's horn. Psalm 98:5, NIV.

Jesus gave me a terrific talent. You may not think it's so great when you hear it, but don't worry—my dad says some things get better with time.

My talent is making music. When I'm alone, hanging out in my room, I sing. I remember the songs I heard in Sabbath school and sing them to my cat, my goldfish, and my favorite doll.

For my birthday, dad bought me an electronic keyboard. It doesn't have a lot of notes on it, but it's fun to play. I press one key at a time and listen to the sound. Then I try to sing along.

Playing my keyboard and singing make me excited inside. I pretend I'm hearing violins and trumpets playing. I imagine choirs singing and pipe organ melodies echoing all around.

Sometimes when I'm singing to myself, my mom will say, "That's a lovely tune. Will you share it with me?" I stand straight and tall and try to make every note as pretty as possible. My mom always says, "Jesus gave you a wonderful talent. Remember to use it to bring joy to others."

I smile. It won't be hard to do that, because making music always brings joy to me.

–Trisha

16
MAY

A friend loves at all times. Proverbs 17:17, NIV.

MY TALENTS FOR JESUS . . .

Making Friends

Jesus gave me a special talent. Would you like to know what it is?

Pretend that you've never been to my town before. You come to Sabbath school on Sabbath morning and don't know anybody!

Then you hear someone say to you, "Hello, my name is David. Would you like to sit with me? I can show you how to make a horse out of clay."

That person is me, and my talent is making friends.

My teacher always brings visitors to my table because she knows I'll make them feel welcome.

Sometimes a new family will move into our neighborhood. If they have any kids my age, I'll walk right up and say, "Would you like to see my new computer game?" Usually they do. Other times they're shy and run away, but that's OK. Making friends sometimes takes a few days.

My dad told me the secret of making friends. Whenever you see a boy or girl who looks like they need a friend, think to yourself, *What can I do to make that person happy?* When you figure it out, do it.

Hey, maybe you have that talent, too. You'll never know unless you put it into action!

Jesus was a friend to everyone, and we want to be just like Jesus, right?

–David

MY TALENTS FOR JESUS . . .

I'm Neat and Clean

A few months ago my dad said to me, "I think you have a special talent. You always keep your room straightened up with your toys put away and bed made. And I notice that you wash your hands before every meal. God has given you the talent of being neat and clean."

I'd never heard of a neat-and-clean talent before, but my dad is pretty smart. He should know a talent when he sees one.

Since he told me that, I've watched myself very carefully. And you know, he's right! I like to see things where they're supposed to be. I like to have my face and hands clean (except when I'm playing trucks in the mud with my friend Debbie).

My dad said having a neat-and-clean talent will help me all my life, no matter what kind of work I do. He says being neat and clean fights sickness, makes people enjoy being around you more, and puts a smile on Jesus' face, too.

Jesus was always neat and clean. He took special care of the things that belonged to Him, and He wants us to do the same with our toys, books, beds, and bodies. By using our neat-and-clean talent, we're saying "Thank You" for what He has given us.

–Tara

Who may stand in his holy place? He who has clean hands and a pure heart. Psalm 24:3, 4, NIV.

18
MAY

May the words of my mouth and the meditation of my heart be pleasing in your sight. Psalm 19:14, NIV.

MY TALENTS FOR JESUS . . .

I Like to Talk

Talking is a talent. I don't mean silly, loud, or just-making-jokes-all-the-time talking. I mean the kind in which you teach someone something they didn't know before.

My dad says I could talk a duck out of water, but I've never tried it.

Some kids are afraid to get up in class and say something. Not me. Whenever my teacher asks if there's someone who'd like to read out loud from a book, I'm there!

When I talk, I speak carefully, not going too fast or too slow. I want everyone to understand what I'm saying.

My teacher says I can use my talent when I grow up too. She says I can be a preacher, teacher, businessman, or maybe a lawyer. All these people do lots of talking.

The best kind of talking is when you say things that help people . . . as Jesus did. He told stories, spoke about heaven, read out loud from the Bible, and explained many important things to the people who wanted to listen.

Whenever He talked, people paid attention because He told them things they needed to hear. That's what I want to do. I want to say important things that people need to hear.

Do you think you have this talent? Let's talk about it.

–Jason

MY TALENTS FOR JESUS . . .

I Can Pray

19
MAY

The prayer of a righteous [man or woman] is powerful and effective. James 5:16, NIV.

I have a talent no one knows about—except God.

Each night I kneel by my bed and pray. I talk to God as though He's my friend and ask Him to watch over all the people in the world and thank Him for my blessings.

Then I tell Him about my friends—how Peter's mom and dad fight all the time, how Karen's sister is sick, and how the new boy in school needs a friend. I mention that I saw Mrs. Lawson, my teacher, crying the other day. Then I ask God to show me what to do.

I also ask Him to help me be kind to the kid in school who says he doesn't like me. And before I'm finished, I pray for a good night's sleep so that I can study hard the next day.

I figure God already knows about the problems my friends are having. But I want to make sure He knows *I* know about them. Then we can work together to help fix them.

Prayer is just a quiet talent, but I think it's important. I always try to make my friends a little happier after I've talked to God about their problems. That makes me feel good inside.

Why not use your prayer talent right now?

–Jon

20
MAY

They found [the boy Jesus] in the temple courts, sitting among the teachers, listening to them and asking them questions. Luke 2:46, NIV.

MY TALENTS FOR JESUS . . .

I Like to Learn

I like to learn things.

Each day my teacher brings me more and more stuff to study. She tells me about faraway countries and describes people who live there. She lets me draw pictures from a book, and then we talk about what I've drawn. Yesterday I drew an elephant. Did you know that elephants can make a noise that can be heard by other elephants miles away, but humans can't hear it? I was amazed!

Last month I learned how to add and subtract numbers. I read a story about a beaver and one about a little boy who lives in a desert. Fun stuff!

Mom says learning is a talent. She says Jesus wants us to learn how to read, add numbers, and be friends with people all around the world. She says we have to learn how to do many things so we can help others discover God's love.

Jesus liked to learn. When He was little, His mother taught Him about nature and getting along with people. His father taught Him how to work as a carpenter. When He grew up, He used what He'd learned to love everyone, even those who hurt Him.

Want to know how to use this talent best? Simple. Learn to love like Jesus.

–Andrew

MY TALENTS FOR JESUS . . .

I'm Kind

21
MAY

Show mercy and compassion to one another. Zechariah 7:9, NIV.

God has given everyone special talents. Mine is kindness.

Being kind means that if you see someone having a problem, you want to help.

When my friend Erin got sick last week, I picked some colorful flowers in the field by my house and gave them to her. She said they were pretty.

Yesterday a new boy came to our school. The other kids made fun of him and laughed at his red hair. I didn't laugh. At lunchtime I sat with him so he wouldn't be lonely. My teacher says that's how kindness acts.

Using your kindness talent means helping animals, too. I always make sure our cat has food to eat and water to drink. I play gently with her and *never* pull her tail. She purrs and purrs. Kindness makes both animals and people happy.

My teacher says Jesus was always using His kindness talent. He listened to people's problems and helped them whenever they asked Him to.

Jesus never was unkind. Even when soldiers hurt Him, He just asked God the Father to forgive them.

Kindness is a talent everyone who loves God should have. When you're kind, you're doing what Jesus would do.

Look around today. See how you can put your kindness talent into action!

–Natalie

22
MAY

Blessed are the peacemakers, for they will be called sons of God. Matthew 5:9, NIV.

MY TALENTS FOR JESUS . . .

I Help Stop Fights

My friend Jimmy got into a fight. Kirk said he was a crybaby, and Jimmy said he was *not.* Kirsten said he was. Jimmy said he wasn't. Kirk said . . . well, you get the idea.

Suddenly Kirk pushed Jimmy down. There was yelling and punching and all sorts of stuff going on.

I tried to stop it. Let me tell you right now that stopping a fight can be painful. I hurt my arm and my ear.

I asked Kirk why he called Jimmy a crybaby. Kirk said it was because he'd gotten in front of him at the drinking fountain. I know this doesn't make sense, but most fights don't.

Jimmy said he didn't know Kirk was waiting in line because he was just standing there talking with Alice Thompson, a fifth grader. And Jimmy said he was very thirsty.

After Jimmy and Kirk talked, they both agreed that they shouldn't have been fighting. They each said they were sorry and went out to play kickball. I went to get a wet rag for my ear.

My teacher says I'm a peacemaker. That's a talent! She said Jesus was a peacemaker too. Hey, if I can be like Jesus, then that's what I want, even if it's hard on my ears.

–Hunter

MY TALENTS FOR JESUS . . .

I Understand Directions

23
MAY

Whether you turn to the right or to the left, your ears will hear a voice behind you, saying, "This is the way; walk in it." Isaiah 30:21, NIV.

Last Friday my mom asked me to help her get the house ready for Sabbath. "Please take out the garbage," she said, "and put new plastic bags in the trash cans. Sweep the sidewalk, feed the dog, and find your sister's yellow socks."

In a flash I was out the door, garbage bag in hand. Fifteen minutes later I went to find Mom.

"Done already?" she gasped, looking around. The garbage was gone, new bags lined the trash cans, the sidewalk didn't have a speck of dirt on it, my sister's yellow socks hung by the washing machine, and our dog Samson was just finishing his supper. "You did all the things I told you to do," Mom said proudly. "You have a wonderful talent."

"I do?"

"Yes. You understand directions. With a talent like that, you'll be a valuable worker for Jesus. He has given us directions on how to live a happy life. Understanding and following those directions are important."

"Thanks," I said. "If you need my talent anymore, just ask."

"Well, there are a couple more things you can do for me. Wash your face, put on a clean shirt, get in the car, and we'll go get some frozen yogurt for tomorrow's dessert."

Sometimes understanding directions is tons of fun!

–David

24
MAY

The man who had received the five talents went at once and put his money to work and gained five more. Matthew 25:16, NIV.

MY TALENTS FOR JESUS . . .

I'm Learning to Manage Money

Money doesn't grow on trees. I know. I've checked. But I do know where money comes from. Hard work!

Many of my friends earn an allowance or do jobs for neighbors. Then they spend their money as fast as they earn it. When something really neat comes along, like a sale on bicycles at Sears, they're broke.

I manage my money by putting it in my bank account and keeping records of my dollars and cents so I know how much I've saved. And if I see something I want to buy, I don't ask, "Do I need that?" Instead I ask, "Can I possibly do without it?" I've saved lots of money that way.

There's another thing I do with my money. I return to God one penny for every 10 I earn. That's called tithing. When you put your tithe envelope in the offering plate at church, you're saying to Jesus, "Thank You for helping me earn my money. Now please help me spend the rest of it wisely."

The other day my mom was sick. I went to the store and bought her some flowers. She put them in a vase right beside her bed. The best thing about managing money is using it to make others happy.

–Jason

MY TALENTS FOR JESUS . . .

I Appreciate People

25

MAY

Let another praise you, and not your own mouth; someone else, and not your own lips. Proverbs 27:2, NIV.

"What's the matter?" my dad asked.

"I don't have a single talent," I said. "All the other kids at school have at least one, but me? Zero. Take Wilton, for instance. He can sing and play the piano at the same time. I like to sit and listen to him. Jessica can add numbers almost as fast as you say them. I gave her four numbers, and *zap,* she added them up. I told her she should be a schoolteacher or a scientist. And Michael paints pictures that look real. He gave me a painting of a horse jumping over a fence. I stuck it on my desk so I could see it every day. He's always giving me pictures."

Dad began to smile. Then he laughed.

"Don't make fun of me," I moaned. "I can't help it if I don't have a talent."

"But you do!" Dad said. "All these other kids like to show you *their* talents because you appreciate them. It makes them happy."

"Appreciating other people's talents is a talent?" I gasped.

"Of course. Jesus said we should be kind and loving. Appreciating others is a wonderful way to do that."

I began to laugh too. "I guess I'd better start appreciating my own talent, now that I know I have one." And I do.

—Trisha

26
MAY

I praise you because I am fearfully and wonderfully made. Psalm 139:14, NIV.

MY TALENTS FOR JESUS . . .

I'm Coordinated

What do pouring a glass of milk, catching a fly ball, and getting an A in handwriting all have in common? The answer is a talent from God. You may have it. I know I do.

That talent is coordination.

Using a coordination talent means being careful when you use your arms, legs, hands, and feet.

My friend Tracy doesn't use it very often. When she pours a glass of milk, she makes a mess. Milk everywhere!

When I pour, I'm careful not to spill.

Baseball is my favorite sport, but I have to work hard at it. I practice and practice. This is helping my coordination talent get better. My feet and hands know what to do when I want to catch a fly ball.

My handwriting teacher says my words look very neat. I have to practice so my fingers know how to form each letter. When I take it nice and slow, my writing looks pretty good.

Good coordination happens when your body and brain work together. When I eat healthy foods and exercise regularly, my coordination improves. God knew this would happen. That's why He wants us to take care of our minds and bodies. After all, who wants to make messes all their lives?

See how coordinated you are today.

–Tara

MY TALENTS FOR JESUS . . .

I'm a Good Leader

27
MAY

When a group of people wants to get something done, they choose a good leader to keep the project organized. That's my talent. I'm a good leader.

Don't think this is because I'm extra smart or anything. I make mistakes. But a good leader knows mistakes are simply ways to learn new things.

When our teacher asked us to make a geography poster at school, I thought about the talents of my classmates and made some suggestions. I said, "Hey, Tony, you can draw, so why don't you paint the picture of South America? Jennifer, you write beautifully, so will you print the country names? And Jason, you're the tallest. Would you hang the poster on the wall?"

Then I held the paint jar for Tony, made sure Jennifer had room to work, and found a hammer and nail for Jason. Together we got the job done.

Good leaders don't do everything by themselves. They need the talents of other people to succeed. And they always say "Thank you" to those who helped.

I believe that Jesus needs everyone's talents in order to tell others how much He loves them. Will you help? I'll show you how, because that's what good leaders do best.

–Jon

I [Nehemiah] stationed some of the people behind the lowest points of the wall . . . with their swords, spears and bows. . . . Half of my men did the work, while the other half were equipped with spears, shields, bows and armor. Nehemiah 4:13-16, NIV.

28
MAY

"Come, follow me," Jesus said. Matthew 4:19, NIV.

MY TALENTS FOR JESUS . . .

I'm a Good Follower

I'm shy. I get embarrassed a *lot.* Whenever my teacher asks me to do something, it makes me nervous.

The other day I discovered something neat about myself. I have a talent!

One of the fourth graders named Lisa was building a fort. She needed someone to get branches for the walls, so she said, "Hey, Shawn, will you please get those branches over there and help me build a wall?"

"Sure!" I said.

Soon we had a great fort. Lisa said, "Hey, thanks for helping. You did everything just as I asked. I thought you were a shy person, but now I know that you're a good follower."

She was right. I was a good follower! I worked hard doing what I was told to do. I didn't complain or fuss and had a great time.

Later that day during Bible class my teacher read a story about Jesus and His disciples. It told how the disciples helped Jesus do His work of healing people and preaching in the villages. They were good followers too.

I'm still shy. But I know something about myself that makes me happy. When a job needs to be done, I'll help any way I can. This is one talent I'm going to use all my life.

–Shawn

MY TALENTS FOR JESUS . . .

Cooking for Health

29
MAY

And the Lord God made all kinds of trees grow out of the ground—trees that were pleasing to the eye and good for food. Genesis 2:9, NIV.

Everybody likes to eat. But not everybody is careful about what they eat.

I learned in school that choosing fruits and vegetables instead of meats, candy, or foods packed with chemicals can actually make you healthier. That made sense because God created fruits and vegetables and He certainly should know what we need to stay healthy.

When I told my dad what I'd learned, he said he'd grow a garden if I learned to cook. Mom said she'd help. That's how I got my cooking-for-health talent.

As the garden grew we collected recipes from friends, neighbors, and magazines. The library had a whole bunch of books on cooking naturally.

Then, when the vegetables were ready, Mom and I practiced until we could make delicious dinner dishes from carrots, squash, potatoes, tomatoes, onions, corn, and cucumbers. We seasoned everything just right so their natural flavors would tickle the tongue. Dad was impressed.

Now whenever I cook something, I ask myself two questions—is this food healthy, and what can I do to make it taste great?

Even if you can't grow a garden, you can ask your mom or dad to buy fresh fruits and vegetables at the store. Then you can have a cooking-for-health talent too. It'll make you feel great!

—Natalie

30
MAY

Whatever your hand finds to do, do it with all your might. Ecclesiastes 9:10, NIV.

MY TALENTS FOR JESUS . . .

I'm Enthusiastic

Life can be hard. Home may not be as fun as you'd like it to be, friends may turn their noses up at you, the teacher may give you too many assignments, and your dog may bite your toe.

That's when you need a very special talent from God. It's called enthusiasm.

I use it every day. When something happens that makes me mad, sad, hurt, or troubled, my enthusiasm kicks in. Like yesterday. My friend Terry decided to stop speaking to me. So I went to the library and found a neat book on space travel and enjoyed the silence. (Terry talks a lot when he does talk.) I got so enthusiastic about the book I showed it to Peter. We had a great time looking at the pictures.

Last week Mom and Dad had an argument. I hate it when they do that. I waited until they were finished and then told them both how much I loved them and how much I enjoyed living with them between fights. They looked at each other and started laughing. Enthusiasm means finding good things right in the middle of bad things.

My teacher says Jesus created enthusiasm so we could survive living in a sinful world.

Someday we'll all live in heaven. I'm getting ready to be enthusiastic forever!

–Andrew

MY TALENTS FOR JESUS . . .

I Have Time

31
MAY

There is a time for everything. Ecclesiastes 3:1, NIV.

There's a special talent Jesus gives *everybody*. You have it, your mom and dad have it, the man who sells shoes at the mall has it, all the people driving by in their cars have it too.

This talent is time.

Jesus gives everyone 24 hours every day. It's a great talent to own. You can use time to work, study, play, sleep, eat, talk to your friends, go on a trip, read a book, help out at home, or even write a poem.

Jesus wants us to use our time talent carefully. He wants us to make sure that we don't waste the hours and minutes He has provided.

If we just sit and watch television when we could be helping someone, we're wasting our time talent. If we spend hours arguing with friends, being selfish with our toys, or forgetting to pray to God each day, we're not using this important talent as we should.

But if we always find some time to help others, to teach ourselves something new, or to learn more about God and His love, then we are using our time talent wisely. God will smile and say, "That person is making the best of every minute of every day."

Time is precious. Let's all use it wisely.

–Hunter

1
JUNE

I lift up my eyes to the hills. . . . My help comes from the Lord. Psalm 121:1, NIV.

CAMP HAPPY PATCH . . .

Getting Ready

How would you like to camp at the edge of a deep green forest, on the shores of a sparkling blue lake? Well, pack your toothbrush, your warm jacket, and your Bible. The adventure is about to begin!

But you won't be camping just for fun. Towering above your campsite is a majestic mountain. That mountain is an important part of your adventure. One day you'll stand at the very top, where strong winds blow and clouds rush by. From there you'll see the world like no one has ever seen it before and learn the secret of the mountain.

For this adventure you'll need the King James Version of the Bible. Make sure the Bible you use is the *King James Version.*

As you read the story, you'll notice some of the words are missing. Where each word is missing you'll find a Bible text. Look up the text and find the missing word. This is the only way you'll discover the secrets waiting just for you.

Like any adventure in life, it's always best to have Jesus by your side. Why not invite Him along as you face today. He's a great friend. Just kneel and say, "Jesus, come with me wherever I go. Amen."

So have a wonderful day, my friend. Play hard and stay healthy. Tomorrow we leave for Camp Happy Patch!

–Carlos

CAMP HAPPY PATCH . . .

Setting Up Camp

2 JUNE

"There," you say to yourself as you sit down on a log to rest, "my camp is all finished. What a beautiful place this is. I'm going to call it Camp Happy Patch. That's a good name."

You smile. Hard work always makes you feel happy. You look out over the ___________ (Luke 5:1—word 23) and watch a couple ducks paddling along, leaving silver ripples behind them.

"And isn't this a wonderful lake," you say. "It's so smooth. I can see myself when I look down into the ___________ (Genesis 2:10—word 9)."

"That's it." You clap your hands together. "I'll call it ___________ (2 Corinthians 3:18—word 11) Lake because it's so clear and shiny."

Suddenly you hear a noise behind you. "What was that?" you ask. "Maybe it's a big, hungry ___________ (Proverbs 17:12—word 3) looking for something to eat!"

You begin to run toward your tent. The sound is getting louder. Something is running very fast behind you!

See you tomorrow!

–Carlos

3
JUNE

CAMP HAPPY PATCH . . .

First Visitor

When you reach your campsite, you turn and look behind you. There, at the edge of the forest, stands a tall, graceful mountain ___________ (Daniel 8:5—word 9). The animal studies you carefully, then disappears into the shadows.

"I know where you came from," you shout after him. "You live up there." Your finger points toward the ___________ (Job 30:6—word 5) high on the side of the mountain. "I'll be seeing you again soon."

You busy yourself making your campsite neat and orderly. Your ___________ (Genesis 12:8—word 17) is fastened tightly to the ground, just in case a big ___________ (Psalm 55:8—word 9) roars across the lake.

You make sure that your ___________ (Mark 14:54—word 26) is just big enough to cook supper without getting too big and causing trouble. Being careful is important to you. You know the forest animals depend on you to not destroy their beautiful home.

"I'm hungry," you say to yourself. "I think I'll cook some supper." You head for your food box and smack your lips. "This is going to taste really good!"

See you tomorrow!

–Carlos

CAMP HAPPY PATCH . . .

Chow Time

"Let's see what I have to eat," you say. Opening your food box, you find freshly baked __________ (Exodus 18:12—word 26) and a large jar of __________ (Proverbs 24:13—word 5).

Next you boil some water and add some sliced vegetables and a few __________ (Proverbs 15:17—word 6). The delicious smell makes your stomach growl. You've worked hard. Now you're going to feed your body the good, healthful food it needs.

As you eat your supper you watch the __________ (Luke 4:40—word 4) slowly slip behind the trees and distant mountain. Long __________ (Jeremiah 6:4—word 24) stretch across the lake and touch the shore. Night is coming.

Chewing your last bite, you wash the pots and dishes in the cool water of the lake. Far above, the __________ (Psalm 136:9—word 2) glows bright yellow in the darkening sky. Soon the __________ Psalm 136:9—word 4) begin to flicker. All the animals and birds have hidden themselves in their dens and nests for the night.

You put out the fire with some water and crawl into your tent. Kneeling by your cot, you pray to the God who made you and the world of beauty. Closing your eyes, you quickly fall __________ (Jonah 1:5—word 48).

See you tomorrow!

–Carlos

5
JUNE

CAMP HAPPY PATCH . . .

Alarm Bird

"Caah, caah, caah!" A loud noise wakes you up. It's ___________ (Proverbs 27:14—word 14). The sun is shining brightly outside your tent. But what is making all that noise? "Caah, caah, caah!"

You stick your head out into the cold morning air. There, sitting on top of your tent, is a ___________ (Genesis 8:7—word 6), calling very loudly to all of his forest friends.

"Will you please be quiet?" you say. He doesn't listen. He just keeps calling and calling.

"Go away!" you shout above the noise. "You're hurting my ___________ (2 Kings 19:28—word 14)!"

You pick up one of your ___________ (Amos 8:6—word 16). "If you don't fly away, I'll come running after you."

The big bird looks at you and tilts his head from side to side. It seems as though he's about to ___________ (Proverbs 1:26—word 4). Suddenly, he lifts his strong ___________ (Psalm 18:10—word 16) and flies into the forest.

"What a way to start the day," you mumble to yourself. "But I'd better get up. I have a lot of things to do."

"Thank You for this new day," you pray. Then you yawn and stretch. The air smells fresh and clean.

See you tomorrow!

–Carlos

CAMP HAPPY PATCH . . .

Housekeeping Day

6
JUNE

Like all good campers, you know how important it is to protect your campsite against wild animals.

First you make sure all your ___________ (Genesis 2:9—word 23) is out of reach of any hungry critter that may pass by. You use strong ___________ (2 Samuel 17:13—word 14) to hang the food box high above the ground.

Next you carefully dig a deep ditch around your tent. This will help keep the __________ (Leviticus 26:4—word 6) from flooding in on you.

You also make sure there's no trash lying around. An animal might try to eat what's left on the ground, making it very ___________ (Proverbs 13:12—word 6).

Each day you wash your clothes and hang them up to dry. It's always important to stay ___________ (Numbers 31:24—word 15).

Soon, Camp Happy Patch looks just like home. It makes you happy to live in such a nice place, so you make sure you don't do anything that would mess it up.

"I think the ___________ (Isaiah 40:28—word 16) would be pleased at how I'm taking care of His wonderful outdoors," you say to yourself. "It's as if God and I are partners. He made nature for me to enjoy. And I take good care of it."

See you tomorrow!

–Carlos

7
JUNE

CAMP HAPPY PATCH . . .

Outdoor Classroom

Before you begin to explore the beautiful valley and lake beyond Camp Happy Patch, you study your Guidebook.

"It would be silly of me to try to ___________ (Isaiah 30:21—word 15) around this valley and _____________ (2 Timothy 2:15—word 1) the plants and animals without this book," you say to yourself. "I don't know everything. There's a lot I have to ___________ (Isaiah 1:17—word 1) first.

So you sit down on a log and read all about the exciting ___________ (Ezekiel 3:13—word 12) living nearby.

You read every page of the Guidebook. "I want to know what I'm looking for," you say. "If I see an owl, I don't want to think it's an ___________ (Jeremiah 49:22—word 10). If I see a fish, I don't want to think it's a frog."

Before long you have a pretty good idea of what kind of wildlife you'll find.

"There are so many things to explore in this valley," you say. "I think I'll call this place __________ (Matthew 6:21—word 4) Valley. Yes, that's exactly what I'll call it!"

See you tomorrow!

–Carlos

CAMP HAPPY PATCH . . .

In Treasure Valley

8
JUNE

You've done it! You've set up Camp Happy Patch by Glass Lake in the exciting Treasure Valley.

To make sure you didn't disturb the beauty of nature, you've been very neat and clean. You've been careful with your campfire, hung your food box with strong ropes in a nearby tree, and tried to keep Camp Happy Patch as safe as possible for you and the animals living around you.

You've learned that keeping your camp safe and clean is hard work sometimes, but it's worth it. You feel as though you are a partner with God. He created nature; you care for it.

You've studied your Guidebook every day, learning about the wonders waiting for you to explore. So far, you've met a mountain goat and a very noisy raven. Other animals are close by. You can tell. You hear them deep in the forest. In the early morning, just before the sun rises, you've seen them come to Glass Lake to drink.

Now it's time to start exploring Treasure Valley. You feel ready. You know you'll find many exciting wonders by the shores and in the forest surrounding Camp Happy Patch.

You stand looking out over the valley. "Here I come," you say.

See you tomorrow!

–Carlos

God . . . said to them, . . . "Rule over the fish of the sea and the birds of the air and over every living creature that moves on the ground." Genesis 1:28, NIV.

9 JUNE

CAMP HAPPY PATCH . . .

Clues

It's a beautiful morning. You lift your backpack onto your shoulders and head out of camp, ready to explore Treasure Valley.

You walk into the ____________ (1 Samuel 22:5—word 29). The air is cool.

You notice something on the ground. "I wonder what kind of animal made these tracks?" you ask yourself. "Maybe a couple ____________ (Song of Solomon 2:15—word 4) went by here last night."

Just then you hear something far away. "Ahwoooo," it says. You listen. "Ahwoooo." The sound echoes through the valley.

"The animal making that noise is not the same animal who made these tracks," you say. "Only one wild creature makes a call like that. I think there's a ____________ (Isaiah 11:6—word 2) in Treasure Valley."

You sit down on a log to rest. "I hope he stays away from camp."

Suddenly you hear a *scratch, scratch, scratch* by your foot. A little ____________ (Leviticus 11:30—word 15) hurries by. "Be careful, little friend," you say. "There are dangers in this valley."

See you tomorrow!

–Carlos

CAMP HAPPY PATCH . . .

Nature Walk

10
JUNE

"I wonder what other animals I'll find," you ask yourself as you walk through the forest. "The Guidebook says I won't find a ___________ (Job 4:10—word 5) around here, so at least I won't have to worry about any of them.

"If I were in the __________ (Matthew 24:26—word 13), I might find a _________ (Matthew 19:24—word 12) or two. If I were near a jungle, I'd have to watch out for __________ (Song of Solomon 4:8—word 34).

"The Guidebook says that if there are farms in Treasure Valley, I might see some ____________ (Psalm 50:10—word 11), and maybe even some baby _____________ (Malachi 4:2—word 28). I'd find __________ (John 10:14—word 9), too. No matter where I go, the Guidebook tells me what kind of animals to look for."

Suddenly you hear a noise behind you. You get the feeling that a very large creature is watching you, following your every move.

"I shouldn't be scared," you whisper to yourself. "The Guidebook says there are no dangerous animals in this part of Treasure Valley. But what's behind me? What's watching me?"

You turn quickly and look toward the forest. There, standing by a fallen tree, is a big, beautiful _________ (Revelation 6:2—word 8)!

See you tomorrow!

–Carlos

CAMP HAPPY PATCH . . .

One Very Big Friend

A horse! There in front of you stands the most beautiful horse you've ever seen.

You hold out your ____________ (Deuteronomy 12:7—word 21). "Come here," you say. "I won't hurt you." The animal doesn't move.

"I know what you want." You open your backpack. "How would you like an _______ (Song of Solomon 2:3—word 3)?"

The horse takes a step toward you. "That's right," you say. "Come on. You can have all of it."

Slowly the big animal moves closer. You see him _______ (Philippians 4:18—word 26) the air with his large, velvety __________ (Job 40:24—word 8). His big, dark __________ (Isaiah 32:3—word 3) study you carefully.

"I won't hurt you," you repeat. "I just want to be your friend. I want to be friends with all the creatures in Treasure Valley."

The horse is now right in front of you. He sniffs the fruit in your hand, then slowly puts it in his mouth. "There," you say happily, "doesn't it taste __________ (Psalm 34:8—word 9)?"

The animal chews and chews. Then he turns and walks back among the trees. "Goodbye," you call after him. "I hope you will visit me again." You smile. Making friends in Treasure Valley is the most fun of all.

See you tomorrow!

–Carlos

CAMP HAPPY PATCH . . .

Feathered Friends

"I wonder what kind of feathered friends I can find around Camp Happy Patch," you ask yourself. Looking up into the blue sky, you see a large bird slowly circling among the clouds.

"That bird must be an _________ (Deuteronomy 32:11—word 3), or maybe a red-tailed ________ (Leviticus 11:16—word 13). It flies so easily. Sometimes it doesn't even move its wings at all."

Over by the lake you spot a ________ (Leviticus 11:18—word 3) swimming gracefully through the sparkling waters. Nearby, a mother _________ (Psalm 84:3—word 10) leads her family on a roller-coaster ride through the air, looking for bugs to eat.

High in a tree a bird calls into the breeze. *"Oohoo, Oohoo,"* it says.

"I know what you are. You're a mourning ___________ (Genesis 8:8—word 6). Why do you always sound so sad?"

The bird answers, *"Oohoo, Oohoo."*

Another feathered creature flies up from the bushes and flaps away. "Hi, there, Mr. ________ (Exodus 16:13—word 10)," you cry. "Have a nice flight."

As you're eating supper a little _________ (Psalm 84:3—word 3) sits on a low twig waiting for you to throw him some crumbs. "This is fun," you say. "Camp Happy Patch is very happy when there are birds around."

See you tomorrow! —Carlos

13
JUNE

CAMP HAPPY PATCH . . .

Creepy Critters

You discover many kinds of birds around Camp Happy Patch. There are lots of animals in Treasure Valley too.

One day over by the lake you see a little creature running over a log. When the creature is on something brown, it turns brown. When it sits on something green, it turns green.

"I know what you are," you say with a smile. "You're a __________ (Leviticus 11:30—word 6). The Guidebook says you can change colors."

A *splash!* makes you jump. Then you hear *rih-bit, rih-bit.* Near the shore, on a floating log, sit a couple of big, fat __________ (Psalm 105:30—word 5). And right next to them, enjoying the bright sunshine, sits a colorful ___________ (Song of Solomon 2:12—word 21).

"Ah, the Glass Lake Swimming Club," you laugh. "Out working on your tans, I see."

A tiny ___________ (Leviticus 11:30—word 9) scurries among the reeds lining the lake.

That night as you lie in your sleeping bag, you sigh and say to yourself, "I wonder who enjoys Treasure Valley more—the wonderful creatures, or me?"

An ___________ (Isaiah 34:11—word 11), resting on a limb above your tent, calls out, "Whooo. Whooo."

You yawn and answer, "Me, me."

See you tomorrow! —Carlos

CAMP HAPPY PATCH . . .

Feeling at Home

14

JUNE

Thus the heavens and the earth were completed in all their vast array. Genesis 2:1, NIV.

Congratulations! You've been at Camp Happy Patch for many days now. You've learned about the wonderful creatures God placed in Treasure Valley. You've said hello to a horse, found fox footprints in the dirt, and heard the lonely howl of a wolf.

Many birds have sung their happy songs for you.

Best of all, the animals have learned to trust you. They know you won't hurt them. They know you love each one of them.

The Guidebook has taught you many things about Treasure Valley. You've learned where to find certain animals. You've also learned there are some places where you shouldn't go, and you obey. The Guidebook is smarter than you are!

Your camp is still neat and clean. Your food supply is safe, and you're careful not to leave anything lying around that would hurt one of God's creatures.

Now you must start training for the most important adventure of all. Towering high above Camp Happy Patch is a tall, majestic mountain. You are going to climb that mountain!

But first you must learn how to climb, how to use your skills, how to do your very best. To climb the mountain, you must learn the many secrets that just might save your life. Get a good night's sleep. Training begins in the morning!

See you tomorrow!

–Carlos

CAMP HAPPY PATCH . . .

Learning

Bright and early the next morning you crawl out of your warm sleeping bag. "Lazy people never learn how to climb mountains," you remind yourself as you fix breakfast.

You munch on some __________ (Isaiah 5:2—word 41) and wash them down with cool, sweet ___________ (Isaiah 7:22—word 11). "A person in training needs to eat lots of healthful food," you say.

As you enjoy your meal you watch a _________ (Leviticus 11:22—word 22) pull a leaf along the ground. "You're a strong little fellow," you call out. "A mountain climber needs to be strong like you."

A _________ (Leviticus 11:22—word 28) hops from stem to stem in the tall grass beside Camp Happy Patch. "You move so quickly," you say to your tiny green neighbor. "I'll have to learn how to move like you."

Down by Glass Lake a handsome red _____________ (Nehemiah 4:3—word 18) stops for a drink, then sniffs the air before hurrying on his way. "And I'll have to be smart like you if I'm going to climb the mountain."

You sit and watch the creatures going about their daily lives. "I can learn a lot from the animals," you say with a smile. "They're good teachers."

See you tomorrow!

–Carlos

CAMP HAPPY PATCH . . .

Training

16

JUNE

"There are three important things I must do during my weeks of training," you say to yourself as you straighten up Camp Happy Patch and make sure the fire is out.

"First, I must ____________ (Ephesians 3:4—word 4) the Guidebook very carefully. It will fill my ____________ (Philippians 2:5—word 3) with all the things I need to know about mountain climbing."

You reach down and pick a beautiful ___________ (Song of Solomon 2:1—word 4). It smells sweet. "I must learn from nature, too. The creatures can teach me important lessons."

"The third thing I must do is make my body ___________ (Hebrews 11:34—word 17)." You stand and start ________ (2 Samuel 18:26—word 7) along the path leading around Glass Lake. "By eating the foods God wants me to eat and exercising my muscles, I can have good ______________ (Jeremiah 30:17—word 5). That's very important to a mountain climber."

Each day, you work a little harder, read a little more in the Guidebook, and spend a little more time watching the creatures around Camp Happy Patch. And each day, you feel yourself becoming more and more prepared for the adventure of a lifetime.

See you tomorrow!

–Carlos

17
JUNE

CAMP HAPPY PATCH . . .

Special Lesson

"That's funny," you say to yourself as you sit reading the Guidebook one morning. "It says here that one of the most important parts of training for a mountain climb is taking time to _________ (Exodus 23:12—word 15). But that doesn't make any sense at all!"

You think for a minute. "Why should I do that? Don't the creatures in nature just _________ (Job 14:15—word 16) all the time?"

Looking into the trees, you see birds busily flying about, hunting for ___________ (Leviticus 19:23—word 18) and building ___________ (Psalm 104:17—word 6).

"They sure don't take any time off," you think to yourself.

Just then one of the birds lands on a limb, tilts back its head, and begins to ___________ (Psalm 21:13—word 12) a beautiful melody. The notes rise and fall in a happy tune. The bird looks around for a minute, then tilts back his head and fills the air again with song.

You listen. "That bird has stopped its busy life and is . . . is . . . ___________ (2 Chronicles 6:41—word 9)," you say out loud. "Yes, that's exactly what he's doing!"

You stare up into the tree. "Even the birds do it," you say to yourself. "I need to learn this lesson. This is something I will always need to ___________ (Exodus 20:8—word 1)."

See you tomorrow!

–Carlos

18
JUNE

CAMP HAPPY PATCH . . .

Getting Healthy

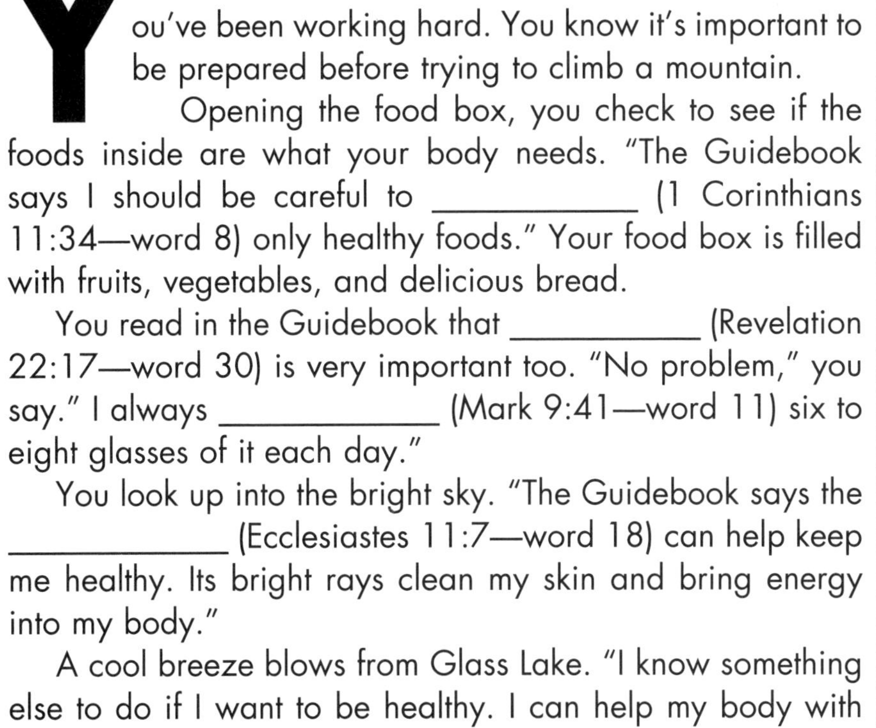

You've been working hard. You know it's important to be prepared before trying to climb a mountain.

Opening the food box, you check to see if the foods inside are what your body needs. "The Guidebook says I should be careful to ____________ (1 Corinthians 11:34—word 8) only healthy foods." Your food box is filled with fruits, vegetables, and delicious bread.

You read in the Guidebook that ___________ (Revelation 22:17—word 30) is very important too. "No problem," you say." I always ____________ (Mark 9:41—word 11) six to eight glasses of it each day."

You look up into the bright sky. "The Guidebook says the ____________ (Ecclesiastes 11:7—word 18) can help keep me healthy. Its bright rays clean my skin and bring energy into my body."

A cool breeze blows from Glass Lake. "I know something else to do if I want to be healthy. I can help my body with every ____________ (Genesis 2:7—word 19) I take. I need to find clean, fresh air every day to keep my blood working hard. Camp Happy Patch has lots of it!"

The sun slowly sinks behind the mountain. "Time for bed," you say. You feel very happy. You like keeping your body healthy, especially in preparation for what's to come soon.

See you tomorrow!

–Carlos

19
JUNE

CAMP HAPPY PATCH . . .

Growing Stronger

Each day, you feel your body growing stronger and stronger. You eat healthy foods, drink lots of water, and remember to rest. You enjoy the bright sunshine and the wonderful fresh air surrounding Camp Happy Patch.

To keep yourself strong, you ____________ (Acts 24:16—word 5) every day. You take a long _________ (Isaiah 2:3—word 40) around Glass Lake in the morning, ___________ (Jeremiah 4:29—word 20) a tree or two after lunch, ___________ (Isaiah 13:2—word 1) fallen branches out of the campsite, and _____________ (Isaiah 28:20—word 11) your muscles often.

As you build up your strength, you notice something else happening to you. What used to be hard ______________ (Jeremiah 31:16—word 17) is now fun. "I like helping my body," you say at the end of the day. "It makes me feel great!"

When evening comes and the shadows are long across the lake, you sit by your tent, listening to the sounds of nature. "All the creatures work hard too," you say. "But I must work even harder. I have a mountain to climb!"

See you tomorrow!

–Carlos

CAMP HAPPY PATCH . . .

Facing the Challenge

20
JUNE

**Trust in the Lord with all your heart . . . ; in all your ways acknowledge him, and he will make your paths straight.
Proverbs 3:5, 6, NIV.**

The sun is hot on your face. You stand at the base of the mountain, looking up toward its cloud-covered summit.

One question keeps popping into your mind. "Can I climb it? Do I have all the strength and knowledge I need?"

Then you think back over the past several weeks and months. You remember the long hours of exercising, the many chapters you've read in the Guidebook, the wonderful things you've seen in nature. Everything you have done has been for this one purpose—to climb that mountain.

"But what if something happens that I don't know about?" you ask yourself. "What if I get scared?"

A voice deep inside you answers gently, "Use what you know. You've learned many things. If a tiny ant can climb a rock, you can climb a mountain. If you need help, just remember what you've learned. What's in your mind cannot be taken away. What you know will help you get to where you want to be."

You look up at the mountain. "I'm going to do it," you say. "I'm going to stand at the very top. If anyone can, I can!"

See you tomorrow!

–Carlos

21
JUNE

CAMP HAPPY PATCH . . .

Getting Ready for the Climb

It's early morning. You slowly open your __________ (Isaiah 40:26—word 4). The air is filled with the sounds of nature waking up. During the last few months your __________ (Psalm 78:1—word 11) have become more alert to the noises in the forest.

"Dear Lord," you pray, "be close to me today. I will need You."

You crawl out of the tent. The grass feels wet on your __________ (Psalm 90:17—word 20). Everything seems clean and fresh in the early morning light.

To protect your __________ (2 Samuel 22:37—word 11) from the sharp stones you'll be walking on, you cover them with thick socks and comfortable hiking boots.

You put on your favorite shirt and pants. A warm jacket keeps away the chill in the air.

Soon the smell of frying eggs and hot herb tea tickles your __________ (Song of Solomon 7:4—word 22). You are hungry. Breakfast will __________ (Psalm 34:8—word 2) very good this morning.

After cleaning the campsite and washing dishes, you read from the Guidebook. Your __________ (1 Chronicles 28:9—word 24) needs to wake up too.

See you tomorrow!

–Carlos

CAMP HAPPY PATCH . . .

On Your Way Up

22
JUNE

You start to climb. All your hard training, daily exercising, and careful learning will be put into action. The mountain will be your test.

Soon Camp Happy Patch and Glass Lake are far below. Treasure Valley looks like a tiny fold in the lap of the mountain. You climb higher and higher.

The path becomes narrow. You want to stop, but you remember how hard the animals worked in Treasure Valley. They never gave up. You will not give up either.

You're getting tired. The climb is hard, very hard.

Stopping to rest, you pull the Guidebook out of your pocket. "Will God help me climb this mountain?" you ask as you open it. You see a sentence underlined with red ink. "What does this say?" you ask yourself, trying not to think about your sore legs.

Slowly, thoughtfully, you read the words one by one.

______________________ (Isaiah 40:29—all words).

"God *is* with me!" you shout into the wind. "I can go on because God will help me climb this mountain."

See you tomorrow!

–Carlos

23
JUNE

CAMP HAPPY PATCH . . .

Fear on the Mountain

The higher you climb, the more rugged the path becomes. Huge stones block your way. Sometimes the ground is slippery. Sometimes you have to walk very slowly so you won't fall over the edge.

Suddenly a thought enters your mind. "What if I get lost? What if I can't find the path anymore?"

You begin to get a little scared. "Maybe God will forget about me up here on this mountain."

You sit down on a rock and open your Guidebook. "I need to find the answer to this question," you say as you flip through the pages, your fingers trembling.

Another sentence has been underlined in red. You read it out loud.

____________________________ (Proverbs 3:6—all words).

You close your eyes. "Thank You, dear Jesus, for promising to show me the path I should take."

Then, with new determination, you begin climbing again.

See you tomorrow!

–Carlos

CAMP HAPPY PATCH . . .

Storm!

24
JUNE

As you climb you notice that the wind has begun to blow very hard. Soon rain splashes on your face. "A storm is coming," you say to yourself. "This could mean very bad trouble when I'm trying to climb a high mountain."

Lightning flashes across the sky. Thunder shakes the mountainside.

"I must find shelter from the storm," you say, trying to climb as fast as you can. "I think I see a small cave up ahead."

With all your might you run, stumble, slip, and crawl toward the cave opening. The clouds swirl around you, trying to keep you from seeing where you're going.

"Lord, help me!" you shout into the roaring wind. "Help me find the cave!"

Just as the storm slams into the mountain with a mighty crash, you slide into the small opening. You're breathing rapidly, your chest heaving. Your arms and legs feel very, very tired.

After catching your breath, you reach into your pocket. "Let's see what the Guidebook says about storms," you say.

You find another sentence underlined in red.

__________________________ (Psalm 46:1—all words).

"Thank You, God," you pray, "for helping me when the storms come." Then you start to wait.

–Carlos

25
JUNE

CAMP HAPPY PATCH . . .

Eyes in the Darkness

The storm grows louder, brighter, and wetter by the minute. You sit in the cave, watching the lightning flash and listening to the thunder roar.

Suddenly you have the feeling you're not alone in the cave. Someone or something is hiding in the shadows.

"Who's there?" you call. No answer. "I said, who's there?"

You hear footsteps coming from the deep, dark center of the cave. You pick up a rock and wait. Maybe a wild animal is coming to attack you.

Two eyes glow in the darkness. You tighten your grip on the rock. Then a tall, handsome mountain goat steps into the light.

"You! I've seen you before." A smile brightens your face. "You visited Camp Happy Patch a while back. Now I'm visiting *your* campsite. Hope you don't mind."

The animal looks at you for a long moment. Then it turns and slowly disappears into the dark shadows of the cave. You sit listening to the crashing thunder. "I guess the goat knows I'm as frightened of the storm as he. I'll just borrow his cave for the night."

Just before you go to sleep, you open the Guidebook and read a beautiful promise.

__________________________ (Proverbs 3:24—all words).

Then you close your eyes and slowly drift into a sweet slumber.

–Carlos

CAMP HAPPY PATCH . . .

Beginning Again

26
JUNE

You wake up. It's morning. The storm has blown away. Only a gentle wind whispers around the rocks.

Crawling to the mouth of the cave, you see a world washed clean by the rain. Above you, the mountain summit stands tall and proud against the blue sky.

"Today, I will get to the top!" you announce.

After eating a light breakfast of fruits and nuts from your backpack, you leave the cave and start climbing once again.

The mountaintop grows closer and closer. With every step, you advance on your goal.

You stop to rest by a large rock. "This mountain needs a very special name," you say to yourself. "What shall I call it?"

Opening your Guidebook, you notice another sentence underlined in red. As you read it, a smile lifts the corners of your mouth.

______________________________ (Psalm 98:1—all words).

"That's it. *That's it!*" you shout. "I know what I'll call this mountain." Looking up toward the summit, you lift your hands above your head and shout to the world, "Because I have depended on God to help me as I climb, I will call this great and noble mountain Mount Victory!"

See you tomorrow!

–Carlos

27
JUNE

I can do everything through him who gives me strength. Philippians 4:13, NIV.

CAMP HAPPY PATCH . . .

At the Top!

You strain at each step. Your chest hurts. Your legs hurt. Your arms hurt. But you must keep going.

You close your eyes. "Lord," you pray. "Please help me."

The path suddenly stops. "What's wrong?" you gasp. "Am I lost? Why is there no more path to follow?"

Then you look up. There is no more mountain above you. You're standing at the top. You've made it! *You've made it!*

No more climbing or stumbling. No more fear of falling. You are standing on the summit of Mount Victory.

Joyful tears fill your eyes. All the work, training, and studying has brought you to the very top of the majestic mountain. Far below, the rivers, forests, cliffs, and rocky paths seem small and fragile. You wonder why you'd ever been afraid of them.

A feeling of peace fills your tired body. It was worth it. It was worth it all.

At the top of the mountain, you learn a wonderful secret. With God by your side, you can do *anything:* handle any problem, unlock the mysteries of nature, find protection from the storms that blow. Yes, you can even climb a towering mountain.

For the first time in your life, you know what victory means. Your journey began in a valley far below and ended beyond the clouds.

–Carlos

GOD IN SCIENCE . . .

Creating With My Camera

28
JUNE

Behold, I will create new heavens and a new earth.
Isaiah 65:17, NIV.

Have you ever wondered how God will be able to perfectly *re*create our friends and family members who have died? After all, they're gone, turned into dust, totally *not* a person anymore!

Well, the answer may be as close as your camera. Let's ask science to teach us something about our heavenly Father.

* * *

Smile! *Click.*

Photographers depend on something God made a long time ago—chemistry. Here's how.

When you take a picture, light travels through the lens of your camera and strikes a piece of film that has been coated with a light-sensitive chemical. The image doesn't appear until those chemicals come in contact with other chemicals when the film is developed. Then, even more chemicals, called fixers, are needed to prevent that great shot of your friend Tom balancing an orange on his nose from fading away.

So the next time you grab your camera, you can thank science for all those colorful memories.

If God can make it possible for us to create images out of light, He certainly knows how to create people out of dust. He did it with Adam. And He'll do it to those we love when He returns. Awesome!

–Uncle Charles

29
JUNE

I will remove from them their heart of stone and give them a heart of flesh. Ezekiel 11:19, NIV.

GOD IN SCIENCE . . .

My Two Hearts

Jesus has promised that He can take our selfish, "stony" heart and give us a new, loving heart. How will he do that?

Let's ask science to teach us something about our heavenly Father.

⁂ ⁂ ⁂

That heart thumping away in your chest is actually two powerful pumps that work hard for as long as you live. It's an amazing muscle machine!

When you take a deep breath, your lungs fill with air. The oxygen in that air is added to your blood, and the heart sends it flowing all over your body. Then when stuff like your legs, stomach, and brain have used up the oxygen, the blood circles back to the heart where it's pumped through the lungs for another load. One pump in your heart draws blood in while the other shoots it out.

When God says He wants to give us a new heart, He means that He wants to give us a new *spiritual* heart, one that works hard to keep our thoughts centered on the needs of others. While our actual heart keeps us alive and kicking, our spiritual heart motivates us to be kind and forgiving.

Hey, Christians have *two* hearts! One keeps you alive. The other keeps you busy loving others. *Tha-dump, tha-dump, tha-dump . . .*

—Uncle Charles

GOD IN SCIENCE . . .

Listening to Jesus

30 JUNE

He who has ears to hear, let him hear. Luke 8:8, NIV.

Seems as if every day someone is telling you to "listen to Jesus" and you'll know what to do. Right? But, how can you listen to Someone you can't see?

Let's ask science to teach us something about our heavenly Father.

* * *

Sound is any movement of air that is heard by an ear. If you've forgotten what an ear is, check the mirror. You've got two!

When something creates a sound, it vibrates molecules in the air. These vibrations, or "sound waves," travel out in all directions until they hit the eardrum of a passing animal or second grader. The eardrum vibrates in response to the movement of the air, and the brain tries to figure out what those vibrations mean.

Loud sounds can damage eardrums, so keep the radio volume down and try not to shout at your friends.

Now if God can figure all of that out and make it work, don't you think He can figure out a way of telling you something? His voice may be in the form of a thought or idea, or He might choose to use a parent or teacher to tell you what He wants you to know.

When facing a problem, listen. God may have a few vibrations ready just for you!

–Uncle Charles

1
JULY

He is like a tree planted by streams of water. Psalm 1:3, NIV.

GOD IN SCIENCE . . .

Growing Like a Tree

The Bible tells us that we can learn a lot about God by studying nature. Really? What are we supposed to learn from a tree?

Let's see if science can teach us something about our heavenly Father.

* * *

Trees grow almost everywhere. Give them a little soil, some sun, and a supply of water, and they'll survive freezing temperatures, blazing fires, and even woodpeckers.

But trees do a whole lot more than stand there and shade you. Their roots keep soil from washing away and store water in times of drought. In their branches you'll find hundreds of species of animals and plants enjoying protection, food, and a place to live. Leaves absorb the fumes pumped out by cars and factories and give off fresh oxygen for us to breathe.

Destroy a tree or a forest, and all of those benefits are lost!

So don't ever think that God made you to just stand around and watch life go by. No way! You've got work to do, such as bringing happiness to old people, helping your mom or dad keep the house clean, making your baby brother giggle, and learning how to encourage those who are sad.

Yes, you can learn a lot from a tree while you stand in its shade.

–Uncle Charles

GOD IN SCIENCE . . .

Splish, Splash!

2
JULY

You will be like a well-watered garden, like a spring whose waters never fail. Isaiah 58:11, NIV.

It's the only thing in nature that can be a gas, liquid, or solid depending on the temperature. It's also great to drink!

I'm talking about *water*—you know, the stuff that gurgles in the creek behind your house or pours hot and cold from your bathroom faucet.

The same bucket of water can become part of a ship-sinking iceberg (solid), coat plants and grasses with morning dew (liquid), or drift high overhead as a cloud (gas).

Not only can water be fun to swim in, it also refreshes the flowers when it rains and cools your lemonade on those hot summer afternoons. And after you've played nine innings of baseball or helped your dad plant a dozen rows of corn, water tastes absolutely delicious!

We need lots of water outside our bodies to keep us clean, and inside where it can flush poisons from our organs. Nothing works as well.

God created water for many purposes. He created you for many purposes, too, such as helping people and making the world a better place in which to live.

So when you sip cool, refreshing H_2O (that's science talk for water) or scrub the dirt from your hands, remember that you too have many things to do for God today.

–Uncle Charles

3
JULY

And hath made of one blood all nations of men for to dwell on all the face of the earth. Acts 17:26.

GOD IN SCIENCE . . .

Blood Brothers and Sisters

All human beings share something in common. Blood. The average adult lugs around four to six liters of the red stuff inside his or her body.

Some scientists want you to believe that since our blood has the same amount of salt in it as the ocean, we came from there. They insist that one day in the misty past, we crawled out onto the land, looked around, and began building shopping malls. Wrong!

Our blood and the ocean share the same amount of salt because the same God created both. He figured, hey, if it works for fish, it will work for people, too.

And did you know that if you were hurt in an accident and needed a transfusion (that's when doctors put new blood in your body to replace what you lost), someone in Japan or South America or Africa or Russia could give you the blood you need and save your life? That's right! People blood is people blood, no matter where they come from.

So the next time you hear someone making fun of another person who may have a different skin color than you or live in a faraway country, say, "Stop! That's my blood brother [or sister] you're talking about."

Outside we may look different, but inside we're all the same.

—Uncle Charles

GOD IN SCIENCE . . .

Cruisin' With Otto

4

JULY

The Lord God formed the man from the dust of the ground and breathed into his nostrils the breath of life, and the man became a living being. Genesis 2:7, NIV.

The next time you go for a ride in your family car, you can thank a German engineer named Nikolaus Otto for the pleasure. In 1876 he figured out a way to mix fuel, air, and a tiny spark to create power. Here's how it works.

Gasoline and air are pumped into a tightly sealed metal enclosure called a cylinder. Another device inside the cylinder, called a piston, rises up and compresses (squeezes) the mixture just as a spark plug creates a tiny spark. *Bang!* The fuel explodes, driving the piston down. This movement spins the driveshaft that is connected to a wheel in your car. As the driveshaft spins around and around, it spins the wheel around and around . . . and off you go to see Grandma!

I'm sure that Nikolaus Otto wasn't thinking about God when he created the car engine. He was probably wondering if his new device could make him rich. Perhaps he wanted to travel from Germany to France, and his faithful old mule just wasn't fast enough. Whatever the reason, we've been blessed by his creative work ever since.

Mr. Otto was smart. God created Mr. Otto. Think about it.

—Uncle Charles

5
JULY

The God of Israel gives power and strength to his people.
Psalm 68:35, NIV.

GOD IN SCIENCE . . .

Powerful Work

Everything in the universe is made up of tiny bits and pieces of matter called particles. Some of these bits and pieces have positive charges, some negative. When you move these particles around or rub them together, you create electricity.

That's exactly what the power company does to manufacture the energy that runs computers and light bulbs.

Electricity makes the light bulb in your bedroom glow each night, plays your favorite tunes on the radio, and helps your computer compute. Without electricity, you'd be studying by candlelight, listening to Uncle Ted play his banjo, and sending notes to your friends by carrier pigeon. Forget about watching television. No electricity; no cartoons.

While electricity is amazing, when handled carelessly, it can kill you! If you stick anything other than a lamp or radio plug into a wall outlet, you'll be in for a very painful surprise. And if you've even *considered* climbing that electric pole outside your house, forget it! You might be alive going up, but you'd probably be dead coming down. That can put a dent in your whole afternoon.

So take care when using electricity. Guard your particles carefully. They're much too important to the universe . . . and to God.

–Uncle Charles

GOD IN SCIENCE . . .

Flying High

Ever watch a bird fly by and wonder, *How does he do that?*

First, you gotta have wings. You can flap your arms all day, but you won't get an inch off the ground. Your friends will think you're crazy, so don't even try.

Birds are built for flight. You're built for eating pizza and playing soccer.

As a bird flaps its feathers, air strikes the bottom of its wings. This pushes the wings, and the bird, up. When he wants to land, he just tilts his wings forward until the wind stops striking them from below, and down he comes. He can fly up and down just by changing how his wings pass through the air. This is called *lift,* and God created it.

When Orville and Wilbur Wright first flew their little airplane over the dunes of North Carolina, they'd been studying birds for a long time. They, and other scientists, had learned that to fly, you've got to control the movement of air over a set of carefully created wings. It took man 6,000 years to figure out what birds know the day they're born!

Today when you see a hawk soaring across the sky or watch a robin zoom by, think of the God who created them and taught them how to fly.

–Uncle Charles

The wings of the ostrich flap joyfully, but they cannot compare with the pinions and feathers of the stork. Job 39:13, NIV.

7
JULY

Your word is a lamp to my feet and a light for my path. Psalm 119:105, NIV.

GOD IN SCIENCE . . .

Danger!

Have you ever watched a science program on television in which men and women in white coats are testing to see if something is "radioactive"? They're looking for stuff that has been changed by coming into contact with dangerous material from a nuclear bomb or nuclear power plant. In their hands, they're holding a machine called a Geiger counter. When it finds a problem, it clicks and clicks as if trying to say, "Watch out. Danger!" Then the scientists work hard to clean away all of the dangerous *radioactive* material.

Did you know that sin has a bad habit of changing people too? That's right. People who live by the devil's rules become sick and weak and have to struggle through life. They're "sin-active" and need immediate attention.

What do you think Christians use to help those people find the dangers hurting their lives. That's right—the Bible. It's filled with good advice and helpful hints on how to remove sin and bring the healing touch of Jesus into your life. It's like a Geiger counter, only this time it's not searching for dangerous radioactive material; it's searching for dangerous sin.

If you want to be one of God's scientists, learn to use your Bible to search for danger. And when you find some, ask your heavenly Father to help you clean it away.

–Uncle Charles

GOD IN NATURE . . .

Spots on the Sun

8
JULY

Your enemy the devil prowls around like a roaring lion looking for someone to devour.
1 Peter 5:8, NIV.

The next time you're listening to the radio and the signal gets all scratchy and begins to pop and crackle, don't be too quick to blame your local radio station. The problem may be the sun!

That big bright ball occasionally falls victim to its own power. Dark, boiling "sunspots" form on its surface. Then solar flares shoot out into space, filling the atmosphere with static, the kind you get when you rub your feet on a rug and then touch something metal. *Ouch!*

When those solar flares strike the earth, your radio snaps, crackles, and pops.

Sometimes the old devil is like those sunspots. He sends anger and jealousy shooting out at you, making you complain and say things you shouldn't. You end up sounding like a radio that's having a problem getting a clear signal. You growl and sniff, moan and groan. Of course, the devil is laughing and laughing at the troubles he's causing.

During these attacks you need to ask God for help. You need to invite Him into your life, where He can fight the devil and keep your mind clear of Satan's noises.

Today, if you begin to snap and crackle, tune out the devil and invite God in immediately!

—Uncle Charles

9
JULY

Then God said, "I give you every seed-bearing plant on the face of the whole earth and every tree that has fruit with seed in it. They will be yours for food." Genesis 1:29, NIV.

GOD IN SCIENCE . . .

Chew on This!

You have up to 32 of them. Without a good, healthy set, you'd have a hard time speaking. Eating peanuts would be impossible. What am I talking about? Teeth!

When God put teeth in your mouth, He had a plan. He wanted you to eat only natural chewy things, such as fruits, grains, nuts, and seeds. Candy bars and cola drinks weren't on the menu in the Garden of Eden. Adam and Eve never had a lollipop. Why? Because God knew that those sugary foods weren't healthy for growing teeth.

Today the grocery store is filled to the rafters with food. Some are great, some harmful. How can you tell the difference? By asking your mom or dad to check what's in the food. Then compare that list with what God gave Adam and Eve. The more natural ingredients you find, the better. The more "unnatural" ingredients—such as chemicals, preservatives, and sugars—you find, watch out. Those foods may be harmful to not only your teeth but your whole body.

So when you eat, chew on foods that are healthy. Your teeth will thank you for years and years to come.

–Uncle Charles

GOD IN SCIENCE . . .

Hello?

10
JULY

It looks and works kinda like an ear, but it isn't.

The telephone has been around since 1876, when an American inventor named Alexander Graham Bell made the first call. No, he didn't order pizza. He asked his assistant for help.

When you speak into a telephone, your voice vibrations are changed into electrical signals that are sent over a wire to the phone that you're calling. There those signals are changed back into words.

Nowadays more and more phone calls depend on satellites. Your voice vibrations are sent as a signal to an orbiting satellite, then beamed back down to your friend and family member in whatever faraway country you're calling. Even if there's an ocean between you, it doesn't matter.

I once called my mom and dad from Japan. They were in Tennessee. We talked and laughed just as if we were sitting in the same room together. Amazing!

Here's a question. Do you know God's telephone number? Of course you don't, because He doesn't have one! If you want to talk to God, you just pray. No telephones. No satellites. No voice vibrations. Just thankful thoughts and secret questions. God's got great ears and can hear no matter where you are or what you're doing.

Take a moment and talk to God right now!

–Uncle Charles

He will call upon me, and I will answer him. Psalm 91:15, NIV.

11
JULY

So then with the mind I myself serve the law of God. Romans 7:25.

GOD IN SCIENCE . . .

The Human Brain

The human brain—that amazing but not exactly attractive organ tucked inside your head—controls everything your body does. Your hands and feet move because the brain tells them to move. It figures out what you're hearing, seeing, tasting, and touching. It also figures out what you're trying to figure out.

Adult brains only weigh 1.3 kilograms, but when they're used properly, they can create very heavy things, such as bridges, office buildings, and sledgehammers.

Kids' brains, while weighing a little less, can do some amazing things too, such as building pretend highways in the mud, learning action songs in Sabbath school, figuring out how to help a classmate who is sad, and writing a poem about a duck. Cool!

I once watched a primary-age boy preach a sermon to an auditorium filled with amazed people. I listened to a junior-age girl play a very difficult song on a piano and saw a video of a bunch of teenagers building a jungle clinic. These teens were using their brains to bring hope and happiness to a lot of people.

By the way, using alcohol, tobacco, and other drugs destroys brain cells. That's why smart people stay away from such poisons. I just thought you'd like to know.

–Uncle Charles

GOD IN SCIENCE . . .

Water Power

Starting a quarrel is like breaching a dam; so drop the matter before a dispute breaks out. Proverbs 17:14, NIV.

Beavers build them. So do humans. They're tall and wide and help you send e-mails. Do you know what I'm talking about? No? Let me explain.

Dams, which are built by busy beavers and hardworking people, do one thing very well. They hold back water. But scientists have figured out how a dam can help them create something that beavers have never heard of. Electricity.

Here's how. The water that's being held back by a human-made dam is sent down long tubes to a large machine at the base. This fast-flowing water strikes a set of blades that rotate a bunch of tightly wound copper coils inside a huge magnet. This turning motion creates electricity that's sent by wires to your house. You plug your computer into those wires, boot up, and bingo—you're sending e-mails and downloading pictures of your cousin Ashley.

I'm very glad that God has taught us how to use science to make our lives better. We can also make the lives of other people better, too. That electricity coming to our house from a dam can help us send words of hope to a friend or make a call to a classmate who is in the hospital. Seems water does a lot more than quench your thirst!

Thank Jesus today for water power.

—Uncle Charles

13
JULY

Many shall run to and fro, and knowledge shall be increased. Daniel 12:4.

GOD IN SCIENCE . . .

Fast Trains

If you want to get from where you are to someplace else, you could walk, ride in a car, or even go by horseback. But if you want to get there fast without leaving the ground, you might jump on board a train.

One train engine can pull more than 100 railroad cars filled with people, corn, or Ping-Pong balls. The engine creates a lot less air pollution and uses a lot less diesel fuel than a hundred trucks. Some trains even run on the electricity they collect from special wires hanging over the tracks.

One of the world's fastest trains can rush you from Paris, France, to Geneva, Switzerland, at 160 miles (260 kilometers) per hour. Let's see the family Toyota do *that!*

When the Seventh-day Adventist Church was very young, our pioneers used trains to go from place to place. They traveled to faraway towns to hold evangelistic meetings and shipped truth-filled magazines to people who wanted to know more about Jesus and His love.

Today we use airplanes and cars to go where we want to go, but trains still chug along, reminding us that God wants us to use every method available to spread the good news of salvation to others.

–Uncle Charles

GOD IN NATURE . . .

Moving Pictures

14
JULY

Jesus said to him, "Away from me, Satan!" Matthew 4:10, NIV.

If you've ever watched a motion picture, I've got some shocking news for you. Half the time you were staring at a blank screen!

A movie camera doesn't take "moving" pictures. It takes *still* pictures—24 of them every second. Later a projector beams those still pictures, one at a time, up on the screen. It shows one picture, closes the lens, positions the next picture behind the lens, and shows that one. This happens 24 times a second.

Your eye thinks you're seeing motion, but you're not. It's only an illusion.

Sometimes the devil says, "Hey, look at this. Watch this. Listen to this." Then he shows us sights and sounds that seem pretty at first. We sit there and smile, thinking, *This is fun. I like what I'm seeing and hearing.*

But the truth is you're not seeing everything. Those beautiful images the devil shows you of people smoking cigarettes, drinking alcohol, or doing drugs hide a terrible danger. You don't see the diseases and body-destroying habits that go along with such activities. "Sin is fun," Satan says. "Enjoy yourself."

But you're smart. You've learned the truth about the devil and his "moving pictures."

"Get behind me, Satan," you say. "You're not going to fool me!"

Always be careful of what you see and hear.

–Uncle Charles

15
JULY

GOD IN SCIENCE . . .

Skyscrapers

Study to shew thyself approved unto God. 2 Timothy 2:15.

Skyscrapers, those very tall buildings you find in cities, can reach to the clouds. But "up" is not the most important part of their amazing construction. "Down" is where the action is.

A skyscraper's foundation is very, very important. If it's built over solid rock, no problem. But if the building is constructed over clay, sand, or moist soil, engineers have to work extra hard to make sure that the foundation won't slip, sink, or even rise when the weather changes or earthquakes rattle the windows.

They build thick concrete floors or create solid supports called footers deep in the ground. Skyscrapers go up only after the "down" is solid and secure.

Have you ever thought of yourself as a skyscraper? Well, you should. God wants you to grow up to be strong and tall in your faith, like David, Daniel, and Moses. But before you go up, you need to build a solid foundation of healthy habits and a strong faith in Jesus.

How do you do that? By studying your Bible, learning from teachers and parents, and asking God to help you each day.

Why not start building that solid foundation today by inviting Jesus into your heart? Then you can grow, grow, grow!

—Uncle Charles

GOD IN SCIENCE . . .

Why Sleep?

16
JULY

He who watches over you will not slumber.
Psalm 121:3, NIV.

It's late in the evening. You've had a busy day filled with schoolwork, ball games, fun times with friends, and constantly going here and there. Suddenly your eyelids feel heavier than before—you can't move as fast or think as clearly. What's going on? Are your batteries running down? Well, kinda.

Your body seems to be saying, "Excuse me. I'm getting a little worn out here. Would you mind taking a break for a while?"

A lot of kids fight that urge, but they shouldn't.

Why? Because you *need* to sleep.

Scientists believe that sleeping is the body's way of fighting diseases, rebuilding damaged or lost brain cells, and basically reenergizing itself. You may think you're sleeping, but your body is actually hard at work doing things it can't do while you're awake.

Everyone needs sleep—from eight to 10 hours each night. So if you start yawning and your eyelids begin to droop, don't fight it. Head for bed. Your body's got some important work to do.

–Uncle Charles

17 JULY

When your eyes are good, your whole body also is full of light. Luke 11:34, NIV.

GOD IN SCIENCE . . .

Camera in Your Head

Some are blue. Some are brown. They're no good in the dark, and some people put glass in front of theirs. You've got two.

What am I talking about? The human eye—those wonderful devices resting proudly on each side of your nose.

Anyone who's ever used a camera should have no trouble figuring out how the human eye works. Like a camera's lens, your eyes allow light to enter your head. But at the back of the eye you won't find any film. Instead you've got something called a *retina*. From here, the image of your best friend making a silly face or that tall tree by the back door is quickly sent to the brain so it can tell you what you're looking at. That way you won't invite the tree in for supper or try to climb your friend.

Jesus says we should always guard what we look at, that we should allow our eyes to see only those things that are true, important, and helpful. Violent television programs with ugly scenes of anger and hate shouldn't be watched by Christian boys and girls. Instead we should focus the cameras in our heads on scenes of caring and compassion.

Guard your eyes today.

–Uncle Charles

GOD IN SCIENCE . . .

Hot and Cold Planet

18
JULY

My own hand laid the foundations of the earth, and my right hand spread out the heavens. Isaiah 48:13, NIV.

It's smaller than our earth, has a couple moons, and enjoys a daytime temperature of 60° Fahrenheit (15° Celsius). This wouldn't be so bad except that at night, the temp drops down to around *minus* 225° Fahrenheit (*minus* 140° Celsius). That's a wee bit chilly, especially if you're not wearing long underwear!

I'm talking about Mars, the fourth planet from our sun. It's named after the Roman god of war because it appears fiery red in the night sky.

Why would God create such a cold and lifeless planet? No one lives on the sun, either. (Too hot!) As a matter of fact, most of the stars we see in our night sky are actually boiling suns.

However, most of those suns are part of star systems where life could be found if we knew where to look. But don't expect little green men or violent monsters on the planets circling those suns. Out there, beyond the reach of sin, are perfect beings created by a loving God, beings eagerly waiting to greet us when Jesus takes us home to heaven.

Won't it be fun to live with our heavenly Father and those perfect beings among the stars?

–Uncle Charles

19
JULY

Even the sparrow has found a home, and the swallow a nest for herself, where she may have her young. Psalm 84:3, NIV.

GOD IN SCIENCE . . .

Long Journey

Some of the residents of my hometown leave every autumn and return every spring. No, they don't pack up the station wagon or hop on a train. They fly, but not in an airplane. They use their wings.

Outside my home office window is a many-room birdhouse sitting atop a tall pole. Inside one of those rooms are some little pink eggs faithfully guarded by a mother and father tree swallow. But a few weeks ago, when snowflakes filled the air and cold winds blew up the valley, those swallows were nowhere to be seen. They were in South America, enjoying warm, tropical breezes.

When birds travel from one area to another, it's called a migration. Scientists aren't sure why they make the journey or how they find their way over thousands of miles of oceans and lands and end up right where they wanted to go. All I know is that each spring, my tree swallows return, build nests, raise young tree swallows, then fly away again. Birds have been doing this for thousands of years.

I guess we'll just have to wait and ask God how it's possible. He should know. He created birds . . . and us. And the same God who guides my tree swallows to their summer home can surely lead us to heaven.

–Uncle Charles

GOD IN SCIENCE . . .

Breathing Lessons

20
JULY

As the deer pants for streams of water, so my soul pants for you, O God. Psalm 42:l, NIV.

Have you ever tried to breathe underwater? Don't bother. You can't . . . unless you're a fish.

Fish breathe by drinking. They use gills instead of lungs. Water flows over their gills, and oxygen is absorbed into their bloodstream. That's why fish can't live on land and we can't live in a pond.

Both fish and humans need oxygen to stay alive. We just breathe it in different ways.

If you've ever wondered how important oxygen is to your body, try holding your breath. At first everything is fine because your body has some extra air stored inside. But very soon, you'll notice that your chest begins to hurt a little as your lungs try to expand. "Give us some air!" they seem to cry harder and harder.

You might start to feel a little dizzy as your brain slowly loses its power to think clearly.

Before long your whole body is in a panic. It needs air right *now!*

Then you breathe again and, oh, how happy your lungs and brain and body are. They relax as oxygen seeps into every cell. Before long, you're calm again. *Whew!*

Here's something to remember. Your mind needs Jesus as much as your body needs oxygen. Think about that today.

–Uncle Charles

21
JULY

GOD IN NATURE . . .

Computer Talk

We do not know what we ought to pray for, but the Spirit himself intercedes for us with groans that words cannot express. Romans 8:26, NIV.

Computers have a language all their own. But they don't speak words. They talk with numbers!

Everything a computer does, every command it follows or piece of information it gives us, is originally made up of two numbers: zero and one. The programs running in the computer's electronic brain translate those collections of numbers into letters for word processing, colors for pictures, and even sounds for hearing.

Aren't you glad that people don't use numbers to communicate? You'd ask a friend if he wanted to go to the store, and he'd say, "Zero one one zero zero one." How confusing!

Did you know that God has a language too? Don't worry—you already know how to speak it. You always have. And don't think you have to use only certain words or say things in certain ways. God hears you whenever you speak, even if you're using words filled with anger or fear. He understands because He loves you very much.

So when you kneel to pray, just talk. Say the things on your mind. Tell Him about your day and about your problems. He's listening and knows exactly what you're saying.

Why not practice your God-language right now!

–Uncle Charles

GOD IN SCIENCE . . .

Bodyprint

22
JULY

How great is the love the Father has lavished on us, that we should be called children of God! And that is what we are! 1 John 3:1, NIV.

Everyone who has a finger has a fingerprint, right? Well, everyone who has a body has a bodyprint, too. It's called DNA.

DNA is found in every cell in your body. It's like an *inside* fingerprint of you. The DNA in your hair is exactly the same as the DNA in your big toe, your blood, and even your sweat. That's how scientists are helping police catch criminals. If a bad guy leaves a hair or two behind at the scene of the crime, they can match the DNA from those hairs to ones on his head and say, "Hey, you were there. Gotcha!"

I like to believe that God has put some kind of bodyprint in you and me. This print tells Him that we belong to Him. No matter what the devil does to us, no matter how filled with sin we become, God can look inside us and say, "Yup, that's *My* boy or girl. There's *My* bodyprint on his or her heart. That proves this person belongs to *Me.*"

So when Satan says, "You're mine," you can say, "Nope. I belong to Jesus because I invited Him into my heart and He has put His print in me."

Why not thank God for leaving His print in you today?

—Uncle Charles

23
JULY

My help comes from the Lord, the Maker of heaven and earth. Psalm 121:2, NIV.

GOD IN SCIENCE . . .

Gravity

Gravity is the force that draws two things together. It's what keeps the moon orbiting the earth and the earth orbiting the sun. It's also what keeps you from floating off into space.

Ever watch an ocean tide rise on a beach? A few hours later it settles down again. That's gravity from the moon pulling and then releasing the ocean. Strong stuff, huh?

Gravity may control us, but God controls gravity.

Have you ever seen pictures of astronauts working in space? Weird! They float around all over the place. They eat dinner hanging upside down on a wall, sleep sideways in their sleeping bags, and work on scientific experiments while sitting on air! That's because in space their bodies aren't being pulled by gravity like here on earth.

Allowing Satan into your heart is sorta like living without gravity. He can push you around and make you go places you usually don't choose to go. You can't run, and you can't fight back. All you can do is float.

Then, when invited, God steps in and switches on the power of His love. Suddenly you can run from sin; you can turn and fight it with all your might. Now *you're* in control!

Why not use some of God's power today?

–Uncle Charles

MY CHAIN OF LOVE . . .

Thankful Link

24
JULY

Hello. My name is Stevie, and I'm doing something really neat.

I'm making a chain out of paper. But not just any chain! On each link I'm going to write something that I learned about Jesus. I'm calling it my chain of love. You can make one too!

Today Jesus did three special things for me, so I'll make three links. Here's what happened.

First He gave me a delicious breakfast. "Hey," you may say, "your mom did that!" True. But she told me how Jesus helped her find a job so she could buy the groceries to make the meal.

Then my teacher, Mr. Mattingly, showed us how one bee can make a whole field of flowers grow. I know God made the bee, and I like flowers, so I'm thankful for nature and how even a little bee can make lots of people happy.

Next my dad finished painting the inside of the house. He once told me that some kids don't have a home to live in. Dad said, "Jesus helps me work hard to earn the money for our warm, safe house with the big tree in front." So I'm thankful again.

Now I have three links in my chain of love. There will be many more soon. I'll tell you about them each day.

–Stevie

Praise the Lord, O my soul, and forget not all his benefits. Psalm 103:2, NIV.

25
JULY

MY CHAIN OF LOVE . . .

Praise Link

Love your neighbor as yourself. Leviticus 19:18, NIV.

How's your chain of love coming along? Today I'm putting a link in my chain called "kind neighbors."

Mr. and Mrs. Appleby have been married for a long, long time. They have also lived in the same house on the same street in the same town ever since their wedding day. That's incredible!

They're very nice to me. In the summer when it's hot, Mrs. Appleby always asks me if I would like a cool fruit drink. I say yes because then I can sit on the porch and listen to Mr. Appleby tell stories about when he was a little boy.

He said he once fell out of a tree and broke his arm. He landed on his sister. She didn't get hurt at all, except she was mad at him for 10 years. Mr. Appleby says that sometimes, when it rains, his arm still hurts a little.

I love to sit on the porch with my friendly neighbors and listen to them remember happy times of the past. They always give me some good ideas on how to be kind to others and keep out of trouble.

Mr. Appleby likes to tease his wife, and they laugh a lot. Maybe that's why they have stayed together for so long.

I thank God for giving me kind neighbors.

–Stevie

MY CHAIN OF LOVE . . .

Listening Link

26
JULY

My brother David is in the Army. He has to live in a faraway country so he can keep people from fighting each other. His job is dangerous, and I worry about him every day.

Each month David sends me a cassette tape. When it arrives, I quickly slip it into my tape recorder, and then something wonderful happens. I hear my brother's voice talking to me.

David knows I'm worried, so he tells me about the country he lives in, the nice people he sees every day, and the birds that sing in the woods behind the Army base. It makes me feel a little better.

I listen to every word because I love my brother. Last week David told me something interesting. He said Jesus likes for people to listen to Him, too, so I should read the Bible every day. My brother said it's just like getting a cassette tape from Jesus, only I have to say the words.

He said Jesus wants to tell me how to be kind and loving. David said if more people would take the time to listen to Jesus, there would be no wars, and he could come home.

On today's link in my chain I'm writing, "I'm glad Jesus wants me to listen to Him." Aren't you glad too?

–Stevie

He who has ears, let him hear. Matthew 11:15, NIV.

27
JULY

Jesus said, ". . . This poor widow has put more into the treasury than all the others. They all gave out of their wealth; but she . . . put in everything—all she had to live on." Mark 12:43, 44, NIV.

MY CHAIN OF LOVE . . .

Party Link

Last week was my birthday, and Mom gave me a party. As I was opening my gifts, a boy from school named Peter asked me to come into the kitchen so he could talk to me. "My dad can't find a job," he said, "and we don't have any money, so this is the only gift I have."

He handed me a little truck with a wheel missing. "It's all I've got," Peter whispered, "but I want you to have it for your birthday." Then he ran back into the living room.

I stood looking at the little truck for a long time. It wasn't new. Someone had played with it a lot.

Mom came in and asked me what I was doing. I told her what had happened. She knelt beside me and said quietly, "I think Peter has given you the best gift of all."

Today when I played roads and bridges in the backyard, I asked Peter to join me. I let him use the little truck with only three wheels. We laughed and had a good time.

I wrote a new link in my chain of love today. It says, "I'm thankful God has invited me to His big party in heaven." Now I know that God will be happy with whatever gift I bring.

–Stevie

MY CHAIN OF LOVE . . .

Lost and Found Link

28
JULY

Rejoice with me; I have found my lost sheep. Luke 15:6, NIV.

Something happened to me that was kinda scary.

Sunday afternoon my mom and dad took me on a picnic. We played catch, ate sandwiches, and fed the ducks.

Then we played hide-and-seek. That's when the trouble began.

I decided to hide in the woods where no one would find me. Well, I did a good job, because no one could find me. And I couldn't find my mom and dad, either. I was lost!

My dad always told me that if I got lost, I was supposed to stay put and wait for someone to come. So I sat on a log and waited . . . and waited . . . and waited.

The sun dropped behind the trees and frogs began to chirp. An owl hooted somewhere up in the leaves. "Whoooo. Whoooo."

Then I heard my dad calling. "Here I am!" I shouted. "Over here!"

Dad gave me a big hug. "You're not lost anymore," he said. "Let's go home."

My Sabbath school teacher once said, "Jesus came to save us in this sinful world. Because He died for us, we can someday go home to heaven."

The newest link in my chain of love has these words written on it: "I'm thankful God sent Jesus to save me."

Believe me, it's scary to be lost!

—Stevie

29
JULY

MY CHAIN OF LOVE . . .

Forgiving Link

Forgive us our sins, for we also forgive everyone who sins against us. Luke 11:4, NIV.

This morning, before I went to school, I said something I shouldn't have.

Mom was getting ready to go to work, and I asked her if she could drive me to the baseball game later that afternoon. She said no because she had to work on a project until after suppertime. Mrs. Anderson would drive me instead.

I guess I got mad. "You don't love me!" I shouted. "All you do is work. If you loved me, you would take me to the ball game."

Mom looked sad. "I *do* love you," she said, "but I have to work."

Well, I just ran out of the house and jumped onto the school bus without even waving or anything.

That night when Mom got home, I was waiting. "Mom," I said softly, "I said unkind things to you this morning. It made me feel sad all day long. Will you forgive me?"

Mom put her arms around me. "I felt sad too," she whispered. "I'll be happy to forgive you. I want to be like Jesus. He always forgives us when we make mistakes."

The new link in my chain of love says, "I'm thankful Jesus and my mom forgive me when I do something dumb." Forgiveness makes me feel happy inside.

–Stevie

MY CHAIN OF LOVE . . .

Witnessing Link

Giving thanks always for all things. Ephesians 5:20.

"How many of you are *thankful* today?" the preacher at my church asked last Sabbath.

Lots of hands went up, including mine. I was thankful that my cousin Nathan was getting better in the hospital. He got very sick two weeks ago, and my dad said he might die. But he didn't.

"How many of you would like to share your thankfulness with the congregation?" the preacher called out.

Wait a minute. Raising my hand was one thing. Standing up there in front of all those people was something else.

But then I remembered the story of the blind man who was healed by Jesus. He wasn't scared to share with others how thankful he was. He ran around telling everyone what Jesus had done for him.

I stood and walked to the front of the room. Taking a deep breath, I told about Nathan and how he was feeling better and would be coming home soon. People nodded and smiled. Then they said "Amen" when I was finished.

Last night I made a new link for my chain of love. On a strip of paper I wrote, "I'm thankful that God helped Nathan get better."

My chain is growing longer every day. How's yours coming?

—*Stevie*

31
JULY

For the Lord himself will come down from heaven, with a loud command, with the voice of the archangel and with the trumpet call of God, and the dead in Christ will rise first. 1 Thessalonians 4:16, NIV.

MY CHAIN OF LOVE . . .

Uncle John Link

I want to tell you about my uncle John. He died three weeks ago, and I'm still very sad.

Uncle John made my mom and dad laugh all the time. He told funny stories and gave Mom terrific presents sometimes.

He would play football with me. I would run and run, but he would always catch me. "You're out," he'd say.

"This is *football,* Uncle John," I'd tell him. "You call 'You're out' when you play *baseball.*"

"Oh," Uncle John would say. "Then let's play baseball so I can hit a touchdown."

Last month he got sick and had to go to the hospital. The doctors operated, but he died anyway. Now I don't feel like playing football anymore.

Mom and Dad told me that Jesus is watching over Uncle John as he sleeps in the ground. They said that someday Jesus will come and wake Uncle John up, and we'll all go to heaven together. We'll be able to play again. I wonder if heaven has a football field.

The newest link in my chain of love has only two words written on it—Uncle John. Jesus knows what it means.

–*Stevie*

MY CHAIN OF LOVE . . .

Dad and Jesus Link

1

AUGUST

Give ear and come to me; hear me. Isaiah 55:3, NIV.

My dad is a busy person. He's always running around saying he's late or he's forgotten something or there's someone waiting for him. Just watching him makes me tired.

The other day I was sitting on the steps of our house, thinking. My best friend Jerry was mad at me, and I didn't know why.

"What's the matter with you?" Dad said when he came home from work. "You look like you've lost your best friend."

I blinked. "How did you know?"

Dad spread his hands. "Just a talent I have. You want to talk about it?"

"Aren't you busy?" I asked. "Aren't you late or didn't you forget something or isn't someone waiting for you?"

"Probably all of those things," he sighed. "But you and Mom are the most important people in my life, so I'll just sit here and talk to you, OK?"

I told Dad about Jerry. He gave me some good ideas, and the next day I tried them out. Jerry's my friend again.

Whenever I read about the life of Jesus, I discover that He is a lot like my dad. Both take time to listen to other people's problems, even when they're busy.

The new link in my chain of love says, "I'm thankful that Dad and Jesus listen to me."

–*Stevie*

2
AUGUST

MY CHAIN OF LOVE . . .

Treasure Link

Store up for yourselves treasures in heaven. Matthew 6:20, NIV.

I wish I had a million dollars instead of just seven," I said one day as I was sitting at the dining-room table counting my money.

"What would you do with a million dollars?" Mom asked.

"Well," I said scratching my head, "first, I'd buy you a new refrigerator because the old one roars like a lion. Then I'd buy Dad a new car so he wouldn't have to mumble under his breath every time he tries to start our old one. Then I'd buy myself a skateboard, a radio-controlled airplane, and a laptop computer."

Mom smiled. "When we go to heaven, we won't need a new refrigerator or car or skateboard or airplane or laptop computer. Don't you think you should store up *heavenly* treasures instead?"

"How do I do that?" I asked.

"By being kind, helping people, thanking your teacher for showing you how to do a tough math problem, or dropping your mission offering in the plate. Those create treasures in heaven. And heavenly treasures won't wear out or stop working."

I thought about what my mom had said. Then I ran to my room and added a new link in my chain of love. It says, "I have treasures in heaven. Thank You, Jesus, for making me rich."

–Stevie

MY CHAIN OF LOVE . . .

Change Link

3

AUGUST

The story of Zacchaeus makes me laugh. Here's this short guy up in a tall tree waiting to see Jesus. Weird!

Yesterday I decided to find out what it was like to be Zacchaeus, so I climbed a tree in our backyard.

I sat on a big limb, thinking. It's easy for me to imagine what it's like to be short because I am. Mom, Dad, and my brother have to look down to find me. Once we went to a parade. All I could see were people's backs and a whole bunch of fanny packs. After Dad put me up on his shoulders, it was a lot better. The marching band looked and sounded great.

As I was sitting up in the tree I thought of something else. Jesus found Zacchaeus even when that old tax collector was in a rather strange place—somewhere most grown-ups wouldn't be. I'm glad Jesus notices us, no matter where we are.

"What're you doing up in the tree?" Dad asked when he walked by.

"Thinking," I answered.

"Well, hurry and come down," he called. "Supper's ready."

Yup. I know just how Zacchaeus felt.

My newest link says, "Thank You, Jesus, for looking for people even in strange places."

–Stevie

When Jesus reached the spot, he looked up and said to him, "Zacchaeus, come down immediately. I must stay at your house today." Luke 19:5, NIV.

4
AUGUST

The gift of God is eternal life in Christ Jesus our Lord. Romans 6:23, NIV.

MY CHAIN OF LOVE . . .

Work Link

Yesterday I was sitting on my favorite log, listening to my Bible story cassettes. I really like the stories about Jesus.

As I was listening, I suddenly realized something interesting. For all the work that Jesus did—you know, healing people, preaching, teaching, traveling from place to place—no one ever paid Him. He didn't get a salary or anything. He worked for free! Amazing.

When my neighbor, old Mr. Martin, asked me if I would help him rake leaves, the first thing I thought was, *How much will he pay me?* But if I want to be like Jesus, I should be happy to help my neighbor because he *needs* me, not because he'll *pay* me.

Now don't get me wrong. Sometimes people have to earn money so they can buy groceries or pay the rent or get a new pair of shoes. My mom and dad work very hard and are glad when they get their paychecks.

But to help someone like old Mr. Martin should be a gift of love. After all, Jesus is going to take us to heaven someday, and that's not going to cost us one penny.

My new link says, "Salvation is a gift from God." From now on, I'll work for Jesus because I love Him.

–Stevie

MY CHAIN OF LOVE . . .

Last Link

5
AUGUST

We love because God first loved us. 1 John 4:19, ICB.

I've had a good time making my chain of love. I've hung it in the shape of a heart and written a Bible verse in the middle that says, "We love because God first loved us."

When I think of all the things Jesus has done for me, I'm amazed. Imagine, the God of the universe cares about me down here on this little, old earth. He sees what I do, laughs when I laugh, cries when I cry, and knows when I'm having problems.

My chain of love reminds me that I'm never alone. Jesus cares about me and wants me to be happy. That's why He helps me.

I'm going to take my chain to school next week for show-and-tell. I think many of my friends would like to see how much God loves us. I'll teach them how to make their own chains.

Each night before I go to sleep, I kneel by my bed and pray, "Thank You, Jesus, for loving me so much. Thank You for showing me, every day, that I'm important to You. Now I know that when I wake up, You'll be waiting to help me through the day."

Why not close your eyes right now and thank Jesus for His wonderful gift of love?

–Stevie

6 AUGUST

I WITNESS BY . . .

Choosing Good Things

Whatever is true, . . . whatever is right, . . . whatever is admirable . . . think about such things. Philippians 4:8, NIV.

Every day, I try to do something to show my friends and family how kind Jesus is. That's called *witnessing.*

I even use my television to witness! Here's how.

Each week I look through the *TV Guide* and carefully pick out programs I think will be fun to watch—shows that teach me something useful or help me become a better person. My favorites are nature programs and stories about people who did nice things for others.

I put a little red check mark next to the programs I think are OK. When I'm finished, I show the list to my mom or dad. They're happy I'm being careful about what I look at. Then when friends come to visit and we want to watch TV, I get out my list. If there's a good program on, we enjoy it together. If not, we play trucks or swing in the backyard.

Sometimes I think a program will be all right, and we start to watch it. Then the people in the show begin to hurt each other or say bad things. I switch the TV off right away! I want only good things to go into my mind. I want my friends to know I'm being careful, because that's what Jesus expects me to do.

–David

I WITNESS BY . . .

Obeying

7 AUGUST

Children, obey your parents . . . for this is right. Ephesians 6:1, NIV.

"Trisha, it's time to come in," my mom called from the back door.

"Oh," I moaned to my friend Jessica. "My road isn't finished."

"Stay a little longer," she whispered. "Your mom will call again."

I thought for a moment. I did want to finish my road. It was a beautiful highway with trees and flowers down the middle and buildings on each side.

But then I thought about how Jesus wants us to obey our parents, even if we're busy doing something. I also wanted to show my friend Jessica that I love Jesus more than my new road.

"I'm coming," I called toward the house. Then I started gathering up my trucks and earthmovers. "I should obey my mom," I said with a smile. "I can finish the road some other time. See ya."

As I walked away, I had a good feeling inside. Not only was I doing what my mom told me to do, I was witnessing to Jessica. I was showing her that, no matter what, I was going to be the kind of person Jesus wants me to be.

Jessica jumped to her feet. "I guess I'd better get home too," she said. "My mom just called. See you tomorrow."

I smiled and waved. Witnessing can even teach others to obey their parents. —Trisha

8
AUGUST

Each helps the other and says to his brother, "Be strong!" Isaiah 41:6, NIV.

I WITNESS BY . . .

Showing God's Kindness

My fingers aren't as strong as they used to be," Mrs. Jackson said as she handed me a big glass of fruit punch. "Must be my old age. Guess I can't grow pretty flowers in my garden anymore."

I swallowed a mouthful of the cool juice and wiped my lips with my sleeve. "I think you need some new fingers. How about mine?"

Mrs. Jackson looked surprised. "Whatever do you mean?"

"Well, if you'll teach me how to pull those weeds and dig the ground, I'll help you grow pretty flowers. I've got strong fingers, see?" I opened and closed my hand. "I don't want your garden to die."

And that's how I witnessed to my neighbor. Each week during the summer I spent an hour pulling weeds, digging in the soft dirt, and sprinkling water on the plants using the big bucket from the garage. And, oh, how beautiful the flowers were!

Mrs. Jackson asked me why I was so willing to help. I told her that Jesus always helped people, and so should we. She smiled. "Thank you for showing me how much God loves me. It makes me happy to think He cares about us, even when we're old."

–Jason

I WITNESS BY . . .

Honoring

9

AUGUST

Rise in the presence of the aged, show respect for the elderly and revere your God. Leviticus 19:32, NIV.

My dad came home from work yesterday and sat down in his favorite chair. "What a day," he said with a sigh.

Usually my dad is a happy person. He laughs a lot and likes to do fun things. But not yesterday. He just sat in his chair and sighed.

He works hard. Sometimes he works *too* hard.

I ran up to my room and got a big piece of paper and a red marker. Carefully I wrote, "Jesus and I love you very much." I drew a picture of a cow and a tree on it, too. Then I hurried downstairs, taped my picture to the front of the television, and hid in the hall closet.

When Dad went to watch the news, my note was hanging right there for him to see.

"Look at this," I heard him say. "A note just for me. And there's a picture of a dog and a rocket on it." (I write better than I draw.) I jumped out of the closet and gave my dad a big hug.

"Thank you for reminding me how much I'm loved," he said. "Now I don't feel so sad. You're a good witness."

I ran off to play wearing a big smile on my face. Witnessing makes people happy—even dads who sometimes sigh.

–Jon

10
AUGUST

If any of you lacks wisdom, he should ask God, who gives generously to all without finding fault. James 1:5, NIV.

I WITNESS BY . . .

Sharing Wisdom

"I'm so dumb!" my friend Barbara said as she buried her face in her hands and moaned an angry moan. "I'll never figure it out. I'm going to be in second grade until I'm 90 years old!"

"No, you're not." I giggled. "You just need someone to help you."

Barbara lifted one eyebrow slightly. "Who wants to help a dummy like me?"

"I do," I said with a smile. "Jesus wants everyone to be wise. That's why He told us to share what we know with each other. I just happen to know how to do that addition problem, so I'll share my wisdom with you if you want me to."

Barbara's face turned from sad to glad. "Really? Hey, thanks," she said. "You're a good friend."

I went to the blackboard and wrote the problem in big numbers. Then I carefully explained how to solve it. Barbara figured out the next addition problem all by herself.

Sharing wisdom is a fun way to witness for Jesus. It shows our friends and family that we think they're important. By helping people solve little problems, we're showing them that God wants to help them solve their big ones, too.

–Tara

I WITNESS BY . . .

Encouraging Others

Encourage one another daily. Hebrews 3:13, NIV.

"Hey, Jared, that's a terrific picture. Did you paint it all by yourself?"

Jared nodded and held up the artwork so it would catch the light from the window. "Yup. It's a seashore with a lighthouse on it."

"I know," I said, moving in for a closer look. "And you've got four seagulls flying overhead and everything. I really like the waves crashing on those rocks. Very dramatic." I paused. "You know, Jesus sure could use your talent."

"Jesus?" Jared asked, looking at me in surprise. "He wants to use my painting talent?"

"Sure," I said as I sat down beside my friend. "You could paint cool pictures to hang in the Sabbath school room or our church lobby. Then the people coming to worship on Sabbath could see them and enjoy the beautiful scenes. What do you think?"

"I guess I could do that, if you think I'm a good enough artist."

Jared got busy making more pictures. But this time he was painting them for Jesus.

When I encourage my friends to use their talents to help make other people happy, I'm witnessing. I'm reminding them that all good talents come from Jesus. And my friends are sharing their best work with others.

–Andrew

12
AUGUST

Whatever you did for one of the least of these brothers of mine, you did for me. Matthew 25:40, NIV.

I WITNESS BY . . .

Caring for Others

Last week I witnessed with my clothes. Sounds funny, doesn't it? Let me explain.

A woman at church told about a country far away that had lots of people who were cold when winter came. They didn't have enough coats and hats to wear. Imagine—a country filled with people who are cold during the winter. It made me sad.

Then the woman invited us to help. She said that if we'd bring some of our coats, gloves, and hats to the community service center, they'd send them on a boat to the people in that country.

Well, the very next day my mom and I went to our closets and began picking out coats, gloves, hats, thick socks, and even a pair of ski pants. I found some earmuffs and fur-lined boots, too.

Then we hurried over to the community service center and gave the man working there our big bundle. "Thank you," he said with a happy smile. "This is a beautiful witness for Jesus. You're showing those faraway people that you care about them. You want them to be warm in the winter just as Jesus wants them to be warm and safe too."

I grinned all the way home. Witnessing can make people feel warm on the outside, while you feel warm on the inside.

–Natalie

I WITNESS BY . . .

Saying No

Do you not know that your body is a temple of the Holy Spirit? 1 Corinthians 6:19, NIV.

The boy held out his hand. "Here," he said. "Try one of these little blue ones. They're great."

"No," I said, backing away.

"Ah, come on," he encouraged. "Take just one. *One* won't hurt you." He shoved his finger through the pile of pills in his hand. "Bryan and Sarah took some. Don't you want to be cool like them?"

"No. No. *No!"* I turned and ran as fast as I could toward the school building. The boy laughed at me, but I didn't care. My witness was over, and I wanted to get out of there fast.

My witness? Yes. By saying no to the boy with the drugs, I was showing him that I wanted to care for my body and mind and not hurt them. Even though he laughed at me, I knew he understood.

Saying no to bad things shows other people that you love God and want to obey Him. Even if everyone else says it's OK to take drugs or smoke cigarettes or see videos in which people hurt each other, I know better. I'm always going to witness with a great big "No!"

When I do that, I make Someone very happy. That's right. Jesus!

–Hunter

14
AUGUST

Look, Jesus is coming with the clouds! Everyone will see him. Revelation 1:7, ICB.

I WITNESS BY . . .

Sharing Hope

"See that?" I said to my friend as we were walking home after school.

"What?" she asked, looking in the direction I was pointing. "All I see are a bunch of clouds."

"Exactly." I smiled. "That's the way it's going to look when Jesus comes again."

"It's going to look like it's about to rain?" she said, scratching her head.

I laughed. "Well, maybe a little. But I'm sure it will be very beautiful. You see, I learned a Bible verse in Sabbath School. It says, 'Look, Jesus is coming with the clouds! Everyone will see him.' " I pointed toward a big, bright cloud above our house. "Every time I look up at the sky, I think about when Jesus will come again and invite us to go to heaven with Him. He promised. It will be an exciting day!"

My friend nodded. "Hey, you're right. Clouds can remind us of when Jesus comes again. I thought all they did was rain."

We stood looking up at the clouds, watching them move across the sky like billowing sails. When Jesus does come, I want to be watching and waiting for Him. Don't you?

–David

I WITNESS BY . . .

Being Friendly

15
AUGUST

A friend loves at all times. Proverbs 17:17, NIV.

Tammy's voice sounded a little tired on the phone. "I have a bad cold," she sniffed. "Mom says I can't go back to school for a whole week!"

"I'm sorry you're sick," I said softly. "But I'll tell you everything that happened today. First, our teacher bumped his head on the map. Gave Europe a good jolt. Then Terrance got a bean stuck in his ear. Had to call the nurse.

"At lunchtime Lori and Belinda wouldn't talk to me, because I said Lori had big feet, which, as you know, she does. And then guess what happened . . ."

I told Tammy all about my day at school. She listened between coughs.

When I was all done, she said, "Thank you. I feel a little better. Will you call me again tomorrow?"

I promised I would, because talking to a sick friend is a neat way to witness for Jesus. Tammy feels sad, having to stay at home while she is sick. When I call her, it makes her happy, at least for a little while. I'm showing her God's love.

Now if only I could get Lori and Belinda to talk to me again. I guess I'll have to tell Lori I'm sorry for hurting her feelings. Tammy will love it!

–Trisha

16

AUGUST

Love one another, as I have loved you. John 15:12.

I WITNESS BY . . .

Sharing

"You build the road, and I'll make the mountain," I said. Bobbie nodded and started digging. "And if you need a dump truck, use mine."

Bobbie smiled and drove my new dump truck over to her road. *"Roarrrrr! Roarrrrr!"* she said as the big wheels dug into the sand.

I learned something a long time ago when I was 5. Sharing my toys is a great witness for Jesus. Why? Because we're showing others how Jesus wants to share His love with us.

"Oh!" Bobbie called out. "Look what happened. The wheel on your dump truck came right off. I was making an on-ramp by the factory, and it snapped. I didn't mean to break it."

Sure enough, there was my poor dump truck with its right front wheel lying flat on the ground.

"That's OK," I said, even though I felt a little sad. "My mom will fix it when she gets home. Just pretend there's a wheel there for now."

Bobbie smiled. "You're not mad at me?"

"Hey, it was just an accident. You didn't do it on purpose."

My friend nodded and began working on her road again. When you share your toys, sometimes they get broken. But a good friend is more important than all the truck wheels in the world.

–Jason

I WITNESS BY . . .

Helping

The sea is his, for he made it, and his hands formed the dry land. Psalm 95:5, NIV.

"Here, I'll carry that big bag for you," I said. Mom smiled and handed me the grocery sack. It was heavy.

We walked into the house, and I carefully placed the bag on the counter. "I'm using my power to witness to you about Jesus," I said.

"Well, you certainly did a fine job," Mom nodded. "You're getting stronger every day."

I sighed. "But I can't figure something out. I can see the muscles on my arms and legs. But how can we see God's muscles?"

Mom opened the refrigerator door and lifted two white milk cartons onto the shelf. "God shows His power everywhere—in the wind, the tall mountains, even the rain that falls. It's His loving power that makes the flowers bloom and the trees grow new leaves each spring."

I thought for a minute. "So when I see things in nature, I can pretend I'm looking at God's muscles?"

"I suppose so," Mom said. "You're seeing God's power in action. It's just like I know you love me by your action of helping with the grocery bags."

I flexed my muscles as hard as I could. I'm not as strong as God, but for a little kid, I can be a powerful witness.

–Jon

18
AUGUST

Guard what has been entrusted to your care. 1 Timothy 6:20, NIV.

I WITNESS BY . . .

Being Trustworthy

"Seventy-five . . . 76 . . . 77." I carefully counted the money as I dropped the coins into my mother's hand. "Seventy-eight . . . 79 . . . 80!"

"Good for you," Mom said with a nod. "You brought back all the change. Thank you for being trustworthy. That's a nice witness."

"It is?" I asked.

"Sure," Mom said. "You're reminding me how trustworthy God is. When I ask God to help me with a problem, He promises He will. When I ask Him to help me take care of my family, He gives me wisdom to make the right choices or figure out how to make the best of a bad situation."

I looked at the coins in my mother's hand. I had been very careful with her money. I'd hurried home from the store so I wouldn't lose any along the way. I did it because I love her.

Since I know God loves me, I can also trust that He's working hard to keep me safe and do what He has promised to do.

"I'm going to be trustworthy for as long as I live," I said. "I want people to see how trustworthy God is, too."

Mom smiled and gave me a hug. "That's a beautiful witness!" she said.

–Andrew

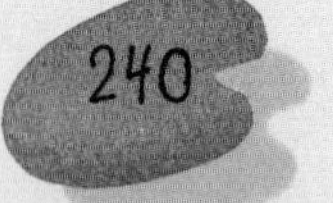

I WITNESS BY . . .

Playing Happy Tunes

19
AUGUST

Make sweet melody, sing many songs, that thou mayest be remembered. Isaiah 23:16.

I'm no concert piano player, that's for sure. But I can make my parents happy with my music. Here's how.

It's 6:00. Mom and Dad stumble in from work. They're very tired.

"Welcome home," I say with a smile. "Before we all get busy with supper and chores, may I play you a song?"

They gladly sit down on the couch and wait as I open my favorite music book and limber up my fingers. Then I begin.

Sometimes I choose a fast song. They tap their toes on the rug. Sometimes I play a slow song and sing the words. Mom and Dad smile and sigh. They think I'm the best music maker in the world. It makes me feel important when they say I play better than anyone they've ever heard on television or the radio. I know they're just kidding, but I like it anyway.

Sharing my talents with my family is one way I show God's love to them. Mom says it's a sweet-sounding witness. She insists that she can hear the angels singing right along with me. Mom has a very vivid imagination. But who knows? Maybe my guardian angel does join in.

Do you have a musical talent? Why not use it today?

–Tara

20
AUGUST

There shall not an hair of your head perish. Luke 21:18.

I WITNESS BY . . .

Telling a Story

Valerie's eyes open wide as I clear my throat. "Then what happened?" she gasps.

"Well," I continue, holding my arms out in front of me and pressing my foot on an imaginary brake pedal, "Dad spun the wheel of the car like this, and we skidded to a stop inches from the big stone wall. I thought we were goners for sure!"

"Ohhhh." Valerie nods. "You were lucky."

"It wasn't *just* luck," I say. "It was God protecting us. He helped my dad remember to buy new tires when the old ones got bare. It could have been a whole lot worse."

My friend thinks for a minute. "Does God help everyone?"

"Sure," I say, "He tries hard to keep people safe by giving them safe thoughts. Even when someone gets hurt, God is right there ready to help the doctors and nurses make that person feel better again. He never leaves us alone, no matter what happens."

Valerie smiles. "I like your stories," she says, "especially when you talk about how God helps you. Do you have another one?"

I begin to tell her about our trip to the ocean. Sharing how God has helped keep my family safe is a great way to witness.

–Hunter

I WITNESS BY . . .

Sharing God's Words

21
AUGUST

Come to me, all you who are weary and burdened, and I will give you rest. Matthew 11:28, NIV.

Sometimes my Sabbath School teacher gives me a pretty picture to take home and put on my wall. But I do something else with my gift. Let me explain.

First I find a big piece of paper and write a memory verse on it. I work carefully so each word is easy to read.

Then I tape the picture and the memory verse together. Next I go find my stepfather and ask him if I can show him something. If he's not too busy, he says OK.

I hold up the picture and memory verse and say the words slowly and clearly. He looks at the picture while I read.

"That's nice," he says. "I like the verse you chose to put with the picture. It makes me think of Jesus and how much He loves our little family."

Then I put my picture-verse on the refrigerator with Mom's little magnets so she can see it when she comes home.

Sharing God's words with other people is a wonderful way to witness. Since Jesus doesn't live here on earth anymore, He likes it when we speak His words and tell others of His love.

Why not try my idea this week for someone you love. Here's a great Bible verse to use: Matthew 11:28. Adults really like that text!

–Natalie

22
AUGUST

If a man borrow ought of his neighbour . . . he shall surely make it good. Exodus 22:14.

I WITNESS BY . . .

Asking Forgiveness

Last week I did a dumb thing. I took my friend Calvin's pencil without asking. Then to make matters worse, I lost it! Calvin was not happy.

My pastor told us always to ask forgiveness when we've done something wrong. I was embarrassed, but I knew what I had to do.

"Calvin," I said at recess. "I'm sorry I took your pencil."

"And lost it," he added.

"And lost it," I repeated. "I was wrong to do that. Will you forgive me? Here, you can have this brand-new pencil my mom bought for me. It has a big eraser on it and everything."

Calvin thought for a minute. He looked at the new pencil, then at me. Suddenly a big smile spread across his face. "OK," he said. "I'm glad we're friends again."

I smiled too. Calvin and I have known each other forever. I didn't want my dumb mistake to hurt our friendship. Also, by asking forgiveness, I was showing how Jesus wants me to act when I've done something wrong.

Oh, I found Calvin's pencil two days later. He said I could keep it, which was good, because I didn't have one.

—David

I WITNESS BY . . .

Choosing to Be Healthy

23 AUGUST

Whether you eat or drink or whatever you do, do it all for the glory of God. 1 Corinthians 10:31, NIV.

I've got a secret to share with you. Promise not to tell? OK, here goes. I love chocolate. I mean, I *love* chocolate.

I'd eat every candy bar in the whole world if I could. But since that would make me sick and die, I guess I won't.

There's nothing wrong with loving chocolate. It's a great treat to enjoy once in a while, like at birthday parties or other special occasions.

The rest of the time, I'm very careful about what I eat. When I have to choose between a candy bar and, say, an apple, I'll choose the apple even though I may want the candy bar more.

Why? Because choosing to be healthy shows my friends that I care about the body God gave me. I want to fill it with foods and treats that help it run strong. Chocolate may taste great, but it doesn't do a thing for my bones and teeth. A candy bar might be tempting, but a sweet-tasting piece of fruit will help my body fight disease and sickness.

So when I have a choice, I pick healthy foods. But on special occasions I choose chocolate!

–Jason

24
AUGUST

May the God of hope fill you with all joy and peace as you trust in him. Romans 15:13, NIV.

I WITNESS BY . . .

Helping My Friends

Yesterday I found my friend sitting alone on a stump.

"What's the matter with you?" I asked. "You look sad and worried."

"I am," my friend sighed. "Did you watch the news last night? The world is in an awful mess. People are hurting each other, stealing stuff that doesn't belong to them, and saying hateful things to their neighbors. It makes me worried. What's going to happen to us in such a terrible world?"

I sat down beside my friend. "Not everyone is bad," I said. "The news shows just the trouble in the world, not the kindness and love. I mean, you and I are good friends. I don't see us on the evening news."

My friend nodded. "Hey, you're right."

"Besides," I continued, "God is watching out for us. He's willing to help anyone who is in trouble. And He wants us to teach our friends and neighbors how to love each other and not fight and steal. Then the world would be a better place for everyone."

My friend smiled. "I'm going to show people what a kind person is like."

I chuckled. "That's what this old world needs—some good news for a change!"

Do you have some good news you can share today?

–Jon

I WITNESS BY . . .

Helping Friends Say No

25 AUGUST

They trusted in [God] and defied the king's command and were willing to give up their lives rather than serve or worship any god except their own God. Daniel 3:28, NIV.

Megan needs help. Some of her friends are trying to get her to cheat on next week's English test. She doesn't want to, but she doesn't want to lose her friends, either. So I'm drawing her a picture.

My Sabbath school lesson this week is about three men who wouldn't bow down to the king. The king got mad and said, "If you don't bow down and worship me, I'll throw you into the fiery furnace." And he meant it!

Well, those three men said, "We bow down only to the true God in heaven." So in they went, right into the furnace.

Guess what? They didn't burn up. As a matter of fact, Jesus Himself came down and stood in the hot fire with them. Scared the king half to death.

God rescued those three men because He wanted to teach that wicked king a lesson. When people say no to sin, Jesus is right there to help them.

That's why I'm drawing this picture of a fiery furnace. I'm telling Megan that God will help her say no to her friends. And I'm going to tell her that if she'd like a friend who won't ask her to cheat, I'm available.

–Trisha

26
AUGUST

Give your worries to the Lord. He will take care of you. Psalm 55:22, ICB.

I WITNESS BY . . .

Writing Letters

My sister lives in a city far away. She used to work in a big office building with a fountain in front of it. But she lost her job because the company ran out of money.

When I talked to my sister last night on the phone, she sounded sad. She's been looking for another job for weeks and weeks, but no other company has any money to hire her.

That's why I wrote her a letter. Here's what it says:

Dear Shelby,

How are you? I'm fine. I'm sorry you can't find a new job. I just wanted you to know that I still love you and Jesus loves you too.

I learned a verse in the Bible this week that might make you feel a little better. I'll write it here for you. "Give your worries to the Lord. He will take care of you. He will never let good people down." That's Psalm 55:22 in my International Children's Bible.

So don't worry anymore. I believe Jesus will help you find a new job soon.

Love, JJ.

I hope my letter makes my sister happy. I want to remind her that, even when she doesn't have a job, God is watching out for her.

—JJ

I WITNESS BY . . .

Hoeing

27
AUGUST

For this God is our God for ever and ever; he will be our guide even to the end.
Psalm 48:14, NIV.

Tim grows beautiful tomatoes in the garden by his house. He also grows lots of weeds. Tomatoes are great. Weeds are a pain.

Since we both love tomato sandwiches, we have to pull up the scratchy, itchy weeds so the plants can grow strong and healthy.

I help him each Tuesday after swimming class. We put on gardening gloves and attack the weeds together. Sometimes the sun is hot, and the wind doesn't blow. As I said, weeds are a pain!

While we're working we talk about stuff. Tim has a lot of worries. His mom and dad fight all the time, and his brother drives his motorcycle too fast. He says he's afraid of what will happen to his family.

I tell him that Jesus understands the problems and wants to help. Then I tell Tim about when my mother was in an accident. I prayed and prayed. The doctors were able to make her get better. It was a close call.

Weeding the garden is a good time for two people to talk about important stuff like moms and dads and brothers. It's a great time to witness about Jesus' love. It's also a really good time to dream about delicious tomato sandwiches—and snow!

–Andrew

28 AUGUST

Make music to the Lord . . . with trumpets and the blast of the ram's horn. Psalm 98:5, 6, NIV.

I WITNESS BY . . .

Playing My Trombone

I play the trombone in the school band. We're not very good, but we have a great time making lots and lots of noise. We practice after classes when everyone else has gone home.

Our teacher says we have potential. He must be deaf!

I can play six songs on my trombone. My friend Alex says I sound pretty good if you don't try to remember what the song is supposed to sound like and you eat an apple at the same time. I think he's deaf too.

I'm teaching him to play "When the Saints Go Marching In." He blows and blows and moves the trombone slide in and out.

Last week he played the song all the way through with just three mistakes. I told him he's got talent. He said he was just lucky.

"No, I think we've found a secret talent," I gasped. "You should join the band."

Alex smiles and smiles when I encourage him. Maybe that's why God wants us to help each other discover new talents. He knows it will make us happy.

I hope Alex will join our band. We sure could use someone who can play on key!

Do you play an instrument? Why not use it to witness to someone today?

–Tara

I WITNESS BY . . .

Acting

29
AUGUST

The king extended the gold scepter to Esther and she arose and stood before him. Esther 8:4, NIV.

I stand at our pretend door and knock quietly.

"Who is it?" My brother's voice is deep and gruff.

"It's me, Esther," I say softly.

"Esther who?"

"That's not what the king said," I moan. "He said, 'Come in, my queen. What do you want?'"

My brother adjusts his robe. "Come in, my queen," he repeats. "What do you want?"

I float into the king's throne room, which is really our porch. I bow low. "I must talk to you about Haman. He's up to no good."

My brother the king holds his broom—I mean scepter—out for me to touch. That means he'll listen to me and not kill me with his plastic sword.

That's how we act out the story of Esther and her husband, King Xerxes. It's very exciting, especially the part where we hang Haman on the basketball hoop. We use a Ken doll.

Every time we do that play for our friends, I think about how God wants to keep us safe in the time of trouble before He comes back to earth. We don't have to be afraid or worried. God will save us, just as He saved Esther and her people from the wicked Haman.

Tomorrow it's supposed to rain. We're going to do Noah and the Flood.

–Natalie

30
AUGUST

Be completely . . . gentle; . . . bearing with one another in love. Ephesians 4:2, NIV.

I WITNESS BY . . .

Working in Secret

Shhh. Don't tell anyone. I'm sweeping this floor as a secret surprise for my mom.

She's kinda tired. Didn't sleep good last night, she says. I slept great, I think. Can't remember.

After I'm finished with the floor, I'm going to dust the piano and end tables, empty the trash, and straighten out the bookcase. If I have time, I might even water the plants and clean the closet. We'll see.

I like doing things to help my mom. She does lots of stuff for me.

When I help my friends and family in secret, I'm doing exactly what Jesus does for us. We don't always see how He keeps us safe from Satan's attacks and quietly reminds us to watch out for others and ourselves. He works in secret too.

Jesus wants us to love other people the same way He loves us. That may mean doing good things without anyone finding out. It may mean helping a friend even if he or she didn't ask.

Later if my mom or dad says, "Hey, I wonder who did that for me," I'll just smile and say, "It must have been one of Jesus' helpers!"

Why don't you do some secret work around your house today?

–Hunter

I WITNESS BY . . .

Helping the Homeless

31
AUGUST

Never again will they hunger; never again will they thirst. Revelation 7:16, NIV.

Imagine what it would be like to live on the street. No home. No mom or dad. No food to eat. Scary!

Jesus loves homeless people just as much as He loves those who live in houses, mobile homes, or apartment buildings. He wants us to care for people, no matter where they live, even if it's on a street corner.

"How can I show that family that Jesus loves them?" I asked my dad as we drove to the store. We were watching a homeless man and woman help their little son across the street.

"By *showing* them," Dad said. "Do you want to try?"

"Yes," I whispered. "I don't want anyone to be sad or hungry."

As we shopped, Dad and I collected a special bag of groceries for the homeless family. Then we drove back to the corner.

"Here," Dad called from the car. "This is for you. Please accept it as a gift. We don't want you to be hungry today."

The man smiled as he took the bag. "Thank you," he said softly.

"We'll be praying for you," Dad encouraged.

As we drove away I felt happy inside. We had *shown* the man and his family that Jesus wants to take care of them, no matter where they must live.

–David

1
SEPTEMBER

I am with you, and I will protect you everywhere you go. Genesis 28:15, ICB.

TERRY IN THE CITY . . .

Moving Day

Today was a busy day for my family. We got up early, packed our suitcases, put our furniture in a truck, and moved to our new home in the city.

I miss hearing birds singing outside my window. I miss seeing the clouds above the cornfields and the flowers in the meadows.

But most of all I miss my best friend, Christina. We used to play together in the cool shade of the oak tree in my front yard.

My new room in our apartment building has a little window that looks down on a busy street. I hear roaring engines, honking horns, and footsteps. I didn't hear one bird singing all afternoon.

After supper we had worship, sitting on packing boxes and piles of clothes. We sang one of my favorite Sabbath school songs, and Dad read a verse from the Bible that says, "I am with you, and I will protect you everywhere you go."

It made me glad to know that Jesus moved with us from the country to the city. Now as I close my eyes to sleep I feel a little safer in my room above the noisy street because I know that Jesus has promised to watch over me.

–Terry

TERRY IN THE CITY . . .

Fearful Noises!

2

SEPTEMBER

Don't be afraid, because I am your God. Isaiah 41:10, ICB.

Rrrrr. Rrrrrrr-blam. Bang! What's that terrible noise? *Tat-tat-tat. Screeeeech. Crunch!* I open my eyes and look around. Where am I? *Rrrrrr. Ding-ding-ding. Blam!* I sit up and call out, "Mom! Dad!"

My father appears at my bedroom door, electric razor buzzing in his hand. "What's the matter, Terry?" he asks.

Mom squeezes past and runs to my bedside. "Are you sick? Did something frighten you?"

Clank. Clank. Crunch, crunch. Bang!

Mom and Dad smile at each other. Then they lead me to the window resting beside my dresser. "Is that what woke you up?" they ask. I look down on the street and see a large truck with men running around carrying metal cans and plastic bags. "Don't be afraid," my dad says. "That's just the city garbage truck picking up the trash."

Rrrrrr. Rrrrrrrr. The strange-looking vehicle roars down the street and turns the corner. I sit back down on my bed and sigh. "I miss our home in the country," I say. "I miss Christina and the oak tree and hearing the birds singing each morning."

Dad sits down beside me. "I know," he says softly. "I miss those things too. That's why I'm going to bring you a surprise today after work."

"A surprise?" I ask.

—Terry

3
SEPTEMBER

**If we love each other, God lives in us.
1 John 4:12, ICB.**

TERRY IN THE CITY . . .

New Friend

"Hello," a voice calls from the end of the long hallway. "What's your name?"

"Terry," I say. "What's yours?"

"Nathan. My mom calls me Nat."

I see a boy wearing a red sweater walking toward me. "Do you want to play computer games?" he asks. "I've got a bunch." He kicks a pretend ball, and I catch it. "Or, we could play soccer if you want."

"I gotta ask my mom," I tell him.

We walk into my apartment together. "What a mess!" he says.

"Tell me about it," I laugh.

We find Mom hanging yellow curtains in the kitchen. "Can I go play with Nat?" I ask.

Mom looks down from her ladder. "Hello," she says with a smile. "Are you Mrs. Frederick's son?"

"Yes, ma'am," Nat answers. "My mother's working at her computer and my dad doesn't live at our house anymore."

"I know," Mom says quietly. "I talked to your mother this morning. I'll be happy for you and Terry to play together. Just try not to make too much noise, OK?"

"OK," we say. As we walk down the hallway I think, *Maybe Nat will be my friend in the city.*

—Terry

TERRY IN THE CITY . . .

Telling Everyone

4
SEPTEMBER

[Jesus has] put gladness in my heart. Psalm 4:7.

It's lunchtime. I sit with my mom eating a sandwich. "You know," I say, "Nat has lots of games and stuff, but he's sad. Why?"

Mom pours herself a glass of milk. "I think he misses his dad. How would you feel if your father went away?"

"*Very* sad," I tell her.

"Even if you had lots of toys?"

I think for a minute. "Yes, because I love Dad more than toys."

"That's the way Jesus wants us to love Him, too," Mom says. "He wants to be more important to us than anything."

"Why?" I ask.

"Because loving Jesus is the only way for people to find happiness. Remember the text your father read this morning for worship? '[Jesus has] put gladness in my heart.' That's what He does when we love Him most."

"Then I'd better tell Nat to love Jesus so he can be glad again."

"Good idea," Mom said. "Everyone needs to hear about Jesus."

"Everyone? How can you tell everyone in this city that Jesus wants them to be happy?"

Mom thinks for a minute. "Well, begin by telling Nat. Maybe he'll tell his mom, and she'll tell her friends. Get the idea?"

"Got it!" I say with a smile.

—Terry

5
SEPTEMBER

The Lord gives me strength and makes me sing. Exodus 15:2, ICB.

TERRY IN THE CITY . . .

Singing Surprise

I sit by my window looking down at the noisy street. Everyone seems to be in such a hurry! Cars, buses, and businesspeople scurry about like busy ants. I sigh. Evening is different in the country. When the sun begins to set, the cows walk slowly toward the barn, the ducks take one more flight around the pond, and then everyone settles in for the night.

Even songbirds sing more softly when evening comes. But here in the city I don't hear any birds singing.

"Tweet." What was that? "Tweet, tweet."

Oh, great. Now I'm hearing things!

"Tweet, tweet, trillllll."

I turn and look toward my bedroom door. Dad is standing there with a little cage in his hand and in the cage I see something moving! "Hey, Terry," Dad calls.

"Tweet, tweet, trillllll." "Dad!" I gasp. "You brought me a bird. A real bird. Just listen to it "sing!"

"Tweetle, tweetle, chirp, chirp, chirp." The bird's happy song fills my room with joy. "Oh, this is a terrific surprise!" I shout as I give my father a hug. "Now I can hear birdsongs in my bedroom again, just like in the country."

Dad proudly hands me the cage as the bird sings and sings.

–Terry

TERRY IN THE CITY . . .

First-Day Lessons

6
SEPTEMBER

Be of good courage, and [God] shall strengthen your heart. Psalm 31:24.

My first day in the city has been interesting. I saw a really strange truck take away the trash, found a new friend named Nat, decided to be a missionary right in my apartment building, and got a bird.

Now we're getting ready for family worship. The supper dishes have been washed and put away, and I'm listening to Dad tell Mom about his new job. Suddenly he turns to me and says, "Well, Terry, what did you learn today?"

I think for a minute. "I learned that if you're sad or afraid, just wait a little while and things will get better."

"Great," Dad says. "How about you, Mother?"

"I learned that there are many, many people in the city who need to know Jesus."

Dad opens our family Bible and finds a special verse. "Be of good courage," he reads, "and [God] shall strengthen your heart." Then Dad looks at me. "I learned that no matter what you want to do for Jesus, He'll help you do it."

Together we kneel and pray, thanking God for His love. Yes, Mom, Dad, and I agree that it's been a very interesting day.

–Terry

7
SEPTEMBER

TERRY IN THE CITY . . .

Quick Witness

You will be his witness to all people.
Acts 22:15, ICB.

B*eep, beep*. Our taxi bounces down the street as we ride to the grocery store. *Honk, honk, honk!* Our driver swerves to miss a bus.

Mom and I look out the window and watch the people, trucks, and buildings slip by. At a corner I see a boy standing with his dad, waiting for the light to turn green. "Hello," I call out. The boy waves back. Then we hurry on.

"Isn't much time to talk to people in the city," I say with a sigh. "Everyone is moving around all the time."

"Yeah," Mom agrees. "This is one busy place!"

"Then how am I supposed to tell people about Jesus if I can't even talk to them?"

Mom adjusts her purse. "You're already telling them."

"I am? All I do is smile and wave."

"Exactly. By being friendly and offering a happy smile, you're showing God's love without saying a word."

"Hey," I laugh, "this is fun. I'm showing people God's love with my smile!"

As the taxi bounces down the street, I grin and wave at everybody I see.

–Terry

TERRY IN THE CITY . . .

Happy Advertisement

The grocery store is packed with fruits, vegetables, cereal, soup, bread, milk, and even a few toys. I like toys.

I push our cart down the aisle as Mom places brightly-colored boxes into it. They each have pictures of food on them, making me hungry!

"I know why there are pictures on these boxes," I say. "That's so you'll know what's inside."

Mom nods. "Yup. By looking at the picture, you know what you're buying."

Mom picks boxes of macaroni, beans, and cereal from the shelves and tosses them into our cart. Suddenly I have an idea.

"Mom," I say, "you told me that Jesus wants to live in my heart. Well, I'd better keep a smile on my face so people will know He's there. It's like a picture on a box. When people see my smile, they know Jesus is inside."

My mother stops pushing her cart and looks down at me. "That's a wonderful idea," she says. "I'll smile too. Then people will know Jesus is controlling our actions and our words. That way we can be missionaries everywhere we go!"

"Hey, Mom," I call, "can we be missionaries over there by the toys?"

–Terry

Happy are the people whose God is the Lord. Psalm 144:15, ICB.

9
SEPTEMBER

TERRY IN THE CITY . . .

Sadness on the Street

Anything you did for any of my people here, you also did for me. Matthew 25:40, ICB.

"Look, Mom," I say as we're riding home in the taxi. "Why is that woman pushing a shopping cart down the sidewalk? Is she going to buy groceries?"

"No, Terry," Mom says sadly. "That shopping cart is her home."

"What do you mean?"

"There are many people in this city who have no place to live, no family, or no money to buy groceries. They stay outside on the streets and sidewalks. Sometimes people help them by giving them a meal and a safe place to sleep, but most of the time they have to search for food and shelter."

"Oh," I say softly.

Mom places her hand on my shoulder. "Would you like to help that woman?"

"How?"

She reaches into our grocery sack and pulls out a bag of apples. Then she asks the taxi driver to stop. I watch as she walks over to the lady. "Here," she says, "my son and I would like you to have these apples. And we'll pray for you every day."

The woman with the cart smiles. "Thank you," she says, taking the bag. Then she continues down the sidewalk and disappears into the crowd passing by.

—Terry

TERRY IN THE CITY . . .

Being Thankful

10
SEPTEMBER

Thank the Lord because he is good. His love continues forever. 1 Chronicles 16:34, ICB.

"T*weet. Tweet. Trillllll.*" My bird sits in his cage and sings a good morning song as I open my eyes and discover sunlight pouring through my bedroom window. I lie and listen to the bird and think about our old house in the country.

"Terry. Terry? Are you awake?" Mom calls from the kitchen.

"Yes."

She appears at my door. "Get dressed and come for breakfast. I made your favorite—toast with strawberries on it!"

As I wash my face and put on my shirt, I think about the woman we saw yesterday on the street. Was she going to have a delicious breakfast this morning?

Sitting down to eat, I look at all the food Mom has fixed. There's milk, cereal, toast, nuts, and a bowl of oranges.

"Would you like to pray?" she asks.

I close my eyes. "Dear Jesus . . ." I stop because I'm thinking about the street lady again. "Dear Jesus . . ." Mom puts her hand on mine as I feel a tear drop down my cheek. "Dear Jesus, thank You for my breakfast. Thank You for my room and my bird and Mom and Dad. Thank You for everything. Amen."

I hear Mom say amen too. And then we eat our delicious breakfast together.

–Terry

11
SEPTEMBER

My Father never stops working. And so I work, too. John 5:17, ICB.

TERRY IN THE CITY . . .

Working Dad

The elevator goes up, up, up. Sometimes we stop and people get on or off, but Mom and I keep going higher and higher.

Finally she announces, "This is your dad's floor."

The door opens, and we step into a room filled with big desks and busy people. A woman sitting next to the elevator looks up and smiles. "May I help you?" she asks.

"I'm Terry," I say, "and we've came to see my dad. Do you know where he is?"

The lady blinks. "What does he do?"

H'mm. What *does* he do? He gets up in the morning, shaves his chin, eats breakfast, kisses Mother and makes her laugh, then goes to work.

When we lived in the country, I could see what Dad did just by watching. He didn't hop in a taxi or ride on an elevator. He simply went into the barn or out into the fields.

"Mom," I whisper, "does Dad work even when I can't see him?"

"Sure," Mom says. "Both your earthly *and heavenly* fathers work hard, even though we don't know where they are. Neat, huh?"

I nod. I like having my dad and God take good care of me even if I can't see them working.

–Terry

TERRY IN THE CITY . . .

The Picture

12
SEPTEMBER

So we have been sent to speak for Christ. 2 Corinthians 5:20, ICB.

Mom speaks to the lady sitting beside the elevator. "My husband fixes things—you know, machines, electrical wiring."

"Oh," the receptionist says with a smile. "You must mean Mr. Williams, our new maintenance director. He's a nice man, always kind and helpful." She points. "His office is over there."

Mom and I move through the busy crowd of people, passing a copy machine, a humming computer, and a ringing telephone. At an office door she points at the name painted on the glass. "Here we are. This is where your father works."

When Dad sees us, he waves. "Hey, guys," he calls from behind a box with wires sticking out of it. "Thanks for coming. So what do you think of my new office?"

I look around the room and notice a small picture of Jesus hanging by the window. "I like that picture," I say.

"Me too," Dad nods. "I want everyone to know that I'm a Christian."

Mom and I look at each other and chuckle. "I think Dad wants to be a missionary too, like us," I say.

Mom gives Dad a warm hug. "We're a missionary family," she laughs. "I'm sure Jesus is pleased."

–Terry

13
SEPTEMBER

He has put his angels in charge of you. They will watch over you wherever you go. Psalm 91:11, ICB.

TERRY IN THE CITY . . .

City Angels

My dad's office is high above the city. From his window I see other tall buildings reaching into the sky. Far below, I notice tiny cars and people moving along the streets and sidewalks. The city is such a busy, crowded place.

"Dad," I ask, "can Jesus help everybody down there? I mean, there are so many people. How can He help them all?"

"There *are* a lot of people in the city, Terry," he agrees. "That's why Jesus offers everyone an angel who can help Him take care of them."

"An angel?" I gasp. "Even me?"

"Yes. You, Mom, me, and all those people down there can have an angel by their side."

I study the streets far below. "If the city has so many angels, everyone should feel safe, right?"

Dad shakes his head. "Some people don't want Jesus or His angels to help them. They want to do everything by themselves. So when Satan brings trouble into their lives, they have no one to turn to, no one to help them."

I press my face against the window. How terrible it must be to live without Jesus. "I want my angel with me always," I say softly.

—Terry

TERRY IN THE CITY . . .

Pages on a Menu

14
SEPTEMBER

I have given you all the plants that have grain for seeds. And . . . all the trees whose fruits have seeds in them. They will be food for you. Genesis 1:29, ICB.

It's lunchtime, and Mom and Dad take me to a restaurant to eat. After I check out the pictures on the menu, I say, "I'll have some of this."

"That may look good, Terry, but it's not healthy," Mom says. "Your body should get only nutritious food."

"How do I know which is good for me?" I ask.

"Healthy food has healthy stuff in it like vegetables, fruits, grains, nuts, and tasty beans," Dad tells me. "Some of the things on this menu are filled with meats and sugars. They can make you sick."

"But the pictures look so nice," I moan.

Mom takes a sip of water. "Remember that Bible verse we read this morning for worship? If what you choose is made from those ingredients, great!"

When the waiter returns to take our order, I'm ready. Handing her the menu, I ask politely, "Could you please show me the fruits, grains, and vegetables page? Oh, and do you have any tasty beans?"

I'm going to eat healthfully, no matter what pictures are on the menu!

–Terry

15
SEPTEMBER

A good person has good things in his heart. And so he speaks the good things that come from his heart. Matthew 12:35, ICB.

TERRY IN THE CITY . . .

A Good Heart

After saying goodbye to Dad, Mom and I are riding down in the elevator when I begin to worry.

"Mom," I say, "if people don't go into Dad's office, they won't see the picture. How will they know Dad is a Christian?"

"He'll have to show them another way."

"How?"

Mom presses her fingers against my chest. "Terry, if Jesus lives in here, people will know you love Him. Your hands will work hard, your mouth will speak with kindness and honesty, and your feet will take you only to the places where God would want you to go."

"Oh," I say, "it's like we are pictures of Jesus. When people look at us, they see that He lives in our hearts. Right?"

"That's right," Mom agrees. "The Bible says, 'A good person has good things in his heart. And so he speaks the good things that come from his heart.'"

"I'm going to put a picture of Jesus on my face, right now," I say as the elevator door opens. As Mom and I walk to the taxi I smile broadly.

–Terry

TERRY IN THE CITY . . .

Safe City

16
SEPTEMBER

I will come back. Then I will take you to be with me. John 14:3, ICB.

Mom, Nat, and I sit on the steps of our apartment building, watching people pass by.

"Look," Nat calls out suddenly. "Here comes a police officer!" A shiny black car drives past our building. The driver waves.

"Is he looking for burglars?" I ask, waving back.

"Maybe," Mom says. "Or he might be checking to make sure everything's OK."

Nat sighs. "Wouldn't it be nice if there was a city where no one stole stuff and police officers could play baseball all day?"

Mom nods. "There is."

"Where?"

"It's called heaven. Jesus lives there. Someday we can too if we choose to love God. No burglars, drugs, guns, or knives." Mom ruffles Nat's hair. "In fact, police officers won't have a job, because we'll all be safe with Jesus."

"Can we move to that city now?" Nat asks.

"Soon, when Jesus comes to take us there," Mom says. "It'll be a wonderful place. Children can play without ever being afraid and both kids and grown-ups can learn exciting things about nature, science, and space travel if they want."

Nat thinks for a moment. "Will Jesus play baseball with me?"

Mom grins. "Absolutely!"

—Terry

17
SEPTEMBER

Let the fields and everything in them show their joy. Then all the trees of the forest will sing for joy.
Psalm 96:12, ICB.

TERRY IN THE CITY . . .

Picnic in the Park

"Watch how high I can go," I shout as I swing back and forth above the soft, green grass.

Mom and Dad look up from the picnic blanket, where they're taking food out of a large, brown basket.

I pump my feet forward and backward, swinging higher and higher as I look around at the trees and bushes spreading across the city park. The sunshine feels warm on my face.

"Hey, Terry," Mom calls. "Dinner is ready."

I let my feet drag on the ground and stop the swing. "You know," I say as I plop down beside my father, "city nature is almost like country nature."

"It's exactly the same," Dad chuckles. "God shows city *and* country folk how much He loves them with beautiful flowers, grasses, and trees. I think that's downright friendly of Him. And we must always keep nature clean and protected. That's why we pick up our picnic papers and toss them in the trash barrel when we're finished."

As we bow our heads to pray I say, "Dear Jesus, thank You for this wonderful food. And thank You for Your beautiful nature. We'll take good care of it! Amen."

—Terry

TERRY IN THE CITY . . .

Where Is Heaven?

18
SEPTEMBER

I am going [to heaven] to prepare a place for you. John 14:2, ICB.

Soft, billowy clouds drift high in the sky above our heads. Mom, Dad, and I lie on our backs, watching them move like boats across a blue ocean. In the distance I can hear cars and trucks speeding along the highway that passes the park. Our picnic is finished and our tummies feel full and happy.

I rise up on one elbow. "God lives in heaven, right?" I ask.

"Yes," Mom says with a yawn.

"But where exactly *is* heaven?"

Dad points skyward. "Waaaay up there somewhere, Terry, beyond the clouds, even beyond the stars."

"Can the space shuttle go there?"

"Nope," Mom says, "only the angels. But someday we'll all travel to heaven with Jesus."

I think for a minute. "Where will we live? Do we have a house up there?"

Dad nods. "The Bible says our house is being built right now. Remember what Jesus said in that text I read this morning: 'I am going [to heaven] to prepare a place for you'?"

"Wow!" I gasp. "Jesus Himself is building us a house."

"That's right," Mom says with a smile. "A big, beautiful house . . . in the country."

—Terry

19
SEPTEMBER

I love you . . . with a love that will last forever. I became your friend because of my love and kindness. Jeremiah 31:3, ICB.

TERRY IN THE CITY . . .

The Package

Ding-dong. Someone is at our apartment door. *Ding-dong, ding-dong.*

"Oh, hello, Mr. Collins," I hear Mom say. Mr. Collins is the mail carrier.

"I have a package for Terry Williams," the visitor announces. What? Did he say he had a package for *me?*

Mom walks into my room. "Look," she says. "Grandma sent you a package!"

"Let's open it," I shout. Quickly I unwrap the box and peek inside. There I find some animal books, a cool T-shirt, and a puzzle. "Look at all this neat stuff!"

At worship that night I show Dad the box. "I've never had anyone send me a package before," I tell him.

"Yes, you have. Jesus sends you a package of words every day."

"Really?" I ask. "What did He send today?"

Dad opens our family Bible and reads. " 'I love you . . . with a love that will last forever. I became your friend because of my love and kindness.' "

"See," Dad says, "this is a letter to you from Jesus. The Bible is like a big package of love letters sent daily just for us."

–Terry

TERRY IN THE CITY . . .

Living Forever

20

SEPTEMBER

The grass dies, and the flowers fall. But the word of our God will live forever. Isaiah 40:8, ICB.

"Oh, dear." Mom studies the plant resting on the window ledge. "My beautiful flowers have died. Guess they didn't get enough sunlight."

She dumps the wilted plant into the garbage and sighs, "It's not easy growing flowers in an apartment in the city."

"Why do things have to die?" I ask sadly. "Even people and animals. That's what happened to Grandpa, remember?"

Mom sits down on the couch beside me. "Yes, Terry, I remember," she says. "Things die because Satan makes them die. But God has promised that someday death and Satan will be destroyed and everyone who loves Him, including grandpas, will live forever. If God made that promise, we can believe it."

"Then I'll see Grandpa again, right?"

"Yes, and Aunt Carol and Cousin John. There's a verse in the Bible that says, 'The grass dies, and the flowers fall. But the word of our God will live forever.' Satan can't destroy Jesus, and Jesus has promised that we'll live forever with Him in heaven."

Now whenever I see a dying plant, I'm glad Jesus has promised to stop death. I want flowers—and grandpas—to live forever.

—Terry

21
SEPTEMBER

TERRY IN THE CITY . . .

Pleasing Jesus

Children, obey your parents in all things. This pleases the Lord. Colossians 3:20, ICB.

Terry?" My dad's voice calls from the kitchen. "Would you please come and help me?"

I put my truck in its pretend warehouse and run to where my dad is waiting. "What do you want?" I ask.

"I've got to take the garbage out to the dumpster. Will you carry this bag for me? It's kinda heavy."

"No problem," I say as I lift the bag into my arms. I want my dad to think I'm the strongest kid on the block. He and I head down the apartment steps behind the building and toss our loads into the big metal trash bin. Then we head back upstairs.

"Did you know that God likes it when children obey their parents?" Dad asks. "The Bible says it pleases Him."

"Really? Does He actually see me when I obey you?"

"Sure. He checks on all His children, whether grown up or growing up, and is all smiles when He sees us doing what our parents or teachers or bosses tell us to do."

"I'll keep that in mind," I say. "Jesus does so much for us, it's kinda neat to do something that makes *Him* happy for a change."

—Terry

TERRY IN THE CITY . . .

Doing Something

22
SEPTEMBER

Happy is the person who thinks about the poor. Psalm 41:1, ICB.

I scratch my head and frown. "Dad," I say, "read that text again."

My father looks down at his Bible. "'Happy is the person who thinks about the poor.'"

"I don't understand," I say. "When I think about the homeless woman and about Mr. McFarland who lives above us, it doesn't make me happy. They're both poor."

Dad nods. "You're right. But, Jesus didn't mean for us only to *think* about them. We're supposed to *do* something as well. That's what Jesus did when He was here on earth."

"I think about Mr. McFarland a lot because I see him every day," I say. "His coat is torn, and his shoes have big holes in them. What can I *do* to help him?"

Dad leads me to his closet. "You know, I don't need two coats," he says, "and one pair of good shoes should do me fine. Let's take this extra coat and these perfectly good shoes up to Mr. McFarland's apartment and ask him if he'd like to have them."

"Great idea!" I say, smiling up at my father. "Then when I think about Mr. McFarland, I can be glad because we *did* something."

–Terry

23
SEPTEMBER

My child, sinners will try to lead you into sin. But do not follow them. Proverbs 1:10, ICB.

TERRY IN THE CITY . . .

Following the Wrong People

"What are those guys doing?" I ask as Mom and I walk along the sidewalk.

A man runs to a car and shows something to the driver. Then the driver gives him some money and the man hurries away. Mom shakes her head sadly. "That gentleman is selling drugs that make the other man's body weak."

"How?"

"Those drugs make him feel good for a while. When the feelings stop, the man has to buy more. Every time he uses those drugs his body grows weaker. That driver is what's called a drug addict. The other man is a drug dealer."

I think for a minute. "Does Jesus love drug dealers?"

"Yes," Mom says. "He loves them very much, and so should we. But the dealer doesn't love Jesus. That's why he's doing such a harmful thing. The Bible says that when a person doesn't obey God, he or she is a sinner.

"But," Mom continues, "God longs to forgive him, just as He wants to forgive us when we do wrong."

I watch the dealer walk around the corner and disappear in the crowd. Maybe someday when I'm older I'll tell him about God and His love. He should know.

—Terry

TERRY IN THE CITY . . .

At the Zoo!

24
SEPTEMBER

So God made the wild animals, the tame animals and all the small crawling animals. Genesis 1:25, ICB.

"Look at those huge ears!" Nat and I watch an elephant move back and forth in his cage. "He can probably hear us whisper a mile away!"

Nat tosses a peanut to the elephant, and the animal scoops it up with his long nose and plops it into his mouth. "I like this zoo," I say as we head for Monkey Island. "God sure created some funny-looking critters."

"*God* made these animals?" Nat says in surprise. "Even that hippo?"

"According to the Bible," Dad answers. "It also tells us that God made one special animal to be His friend forever."

"The dog, right? Dogs are good friends."

Dad shakes his head no.

"A cow? A horse?"

"I know. I know!" I call, jumping up and down like a monkey. "God made *people* to be His friends."

"Right!" Dad says with a smile. "And I think we're much better looking than hippopotamuses. Don't you agree?"

We laugh as the big hippo snorts and then dives under the water. He must have good ears too.

–Terry

25
SEPTEMBER

"I will bring back your health. And I will heal your injuries," says the Lord. Jeremiah 30:17, ICB.

TERRY IN THE CITY . . .

Helping God

"Listen," I say to my parents while we're eating breakfast. "Do you hear that siren?"

They stop chewing for a moment. "Yes."

I run to the window and watch as an ambulance hurries down our street, lights flashing and siren wailing. "Somebody somewhere is sick or hurt," I say as I return to the table. "That's sad."

At morning worship Dad reads from our family Bible, "I will bring back your health. And I will heal your injuries."

"How can God help us when we're sick?" I want to know. "He's in heaven. We're on earth."

Dad nods. "It does seem impossible, but He's got help."

"He does? Who—" Then I remember the ambulance. "Wait, I know! Doctors and nurses, the people driving the ambulance—they're His helpers, right?"

"Right," Dad says. "God can send someone to our bedside, or we can head for the hospital or clinic when we're sick or injured. It makes me feel a little safer knowing God, or one of His helpers, is close by. When we pray, God comes running. When we hear a siren, we can know one of His helpers is on the job!"

—Terry

TERRY IN THE CITY . . .

Better Than Being Rich

26
SEPTEMBER

It will be very hard for rich people to enter the kingdom of God! Luke 18:24, ICB.

"Look at that!" I say, pointing at a long, shiny car driving past our building. "Why are all the windows dark?"

Dad glances at the vehicle as it speeds by. "That's a rich person's automobile," he says. "I guess rich people like privacy. They sit in the back seat while their drivers take them where they want to go."

I think for a minute. "This morning you read a verse that says it's hard for rich people to go to heaven. Are they all bad?"

"Oh, no, Terry," Dad answers. "Most are hardworking and honest. But Jesus knows that when you have lots of money, it's easy to forget about Him. You might stop depending on His blessings. Then Satan tries hard to make you forget about God completely."

The long car turns the corner and stops in front of a building. A man with white gloves opens the door, and some people get out. They're wearing beautiful clothes.

"Being rich would be nice," I say, "but I don't want to forget about God and how much He helps me each day."

"Good," Dads says. "Money is nice. But staying friends with God is much, much nicer."

–Terry

27
SEPTEMBER

TERRY IN THE CITY . . .

My Sabbath

The seventh day is the sabbath of the Lord thy God. Exodus 20:10.

Dad steers our car along the busy streets. Finally we reach our church and find an empty space in the parking lot. My city church is big. My Sabbath school class is big. The organ, the seats, and even the bathroom are big.

Nat, who I invited to come along, looks at the people walking about and listens to the music. He watches our teacher tell a story and hears two people play a very loud song on their trumpets. He even walks up front with me for the children's story.

When we're in the car heading home again, Nat says, "I've never been to church on Saturday. Why don't you go on Sunday, like everyone else in our building?"

Mom smiles. "We attend church on Saturday because Jesus asked us to. He said that we should keep the seventh day holy because He created it especially for us and wants us to enjoy special blessings on that day. Saturday is the *seventh* day."

"I enjoyed the songs and stories," Nat says. "May I go with you again?"

"Sure," Dad answers. "Maybe your mom would like to come along, too."

I love my Sabbath, especially when I share it with Nat.

–Terry

TERRY IN THE CITY . . .

Planetarium Day!

SEPTEMBER

When you look up at the sky, you see the sun, moon and stars. . . . The Lord your God has made these things for all people everywhere. Deuteronomy 4:19, ICB.

What is this place?" I ask as Dad, Nat, and I sit down in a dark, round room. In the middle is a large, strange-looking machine.

"It's called a planetarium," Dad says, leaning back in his chair. "We're going to see the night sky in a few minutes."

"But the sun is shining outside!" Nat chuckles.

Just then the lights go out and above us beautiful stars appear. "Oh," I gasp, "this is wonderful. It's like nighttime at our house in the country."

"I know, Terry," Daddy says with a sigh. "That's why I like to come here. In the city you can't see very many stars. So that machine over there projects images of the stars on this ceiling."

We sit and enjoy the program while music plays and a man tells us some of the names of the stars and how far away they are. I remember some from our country home. Dad showed them to me a long time ago.

When the program finishes, we just sit still, thinking about all those beautiful stars. Quietly I whisper, "Thank You, Jesus, for creating them for us."

—Terry

29
SEPTEMBER

I go to bed and sleep in peace. Lord, only you keep me safe. Psalm 4:8, ICB.

TERRY IN THE CITY . . .

Mr. Weatherby's Partner

"Hi, Mr. Weatherby," I say as I climb the steps to our apartment building. "How are you?"

Mr. Weatherby smiles and waves. "I'm fine, Terry."

I sit down beside him and tell him about the planetarium and the beautiful stars. Mr. Weatherby likes it when I talk to him.

"Are you guarding the apartment again tonight?" I ask.

"That's my job," he says. "I'll keep my eyes and ears open for trouble."

"Thanks," I say as I head for the elevator. "I'm glad you and Jesus are watching out for us."

"Me and *who?*"

"Jesus," I repeat. "He guards me too. I learned a verse in Sabbath school that says, 'I go to bed and sleep in peace. Lord, only you keep me safe.' Of course, I know *you're* helping too, so I feel doubly safe when I'm sleeping."

"Well, well," Mr. Weatherby says with a chuckle. "Me and Jesus, huh? Sounds like I've got a good Partner."

As the elevator doors close I see Mr. Weatherby checking his watch and flashlight. He and Jesus have work to do.

—Terry

TERRY IN THE CITY . . .

He Sees Me

30
SEPTEMBER

Yes, I am sure that nothing can separate us from the love God has for us. Romans 8:38, 39, ICB.

Mom, Dad, and I are going to a large store on the other side of the city. Dad says we'll ride on something called a subway under the streets.

We walk to the station and then go down a long flight of stairs. *Rumble. Whoosh!* Trains rush past us. I grab hold of mom's hand, just in case she's afraid.

"Terry, are you OK?" Dad asks.

"Sure," I say, trying to be brave. Then I have a *really* scary thought. "Dad, can Jesus see us way down here under the city?"

My father bends down to talk to me. "Of course He can," he says. "Jesus can see you anywhere and anytime, even in a subway."

I watch the trains rush by and feel the ground tremble under my feet. I see people getting on and off the cars.

Then I think of the tall buildings above us—the streets and cars, buses and trucks. And then I think of the huge sky and the millions of stars.

Finally I imagine Jesus looking down and seeing me, even in this noisy tunnel. And I smile. Yes, Jesus knows where I am. Even in the big city He sees me.

–Terry

1

OCTOBER

John's clothes were made of camel's hair. Matthew 3:4, NIV.

DO YOU KNOW MY NAME? . . .

Desert Train

Do you know my name? I live where hot desert winds blow. If you saw me, you might laugh right out loud, because I'm not the best-looking animal in the world. However, if you needed someone to carry you safely across a desert, I'm your critter!

Some say I have funny feet. But they help me walk on sand day in and day out.

When I take a drink of water, I drink a lot! Why? So I can travel great distances without having to stop to drink more.

In some countries of the world I have a great big hump on my back. In other countries I have *two* great big humps on my back!

God created me special so I could do a special work. Yeah, I may be kinda strange-looking, but I serve a very important purpose for my human masters.

Perhaps people say you're kinda strange looking, with a big nose or floppy ears. Maybe you think you're too tall or too short. Don't worry. Find something you're good at and do it better than anyone else. But don't try walking across a desert without water. That's *my* special skill!

If you haven't figured out who I am, allow me to introduce myself. My name is Camel.

DO YOU KNOW MY NAME? . . .

Striped Pajamas

2

OCTOBER

By him all things were created. Colossians 1:16, NIV.

Do you know my name? I'm a very confusing animal. Some people think I'm black with white stripes. Others say I'm white with black stripes. I say, "Who cares! I'm just me!"

I like to munch on grass and leaves for lunch, so I guess you could call me a vegetarian. If anyone ever tells you that being a vegetarian makes you weak or a sissy, tell 'em to come see me. I'll challenge them to a footrace, up a mountain, in the summer, carrying a heavy pack.

When you visit me, I'll either be out grazing on the plains or enjoying a cool drink down at the ol' water hole. Soda pop or colas? Forget about it! Give me fresh water any day.

Maybe you'd think I'm a horse. Well, I do look like one if it was wearing striped pajamas. But that's not my name.

God made me different from all the other animals on earth. Hey, did God make you different from everybody else too? He did? Cool! Being different makes us special if you ask me.

OK. If you don't know my name, allow me to introduce myself. My name is Zebra.

3
OCTOBER

DO YOU KNOW MY NAME? . . .

Little Eyes, Big Body

Look at the behemoth, . . . which feeds on grass like an ox. . . . What power in the muscles of his belly! His tail sways like a cedar. Job 40:15-17, NIV.

OK, stop giggling. Just answer the question. Do you know my name?

I love to swim in cool water, where the hot sun and hungry bugs can't get to me and make my life miserable. Often I stand on the bottom of a pond or river with just my little eyes and bumpy nose sticking out of the water, which may explain why people in Africa sometimes run into me with their boats. Ouch! That hurts!

I'm not afraid to admit that I'm kinda heavy. No, I'm really, *really* heavy. If I were to step on your bathroom scales, I'd squish them flat as a pancake. I suppose God made me heavy so I could stay under the water and not float away, which would be totally embarrassing if I took a nap and woke up in another country. God knew what I needed to be like and made me just right.

What are some of the things that are just right about you? Oh, come on. Everyone is just right in some way or another.

If you don't know my name, allow me to introduce myself. My name is Hippopotamus, but you can call me Hippo!

DO YOU KNOW MY NAME? . . .

Ice House

4

OCTOBER

The cow will feed with the bear, their young will lie down together. Isaiah 11:7, NIV.

Do you know my name? I live where there's lots of ice . . . no, not in the freezer. On the ground! That's why God gave me a beautiful, thick, furry coat to wear. It keeps me warm even when winter winds blow and snow fills the air.

When it's very, very cold, I head for my house under the snow. Only when it gets warmer do I go out again in search for food. By the way, I have my babies under the ice too. Let's see a human mother do that!

Maybe you think I'm fat. Well, I am. But my fat helps keep me warm and provides nourishment during my long winter naps.

Oh, yes, here's another hint. My fur and the snow that blows about my ice house share something in common. They're the same color.

The Creator made me just right so I can hunt for food and survive in my icy-cold land. If He'd made me any different, without my thick fur and body fat, I'd die.

I'll bet you have things about you that make you perfect for the work God wants you to do. Check it out.

If you don't know my name, allow me to introduce myself. My name is Polar Bear.

5
OCTOBER

The lambs will provide you with clothing, and the goats with the price of a field. Proverbs 27:26, NIV.

DO YOU KNOW MY NAME? . . .

No Kidding!

Do you know my name? I live in many different places like high on mountaintops or in deep valleys. But most of the time, you'll find me living on a farm.

My legs are long and can run and climb fast. I usually have two horns, but they're not for blowing in a traffic jam. And if you like milk, I'm your animal. Many people around the world rely on my milk as a nutritious part of their diet.

By the way, I enjoy eating many kinds of food and will chew on almost anything.

When I have a baby, it's called a "kid." They're so cute and energetic. They run around and play just like human "kids" do.

When the farmer gives me food, water, and a safe, comfortable place to live, I give the farmer delicious milk to drink. We're partners.

Kids like you can be partners with God, you know. He helps you live a healthy, happy life, and you tell others about His love. Pretty good deal for everyone!

If you don't know my name, allow me to introduce myself. My name is Goat.

DO YOU KNOW MY NAME? . . .

On the Prowl

6 OCTOBER

They will neither harm nor destroy on all my holy mountain.
Isaiah 11:9, NIV.

Do you know my name? If you lived in the jungle you would. I can run and climb a tree much faster than any human. Some call me a "giant with stripes."

Sometimes late at night, when the world is silent and still, I'll open my mouth and let out a scream that sends animals running for cover. Other times I'll creep through the shadows, and you won't even know I'm close by, even if you almost step on me in the dark.

Most creatures are afraid of me, and well they should be. I protect my young at all costs, attacking animals much larger than I am if I have to.

If you ever surprised me on a trail, you'd turn and run as fast as you could. But guess what? If you'd happen to look back, you wouldn't find me trying to catch you. No. You'd see me running in the opposite direction as fast as I can! That's right. Even though I'm a fierce hunter, I'm afraid of people. Nothing personal.

In heaven creatures like me won't be afraid of creatures like you. The only running we'll do is having fun playing hide and seek in the meadow.

If you don't know my name, allow me to introduce myself. My name is Tiger.

7
OCTOBER

Everything God created is good. 1 Timothy 4:4, NIV.

DO YOU KNOW MY NAME? . . .

Nuts!

Do you know my name? Please don't think I'm crazy if I tell you that I live in a tree. And I've been seen to jump from limb to limb far above the ground. Hey, it beats climbing down and then climbing up again.

My large, bushy tail helps me keep my balance when I'm scampering high overhead. Sometimes I sit and chatter with my neighbors, but most of the time, I'm working.

Before winter comes, I've got to load up my house with food so that when the snows fall and the ground is covered with drifts, I'll have something for dinner. And not just for me. My family has got to eat too, you know.

I'm glad God gave me a big bushy tail and little, sharp claws. Without them, I'd lose my balance on the limbs and tumble, tumble, tumble to the ground. *Thump!* That's gotta hurt!

God always lets me know when winter is approaching so I can get busy and store nuts in my treetop house. I'd invite you up for dinner but, sorry, you don't have a bushy tail or sharp claws. But I'm sure God made you so you could do some other neat work.

If you don't know my name, allow me to introduce myself. My name is Squirrel.

DO YOU KNOW MY NAME? . . .

Hairy Friend

8 OCTOBER

Abel kept flocks. Genesis 4:2, NIV.

Do you know my name? You should, because I probably help keep you warm when it's cold.

When you head outside to play in the snow, chances are your mom or dad say, "Don't forget to put on your coat." That coat might be made from my hair!

I grow lots of hair. I mean *lots* of hair. Every year, the farmer or rancher who takes care of me carefully clips me with an electric shaver and ships my hair off to a factory that makes blankets, coats, gloves, and pants. No, it doesn't hurt when they do that. It's just like when you visit the barber. Afterward, I look kinda skinny for a while. But my hair grows back in a hurry and I look nice and fat again.

I'm really pleased that God gave me all that wool (that's what my hair is called). It's neat to know that I'm helping to keep people warm. Hey, I'm just a little animal. Maybe God gave you a special talent that you can use to make life better for others.

If you don't know my name, allow me to introduce myself. My name is Sheep.

9

OCTOBER

Do you give the horse his strength or clothe his neck with a flowing mane? Do you make him leap like a locust, striking terror with his proud snorting? He paws fiercely, rejoicing in his strength. Job 39:19-21, NIV.

DO YOU KNOW MY NAME? . . .

Hitch a Ride

Do you know my name? I'm strong, fast, and friendly. People like to hop on my back and go for a ride! But don't think I'm just for fun. I'm a good worker, too. You can hitch me to a wagon or a plow, and I'll pull all day long if you give me a few minutes to rest every once in a while.

Before you were born, I was just as important to people as your family car. As a matter of fact, it was me that took people from place to place, even traveling across mountains and deserts to lands they'd never seen before.

Now machines do the work.

Even though I don't work as hard as I used to, I still get a kick out of helping people enjoy a trip through a forest or across a flower-carpeted meadow. Some even race me against other animals like me. We run like the wind, tossing up clouds of dirt and dust as we thunder around the racetrack.

I always do the best I can, no matter what I'm asked to do. Are you like that too?

If you don't know my name, allow me to introduce myself. My name is Horse.

DO YOU KNOW MY NAME? . . .

Udderly Good

10 OCTOBER

The cow will feed with the bear. Isaiah 11:7, NIV.

Do you know my name? I live on a farm and spend my whole day doing just one thing . . . eating grass. I *love* grass. Sometimes you might see me out in the fields chewing and chewing as you ride by in your family car.

Farmers take good care of me because I make something absolutely wonderful to drink. Each day, the boss (that's what I call the farmer) leads me and my friends into his barn and hooks me up to a noisy machine. *Chugga, chugga, chugga,* it goes. I don't mind. It doesn't hurt. Pretty soon, after he's finished, he's got a truckload of delicious white milk ready to send to market.

Sometimes I'm brown, and sometimes I'm black. I can be both black and white or brown and white. But no matter what color I am, my milk is always creamy white and ready for people to enjoy on their breakfast cereal.

Hey, I just thought of something. No matter what color I am, God created me so I can do something nice. God made you, too. That means you're special no matter what color you are. Awesome!

If you don't know my name, allow me to introduce myself. My name is Cow.

11
OCTOBER

DO YOU KNOW MY NAME? . . .

Pounding Hooves

Save me from the horns of the wild oxen. Psalm 22:21, NIV.

Do you know my name? I live on the prairies, where grasses grow tall and the sun shines brightly.

During the winter, my land becomes uncomfortably cold, but I don't worry because God has given me a warm coat of fur to wear.

I grew up in a large family. When we move from place to place or travel from our summer grazing area to our winter homes, we stay together in large herds, helping to keep each other safe from predators. Sometimes our herd will join other groups, and we'll race across the prairie like a dark wave, shaking the ground with the mighty power of our pounding hooves.

Years ago American Indians lived on our lands, but that was OK, because on the prairie there's room for everybody.

In the winter when snows carpet the ground, we have to dig through drifts to reach the tiny bits of grass waiting underneath. If the summer has been rainy and the grasses have grown healthy and tall, we find enough to eat. But some years when food is scarce, many in our herd suffer and even die. We're very glad when spring returns and the grasses grow tall across the prairie.

If you don't know my name, allow me to introduce myself. My name is Bison.

DO YOU KNOW MY NAME? . . .

Furry Friend

12
OCTOBER

There is a friend who sticks closer than a brother. Proverbs 18:24, NIV.

Do you know my name? I have a tail that swishes back and forth and soft, floppy ears. Sometimes I talk and talk (you call it something else) when danger comes or if I don't know what's going on.

Many boys and girls let me live with them in their houses, sometimes even sleeping in their beds! I love to play with rubber balls and old slippers and can learn tricks that make my masters proud.

Some say I'm "man's best friend," but I like women, boys, and girls just as much. I guess you could say that I want to be a friend to *everybody!*

Occasionally people hurt me, and I get angry. I'll sit around and growl and snap, feeling dejected and lonely. But as soon as someone loves me again, I stop being mad and jump for joy.

I think that God wants you to be "man's best friend" too, just like me. So if you're sitting around feeling angry and lonely, do what I do. Start jumping for joy because Jesus loves you very much.

If you don't know my name, allow me to introduce myself. My name is Dog.

13
OCTOBER

You may not eat . . . the rabbit. Deuteronomy 14:7, NIV.

DO YOU KNOW MY NAME? . . .

Twitchy Nose, Fat Cheeks

Do you know my name? If you saw me you would because I don't look like any other animal on earth. Sometimes I wonder if God made a mistake when He created me because He gave me great big ears, a little tiny nose, two front teeth that stick out, fat cheeks, and a silly white tail.

Have you ever wondered why you look the way you look? Do you sometimes think that you were created wrong?

Well, when I got older, I discovered some things about myself. My big ears help me hear noises better. My tiny nose can smell food and help me find it. I munch on tons of carrots with my funny teeth, and my fat cheeks allow me to carry food home to my family.

When danger comes, my powerful hind legs allow me to run away . . . fast! And my silly tail? I use it like a flag to warn my friends of danger so that they can hide too.

Now I don't mind looking the way I look. God made each part of me for a reason. It's the same for you.

If you don't know my name, allow me to introduce myself. My name is Rabbit.

DO YOU KNOW MY NAME? . . .

Home in a Hole

14
OCTOBER

O Lord, our Lord, how majestic is your name in all the earth! Psalm 8:9, NIV.

Do you know my name? I dig long tunnels under the ground so that I can go from place to place without being seen.

I have a little bushy tail and on my back are several pretty stripes. Sometimes I sit by my front door—a hole in the ground—and watch for danger. If I see any, I go, "Chip, chip, chip, chip!" All my brothers and sisters, and the other animals around my home, run and hide.

I eat nuts and seeds. In the spring, when my mother has babies, she keeps busy finding food for her growing family. But she and my father work hard so the little babies won't be hungry. I'm glad God helps moms and dads work hard for us, aren't you?

I enjoy playing in the bright sunshine. I scamper here and there, jumping and hopping, having a great time. But I always know where my tunnels are and how to get to them fast! I believe that all little animals, including boys and girls, should know how to get home if trouble threatens. When I am in my underground house, I feel safe.

If you don't know my name, allow me to introduce myself. My name is Chipmunk.

15
OCTOBER

God said, "Let . . . birds fly above the earth across the expanse of the sky." Genesis 1:20, NIV.

DO YOU KNOW MY NAME? . . .

Finger Sitter

Do you know my name? I'm little with pretty feathers. Sometimes they're blue, sometimes they're yellow. Or they could be white or green.

I sit in my cage and chatter at the world. Sometimes I'll even sing a little song, but most of the time I just chatter.

I love to eat seeds. That's why God gave me a strong beak so that I can crack them open and enjoy the soft, tasty food hiding inside.

My family originally came from a faraway jungle. However, if you promise to take good care of me and always check to make sure I have plenty of food and water, I will be happy to live with you.

If you're gentle with me, I'll even sit on your finger and chatter. No, you won't know what I'm saying. You'll just tell your friends, "This is one happy critter!"

Even though people and animals can't talk to each other, we can be kind and loving because love is something we all share. Love allows us to be happy together, no matter where we came from.

If you don't know my name, allow me to introduce myself. My name is Parakeet.

DO YOU KNOW MY NAME? . . .

Running Round and Round

16
OCTOBER

Praise the Lord from the earth, . . . small creatures and flying birds. Psalm 148:7-10, NIV.

Do you know my name? My fur is soft, and I have little feet, dark eyes, and whiskers.

I love to run on the exercise wheel in my cage. Around and around and around I go, keeping my heart and muscles strong and healthy.

I came from a big family with 12 brothers and sisters! How'd you like to wake up one morning and find you had 12 brothers and sisters? *Yikes!*

At bedtime, I hide under patches of cotton or piles of shredded newspaper in my cage so I can feel cozy and safe. When I'm sleeping, you may wonder where I went. Don't worry, I'm just hiding. When I wake up, I'll come back out to play and eat.

Even though I'm small, I need love. God knew all the animals in the world would need love so He instructed Adam and Eve to remember to care for each one. Today, God wants you to love all animals, even little guys like me. You see, He loves animals and people no matter how big or small they happen to be. Isn't it great to know that no matter who you are, God cares for you?

If you don't know my name, allow me to introduce myself. My name is Hamster.

17
OCTOBER

God made . . . all the creatures that move along the ground according to their kinds. Genesis 1:25, NIV.

DO YOU KNOW MY NAME? . . .

The Purr-fect Pet

Do you know my name? Many boys and girls enjoy playing with me because I jump around and chase things. And when I want to catch something, I pounce on it with my front paws.

Everyday I clean my fur with my tongue. Hey, doesn't everyone? God gave me a special, scratchy tongue, so I can keep my fur soft and clean.

If you're gentle with me and hold me in your lap, you'll hear me make a little noise. It sounds kinda like I have a motor running inside of me. *Purrrr, purrrr, purrr.* I think it's a nice sound and so do the people who care for me.

I have really sharp claws that help me climb trees. One problem, though. It's a lot easier for me to go *up* a tree than *down* a tree. Sometimes I get stuck high in the branches and have to wait for someone to come get me. How embarrassing is that?

When someone helps me, I say Thank you by going *purrrr, purrrr.* I always say Thank you because I'm a very polite critter. Aren't you?

If you don't know my name, allow me to introduce myself. My name is Cat.

DO YOU KNOW MY NAME? . . .

Golden Scales

18
OCTOBER

God said, "Let the water teem with living creatures." Genesis 1:20, NIV.

Do you know my name? I live underwater and swim around all day, eating food that floats by.

You might think that I have a funny mouth because I always look like I'm about to kiss you. But that's the way I breathe. God made me so I can live my whole life without ever going out of my watery home.

Some of the other creatures in my world have beautiful, silver-colored scales. But my scales are gold. When the sun shines down through the water, they glow.

Because I am such a beautiful color, many people let me live in their homes. They fill a glass bowl with fresh, clean water and put me inside. I swim around as happy as can be.

Every day they drop tiny bits of food in my water. Yum! It's great when people make my glass bowl a fun place to live. They'll even put green, wavy, underwater plants at the base of my bowl with colorful rocks scattered about. My home is just beautiful.

That's the way God cares for people. He puts trees and flowers on this earth to make it a great place in which to live.

If you don't know my name, allow me to introduce myself. My name is Goldfish.

19
OCTOBER

Whatsoever thy hand findeth to do, do it with thy might. Ecclesiastes 9:10.

USING MY HANDS
THE WAY *JESUS USED* HIS HANDS . . .

New Game

Hello. Our names are David and Nicole. We live across the street from each other and are best friends. Have been ever since we were little. We go to the same school, attend the same church, and like to watch basketball games on television.

Today we were hanging out in the backyard when we came up with an idea. Our Sabbath school lesson said we should try to use our hands the way Jesus used His hands—you know, helping friends and neighbors, being kind, and working hard.

So we're starting a new game. For the next couple weeks, we're going to make our hands do what Jesus' hands did when He was here on earth. If you'd like, you can play too.

First, we must find out what Jesus' hands did. Where do you think we should look for that information? Yup. The Bible. It tells all about Jesus' hands.

So the very first thing our hands are going to do is open our *International Children's Bible*s and read what it says in Matthew, Mark, Luke, and John. Our parents have promised to help.

Hey! Jesus read His Bible! We're off to a great start.

–David and Nicole

USING MY HANDS
THE WAY JESUS USED HIS HANDS . . .

David's Healing Hands

20
OCTOBER

I will go and heal him. Matthew 8:7, ICB.

Mom came home early from work today. She parked the car, walked into the living room, and flopped down on the couch.

"David," she called, "my head aches. Please play quietly so I can take a short nap."

"No problem," I said.

My friend Nicole and I are trying to use our hands like Jesus did when He was on earth. So when Mom lay down on the couch, I thought to myself, *What would Jesus do*?

Then I remembered the Bible text we read for worship. A soldier whose servant was sick asked Jesus for help. Let me recite it for you. "Jesus said to the officer, 'I will go and heal him' " (Matthew 8:7, ICB).

Well, my hands can't exactly heal a sickness, but they can help someone feel better. Quickly I ran to the kitchen and found a clean cloth. Then I poured cool water over it.

"Here, Mom," I said. "I brought you a cool cloth for your head."

"Thanks, David." She said with a smile. Then she placed the cloth across her forehead, closed her eyes, and was soon fast asleep. When she woke up, the headache was gone.

"You've got healing hands," Mom said as she hugged me tightly.

"They're just doing what Jesus' hands would do." I grinned.

–David

21
OCTOBER

Jesus taught the people. Matthew 5:2, ICB.

USING MY HANDS
THE WAY *JESUS* USED HIS HANDS . . .

Nicole's Teaching Hands

I love action songs. So does my little brother Andrew except he keeps getting the words and his arms and legs all mixed up. When he's supposed to wave, he stomps. When he's supposed to march, he spins around. I laugh, but he doesn't care. He's only 2.

Yesterday Dad read an interesting text in the Bible. It says, "Jesus taught the people" (Matthew 5:2, ICB). Since I want my hands to do the same as Jesus' hands, I decided I'd better get busy and teach Andrew a thing or two about action songs.

"When the words talk about the mighty ocean, do this," I said, rolling my hands around each other.

Andrew nodded and rolled his hands.

"When you sing about birds flying, do like this." I flapped my arms. Andrew jumped up and down like a kangaroo. He does pretty well with oceans, but his birds need help.

I'm not going to teach Andrew the song about the ark and all the animals, although he won't have any trouble with the kangaroo verse.

Jesus' hands were always busy teaching people about God's love. He told them about heaven and the mansions waiting there.

When I use my hands the way Jesus used His, even Andrew will learn. Maybe.

–*Nicole*

USING MY HANDS
THE WAY JESUS USED HIS HANDS . . .

David's Praying Hands

[Jesus] fell to the ground and prayed. Matthew 26:39, ICB.

My uncle Danny was in a car accident last week. An ambulance rushed him to the hospital where the doctor said he was hurt badly and might die.

I didn't have to think very hard about what Jesus' hands would do in this situation. Once, He was scared about what was going to happen. Mother read about it in Matthew 26:39. The verse says, "[Jesus] fell to the ground and prayed" (ICB).

That's exactly what I did. I knelt by my favorite tree and said, "Dear Jesus, help the doctors know what to do for Uncle Danny. Help the nurses take care of him too. I don't want him to die. And no matter what happens, help me to be strong. Amen."

Now I know why Jesus prayed to His heavenly Father whenever He felt afraid. It makes you feel as if you're not alone.

Now even though my friends at school, who've never met my uncle Danny, laugh and play as if nothing is wrong, I know Jesus is at the hospital, helping the doctors and nurses save my uncle's life.

I know I have a Friend who'll stick by me, no matter what the next few days will bring.

Maybe that's the reason that when Jesus was afraid, He fell to the ground and prayed.

–David

23
OCTOBER

So [Jesus] traveled everywhere in Galilee. He preached in the synagogues. Mark 1:39, ICB.

USING MY HANDS
THE WAY JESUS USED HIS HANDS . . .

Nicole's Preaching Hands

Last Sabbath our pastor told a story about how Jesus hurried to a synagogue and preached. He read a Bible verse that says, "So [Jesus] traveled everywhere in Galilee. He preached in the synagogues" (Mark 1:39, ICB).

Since I want to use my hands the same way Jesus used His, I figured I'd better get busy and do some preaching of my own.

One problem. Getting up in front of a bunch of people makes me so scared that my knees shake.

"Don't worry," Dad said. "Preach to people you know, such as Grandma or even your cousin Sarah." So I got my favorite Bible picture book, found an exciting story about a shepherd who takes good care of his sheep, and then went to see Cousin Sarah. I waved my arms, smiled, frowned, and lifted my book over my head, just like our pastor.

Cousin Sarah was impressed! She said she liked my story about the Good Shepherd, that it made her happy to know how much Jesus cares for people who are hurting.

Next week I'm going to tell her the story about how Jesus forgave the sins of a wicked woman. Some said she was very bad, but Jesus didn't listen. I hope Cousin Sarah likes that one too.

–*Nicole*

USING MY HANDS
THE WAY JESUS USED HIS HANDS . . .

David's Feeding Hands

24
OCTOBER

Jesus said, "I am the bread that gives life. He who comes to me will never be hungry." John 6:35, ICB.

Yesterday I saw a picture in the newspaper that made me sad. It showed a little baby crying. The mother looked worried.

"What's going on?" I asked my mom.

She shook her head sadly. "They're hungry."

"But didn't we give some money to help those people?"

Mom nodded. "Sometimes it takes a while for our gifts to get to faraway places."

"I don't want them to wait," I sighed.

"You know," Mom said, "Jesus cared for people who were all around Him. How'd you like to have feeding hands like His?"

"How?"

Mom hurried to the refrigerator. "Our neighbor Mrs. Perez is old and can't fix nutritious meals very often. Why don't we make her a healthy sandwich and some vegetable soup? You can take them to her for supper."

Mrs. Perez gave me a big hug when I brought her the delicious meal. I sat and watched her eat, knowing I'd used my hands to bring happiness to her day and healthy food to her tummy.

It reminded me of a Bible verse that reads, "Then Jesus said, 'I am the bread that gives life. He who comes to me will never be hungry'" (John 6:35, ICB). My hands can help Jesus keep His promise.

–David

25
OCTOBER

Those who are sad now [will be] happy. God will comfort them. Matthew 5:4, ICB.

USING MY HANDS
THE WAY JESUS USED HIS HANDS . . .

Nicole's Comforting Hand

Last week my friend Shelby came to visit me. We played croquet for a while, but she seemed sad. "What's the matter?" I asked.

Shelby sat down on the grass. "My parents are fighting again," she said. "It makes me worried. I don't want them to get a divorce, but I heard one of them say that word yesterday." She looked at me. "What am I going to do?"

Shelby is my friend. I didn't like seeing her so sad and wanted to do something. Then I remembered a Bible text I learned that said, "Those who are sad now [will be] happy. God will comfort them" (Matthew 5:4, ICB). Yes! I'd use my hands and my words to comfort Shelby.

I put my arm around her shoulders. "I'm sorry these bad things are happening to you," I said. "It makes me sad. But I'll always be your friend."

Shelby smiled. "Really?" she asked. "Even if my mom and dad get a divorce?"

"Sure," I answered. "And if you have to be sad sometimes, I'll understand."

We played more croquet. Shelby beat me four games to one, but that was OK. She knew I'd be her friend no matter what.

–Nicole

USING MY HANDS
THE WAY JESUS USED HIS HANDS . . .

David's Working Hands

26
OCTOBER

Jesus said to them, "My Father never stops working. And so I work, too." John 5:17, ICB.

Today I washed the living room windows, took out the trash, straightened my closet, and dusted the furniture in the den.

"Whatever has gotten into you?" my mom asked as I was carefully watering the plants in the dining room. "I've never seen you work so hard. Is your birthday coming up or something?"

"No, Mom." I laughed, lifting my arms up in front of her. "I'm letting Jesus use my hands today. Don't you remember the text Dad read for worship this morning?"

We went to the living room, where I opened our Bible to John 5:17. "You read it," I invited.

Mom cleared her throat. "Jesus said to them, 'My Father never stops working. And so I work, too'" (ICB).

"Don't you see?" I asked. "I want to use my hands the way Jesus used His. The text said He was always working, just like God the Father. So that's exactly what I'm doing too."

Mom smiled. "Now I understand. But don't forget, Jesus also rested on Sabbath and spent time relaxing with His friends."

"OK," I said. "I won't work so hard that I forget to rest. And like Jesus, I'm always going to work hard when I'm not resting."

–David

27
OCTOBER

You must tell people to change their hearts and lives. If they do this, their sins will be forgiven. Luke 24:47, 48, ICB.

USING MY HANDS
THE WAY JESUS USED HIS HANDS . . .

Nicole's Reaching-out Hands

"Our evangelistic meetings begin next week," the preacher announced. "Everyone in our city needs to know that Jesus loves them. So we're looking for volunteers to help us reach out to the community."

Then he read, "You must tell people to change their hearts and lives. If they do this, their sins will be forgiven" (Luke 24:47, 48, ICB).

As we drove home after church I kept looking out the window. How could I do what the text said?

"I know what you're thinking," Mom called, nudging me with her elbow. "You're wondering how we can tell people about the meetings."

"Yeah?" I moaned.

"Look in the back seat. In that box are invitations to those meetings. We're going to stick labels on them with the names and addresses of all our friends and neighbors, as well as some people we don't even know. What do you think?"

"Great idea!" I said excitedly. "Then I can use my hands to reach out to others—through the mail."

By suppertime the next day we had a big stack of invitations ready to go. "I enjoy using my hands as Jesus did," I said with a tired sigh. "Even if it makes my fingers sore."

–Nicole

USING MY HANDS
THE WAY JESUS USED HIS HANDS . . .

David's Loving Hands

28
OCTOBER

**For God loved the world so much that he gave his only Son.
John 3:16, ICB.**

I have a dog named Wiggles. When I feed him, he wags his tail. When we play ball, he jumps around like a grasshopper. When we go for a walk, he runs here and there as if he's chasing something. Good name, huh?

Wiggles keeps my hands busy. If I'm not getting his food, I'm cleaning up his messes, pulling him out of a mud puddle, or giving him a bath.

"Love keeps you busy, huh?" Dad chuckled. "Remember the Bible text we read yesterday? It said, 'For God loved the world so much that he gave his only son' [John 3:16, ICB]. It was Jesus' job to use His hands to show people how much He and His Father loved them. The Bible is full of stories of how Jesus fed the hungry, played with children, taught His disciples, and chased devils away."

I nodded. "So when I love Wiggles, I'm using my hands as Jesus did?"

"Yes. Your hands show the love that's in your heart."

I gave my dad a big hug. "I just wanted you to know how much Jesus and I love you."

Wiggles rushed into the room and barked. "I think the puppy loves you too," I said. We laughed and laughed as Wiggles wiggled.

–David

29
OCTOBER

Surely your heavenly Father will give good things to those who ask him. Matthew 7:11, ICB.

USING MY HANDS
THE WAY JESUS USED HIS HANDS . . .

Nicole's Sharing Hands

Look!" I said, pointing. "Those people's house burned down."

Dad put on his glasses and stared at the television news program. There were pictures of a family who had just lost everything.

"We're happy to be alive," the father was saying. "But my sons won't have a very happy birthday tomorrow. Their gifts burned up."

That night I kept thinking about those boys with no gifts for their birthday. By morning I had a plan.

"What are you doing?" Mom asked as I was carrying a big box into the living room.

"I'm going to use my hands the way Jesus used His," I said. "That fire on TV didn't hurt my stuff. So I'm going to share what I have."

Dad took the box to the television station, where other people were helping too. A few days later the announcer showed more pictures of the family. This time the father was smiling. His sons had birthday gifts to open after all.

"This reminds me of a Bible text," Mom said. "It says, 'Surely your heavenly Father will give good things to those who ask' [Matthew 7:11, ICB]. Seems He even gives good things to those who might not know how to ask, like that family on television."

"I'm glad Jesus used our hands," I grinned.

–Nicole

USING MY HANDS
THE WAY JESUS USED HIS HANDS . . .

David's Joyful Hands

30
OCTOBER

I want your joy to be the fullest joy. John 15:11, ICB.

My friend Dudley plays the piano. Well, let's just say he tries very hard to play the piano. My mom says it must be heavenly music, because she's never heard anything like it on earth.

Last week we all went to his teacher's home and listened to each of her students play their songs. Then it was Dudley's turn.

He cracked his knuckles, lifted his hands, and dropped them onto the keys. I smiled. My mom smiled. Even Miss Andersen, the music teacher, smiled. Dudley played his recital piece from beginning to end without one mistake—I think. It was kinda hard to tell.

While he was playing, a Bible verse popped into my head. Jesus said, "I want your joy to be the fullest joy" (John 15:11, ICB). I wondered what He'd do if He were sitting here listening to Dudley.

Suddenly the song ended. My friend stood proudly to his feet and bowed. That's when I knew what I had to do. I clapped my hands together harder than I had ever clapped them before.

Dudley bowed again. Then again. I may not have liked how he played the song, but I sure liked how happy he looked when he saw me clapping. Yup. He had the fullest joy.

–David

31
OCTOBER

Jesus took the children in his arms. He put his hands on them and blessed them. Mark 10:16, ICB.

USING MY HANDS
THE WAY JESUS USED HIS HANDS . . .

We Did It!

Wow! We've been using our hands just as Jesus did. We've kept them busy with healing, teaching, praying, feeding, and comforting those around us. We also worked hard, reached out, loved, shared, and brought joy to our friends and family.

Now that the game is over, whose hands are going to do all those things tomorrow or the next day?

Wait! Jesus never finished using His hands. Even now they're getting heaven ready for us. They're building mansions, gathering flowers, planting trees, and forgiving our sins, even before we ask.

So we're starting a new game. It's just like the old one, except this one will last as long as we live.

Hey, why don't you play too? Just bow your head and ask Jesus to show you how to use your hands as He would. It works!

Someday Jesus is going to do something that will make every boy and girl like us very, very happy. Listen to this verse from the Bible. "Then Jesus took the children in his arms. He put his hands on them and blessed them" (Mark 10:16, ICB).

In heaven we're going to hold the hands that did so much for us. That will be the happiest day ever!

–David and Nicole

WHAT I LEARNED TODAY . . .

Jesus Died for Everyone

1
NOVEMBER

For God so loved the world so much that he gave his one and only Son. John 3:16, NIV.

Last night I learned about a picture of Jesus dying on the cross. Maybe you've seen it too. It has a mountaintop, an altar of stones, and a ram caught in the bushes. Remember the story of Abraham and Isaac? That's the picture!

"Jesus was crucified on a mountaintop," Dad told me. "The altar was made of wood, and the sacrifice wasn't a ram. It was Jesus Himself. God was giving Abraham a preview picture of what was going to happen later."

"I want to show Mrs. Benton that picture," I said. "She needs to know that Jesus died for everyone—including her. But," I shook my head sadly, "how can I? She's blind."

"She may not be able to see," Dad said, "but she can *feel.*"

We found two small pieces of wood and some clay. Then we made a little cross and molded an image of Jesus hanging on it. Soon my "feeling picture" was ready.

"Here," I said when Mrs. Benton came to the door. "This shows how much God loves you." Mrs. Benton felt the little statue as I waited.

"Thank you," she said. "What a beautiful picture of God's love!"

I discovered that blind eyes may not be able to see, but they can cry joyful tears.

–David

2
NOVEMBER

I will instruct you and teach you in the way you should go. Psalm 32:8, NIV.

WHAT I LEARNED TODAY . . .

God Will Guide Me

My brother Andrew called yesterday. "I don't know what to do," he said to my parents. "Should I take that good job or stay in college one more year?"

Dad said, "It's your decision."

Recently, I read the story of how God guided Eliezer to find Isaac's new wife, Rebekah. The Bible said that Isaac loved Rebekah very much and was glad Abraham and Eliezer let God help them in this important search. I thought God could help Andrew figure out what to do too.

So I sat down and typed an e-mail on our computer. It took me a long time, because I had to search for the letters, but I wanted my words to be just right. Dad helped. "Dear Andrew," I said. "Remember, God can help you figure out what to do. Pray and read your Bible. Be sure to check out Psalm 32:8. It says, 'I will instruct you and teach you in the way you should go; I will counsel you and watch over you' [NIV]. Remember I'm praying for you.

"Oh, and when you want to find a wife, God can help there, too."

After I sent the message, I felt happy. Now my brother wouldn't have to figure out everything all by himself.

–Jason

WHAT I LEARNED TODAY . . .

To Tell the Truth

3

NOVEMBER

Do not lie to each other. Colossians 3:9, NIV.

I think I know how Jacob felt the night he ran away from home.

No, I didn't run away, but I told a lie. It wasn't even a big lie, but it made my stomach feel sick anyway.

"Your ruler?" I said to my friend Kari. "No, I haven't seen it. Maybe you lost it." But that wasn't true. I *had* seen it. As a matter of fact, it was in my desk.

When Kari went to the bathroom, I put her ruler back fast. But I had lied, just as Jacob in the Bible story had. He tricked his father and ended up running away from home. I ended up with a stomachache.

As I sat on my favorite log by our house a certain Bible verse kept popping into my mind. "Do not lie to each other" (Colossians 3:9, NIV).

"What's the matter?" Mom asked when she saw me.

"I told a lie."

Mom sighed. "The only way to get over that sickness is to ask forgiveness."

I nodded. "I'll go call Kari right now."

Guess what? After my friend forgave me and God forgave me, my stomachache disappeared. The birds sang in the trees, and the air smelled sweet again. I wonder if that's how Jacob felt after he learned to ask forgiveness and tell the truth.

–Trisha

4 NOVEMBER

I am with you and will watch over you wherever you go. Genesis 28:15, NIV.

WHAT I LEARNED TODAY . . .

I Can Love a Bully

Jared is the scariest kid in my school. He eats like a horse (I know, I've seen a horse eat), wears dirty shirts, shouts instead of talks, and calls me "dog face."

"Why do you call me that?" I ask him.

"Because you're ugly and have funny ears!" he said. Jared is not my favorite person.

This morning in family worship we read about Jacob fighting with Jesus. Yesterday, we learned how he had lied to his father and had run away from home. I think Jacob wasn't one of God's favorite people at that moment.

"But listen to what God said to him," Mom stated. "'I am with you and will watch over you wherever you go'" (Genesis 28:15, NIV).

I gasped. "Even though Jacob had done wrong, God still watched over him?"

"That's right. God loves us no matter what we do."

Then I thought of Jared. Maybe he didn't know that. So today I wrote him a note that says, "I just wanted you to know that God is always with you, even when you call me dog face."

He still calls me that awful name, but it doesn't bother me so much. If God loves Jared even when he's being bad, so should I.

—Tara

WHAT I LEARNED TODAY . . .

God Rides With Me

5 NOVEMBER

Surely I will be with you always. Matthew 28:20, NIV.

The trees rushed by our car as I sat silently thinking. Why did I have to leave all my friends? Why did we have to go to a new home in a faraway state?

"Something wrong?" Dad called from the front seat.

"I won't know anyone there," I said.

"What about Jesus? Isn't He your friend?"

"Well, yes."

Dad guided our car down the highway. "Remember when we read the story of Joseph and his long journey? He felt lonely too. He missed his home and family. But what happened when he got to Egypt?"

I thought for a moment. "He worked hard and found some new friends?"

"Right." Dad nodded. "And he also found that God had been right there with him, even as that old camel carried him away from everything he loved."

"So," I said hesitantly, "God is here in our car, riding with me as we go to our new home?"

"Absolutely," Dad said. "And like Joseph, you can work hard to make new friends. Remember the verse you learned this morning?"

"I know it by heart," I answered. "It says, 'Surely I will be with you always' [Matthew 28:20, NIV]." As I sat watching the trees rush by, I felt better. With God riding with me, I didn't have to go anywhere alone! —Jon

6
NOVEMBER

[God] knows the way that I take; when he has tested me, I will come forth as gold. Job 23:10, NIV.

WHAT I LEARNED TODAY . . .

To Work Hard

What are you doing?" my friend Joey called from his porch.

"Picking up gold," I responded.

"There's no gold in your yard."

"I'm just pretending," I said.

My friend shook his head and went back into his house. There really isn't any gold on our lawn, but I like to pretend there is because of a Bible text we read. It says, "[God] knows the way that I take; when he has tested me, I will come forth as gold" (Job 23:10, NIV).

"Joseph worked so hard he became as valuable as gold," Mom told me. "Even though people lied about him and threw him in jail, he served God faithfully."

"If I work hard, will God love me more?" I asked.

"God loves you no matter what you do," Mom told me. "But working faithfully, helping people, and putting others first are wonderful ways to show everyone how much you love God. Understand?"

I thought for a moment. "Yup. I want to be like Joseph."

"Great!" Mom said. "Then people will see how faithfully you do your job. What a beautiful witness."

That's the reason, when I have to pick up the rocks in our yard, I don't think of them as rocks. They're pieces of gold I'm gathering for Jesus.

–Andrew

WHAT I LEARNED TODAY . . .

To Be Faithful in My Chores

7
NOVEMBER

Whoever can be trusted with very little can also be trusted with much. Luke 16:10, NIV.

Did you remember to sweep the basement yesterday?" Mom asked. "Daddy cut some boards and made quite a mess."

"Oh, I forgot," I moaned.

"That's the second time this week," Mom said with a frown. "What if Joseph had kept forgetting to do his duties?"

"Joseph?" I asked. "What's he got to do with our basement?"

"Our Sabbath school lesson said he was always faithful in his duties. God could trust him." Mom sighed. "Maybe you can't be as trustworthy as Joseph."

"Yes, I can!" I cried.

Running to my room, I grabbed a piece of paper. In big letters I wrote, "SWEEP THE BASEMENT." In small letters I added my memory verse. "Whoever can be trusted with very little can also be trusted with much" (Luke 16:10, NIV). I put my new sign on my wall and hurried to the basement. Before the school bus arrived, I had that old cement floor sparkling clean.

"Wow!" Mom said later that day. "The floor looks nice. And you did your other chores too. What happened?"

"I got smart like Joseph," I said. "Every day I'm going to ask God to help me be trustworthy."

"I'm proud of you," Mom said with a hug.

–Natalie

8 NOVEMBER

He kissed all his brothers and wept over them. Genesis 45:15, NIV.

WHAT I LEARNED TODAY . . .

To Forgive

Yes, you did!"

"No, I didn't!"

Mrs. Downing lifted her hand. "Hey, you guys are disturbing the whole class."

My until-a-minute-ago best friend Darlene pointed at me. "This . . . this *person* took my lunch money."

"I did not! You probably lost it like last week."

"Well," she sneered. "Maybe I didn't lose it then, either."

I gasped. "Are you saying I took your lunch money two weeks in a row? I'm never going to talk to you again!"

"Fine!"

That night I read about how Joseph was able to save his whole family from a terrible famine. One thing made it all possible—he forgave his brothers. H'mmm. Maybe I should be like Joseph and forgive my friend for accusing me of something I didn't do. This morning I tapped Darlene on the shoulder. "Here. I want you to have this money," I said. "It's from my allowance. And I forgive you for saying I stole it."

Darlene blinked. "You forgive me even when I didn't ask?"

"Yes," I nodded. "Like Joseph."

"Joseph?"

I sat down beside her and told her about the man who forgave a few and saved many.

–Hunter

WHAT I LEARNED TODAY . . .

God Can Help Me Sing

9

NOVEMBER

The Lord is with me; I will not be afraid. Psalm 118:6, NIV.

Some say I have a lovely singing voice. Maybe I do. But when I sing in front of people, I sound like our cat when its paw got caught in the screen door.

Yesterday Mom read from my primary lesson study, "God can help us in ways we never imagined." We were studying about Moses and how he floated around in a basket while soldiers looked for male babies in Egypt. Scary!

Then I got to thinking. Maybe God can help me with my voice. So I asked Him to see what He could do.

This morning I gathered my collection of dolls, sat them on the sofa, and sang a song I made up about Moses. I pretended the dolls were real people.

"What's going on?" Mom asked when she walked into the room.

"I'm letting God teach me how to use my voice even when I'm scared," I explained.

"Is it working?"

"You tell me."

Mom sat down with my dolls and listened. "Hey, not bad," she said. Then she repeated her favorite Bible text: "The Lord is with me; I will not be afraid" (Psalm 118:6, NIV).

Next month I might tell our pastor that I'm ready to sing a solo for church. Maybe.

–Trisha

10
NOVEMBER

Moses saw that though the bush was on fire it did not burn up. Exodus 3:2, NIV.

WHAT I LEARNED TODAY . . .

To Show Respect

"What would you do if you saw a burning bush?" I asked my older sister Julie.

"Throw water on it," she said. My sister wouldn't have made a very good Moses.

"But what if you found out that God was burning the bush and He asked you to take off your shoes to show reverence? What would you do?"

"Throw water on my feet," Julie said with a smile.

I don't think my sister understands what Moses learned.

Last night while we were studying our Sabbath school lesson Dad said God was trying to teach Moses to show respect when they met at a burning bush. "Where do we go to fellowship with God?" he asked.

"Church," I said quickly.

"And since it's not our custom to take our shoes off at church, how can we show reverence to God while we're there?"

I thought for a moment. "By sitting quietly, listening to the preacher talk, and not waving at our friends."

"Good." Dad said. "And remember, Moses discovered it wasn't the place that was holy. It was God's presence. Even a burning bush is on holy ground when God is there."

"From now on I'm going to be reverent whenever I meet with God," I promised. "Even if it's in a desert, beside a burning bush."

–Nicole

WHAT I LEARNED TODAY

To Obey Even When Afraid

11 NOVEMBER

I will help you speak and will teach you what to say. Exodus 4:12, NIV.

Yesterday Daryl came up to me and said, "Let's go tease Milton."

Milton is kinda strange. He doesn't laugh, sits all by himself at lunch, and falls down a lot during baseball. One more thing. He's tall! Strong, too. We tease him, then run away.

"I don't want to do that anymore," I said.

"Why not?" Daryl asked. "It's fun."

"Because Moses wouldn't."

My friend chuckled. "Man, you're weird." Then he left.

What would Moses say to a really scary guy like Milton? I asked myself.

Then I remembered my memory verse for today: "I will help you speak and will teach you what to say" (Exodus 4:12, NIV). Hey, if it worked for Moses, maybe it would work for me.

Taking in a deep breath, I approached Milton slowly. My legs felt like water balloons. "H-hi, Milton. Wanna eat lunch with me?"

He looked at me in surprise. "You mean it?"

"Sure," I said, my hands trembling. "As long as you promise not to beat me up."

Milton grabbed me and sat me down beside him with a plop. "Deal," he said with a smile.

Now Milton is my friend, all because God told me what to say.

—David

12
NOVEMBER

Like cold water to a weary soul is good news from a distant land. Proverbs 25:25, NIV.

WHAT I LEARNED TODAY . . .

To Look for Good News

"That's terrible!" I gasped, pointing at the newspaper where pictures of a cruel war were spread across the front page.

Dad shook his head. "I wish they would write some good news once in a while."

"Good news?" I asked.

"Sure." Dad smiled. "Remember what our Sabbath school lesson taught us? Even while the plagues were falling on Egypt, the people who obeyed and loved God were safe. That's good news."

I nodded. "Yeah. And even though those people in the paper are fighting each other, there are other people who aren't. That's good news too."

"We should start our own newspaper!" Dad announced.

"How?"

Dad pointed at his computer. "You find good news, and I'll put it into a newsletter. We'll work on it every night after family worship to remind us that God is still in control and there are people who love and obey Him."

All day I collected good-news stories—my friend Stacey getting over her cold, Mom finding her lost pocketbook, my teacher getting married, and my dog almost getting hit by the UPS truck but getting out of the way just in time. "Wow!" I said as our first newsletter came out of Dad's printer. "I'm going to share all this good news with my friends." And I did.

–Jason

JESUS IN MY HEART . . .

"The Boy Jesus"

13 NOVEMBER

And Jesus grew in wisdom and stature, and in favor with God and men. Luke 2:52, NIV.

"What's up?" Mom asked.

"I'm just looking at pictures of my best friend," I said.

Mom sat down beside me and pointed at the book in my lap. "Those are pictures of Jesus," she said.

"Yes," I answered, turning the pages. "See? Here He's helping people who are sad and lonely. On this page He's giving a poor family some food. And look at this; Jesus is healing a sick man by a river."

"Your best friend sure was busy," Mom said. "Do you know why?"

"Why?" I asked.

"When Jesus was a little boy, His mother taught Him about God and nature. She told Him how people are supposed to love and care for each other, just like a mother hen loves her chicks and foxes find safe dens for their families."

"Can I be like Jesus?" I asked.

"Sure," she said. "I've got a book that will help. It's called *The Desire of Ages,* and on pages 68 through 74 are lots of words that tell us what Jesus was like when He was a little boy. We could learn one new word each day. OK?"

"Great. Let's start tomorrow," I pleaded. "You can read to me what the book says. This is going to be fun!"

–Sarah

14 NOVEMBER

Jesus grew in wisdom and stature, and in favor with God and men. Luke 2:52, NIV.

JESUS IN MY HEART . . .

"Busy"

What does *busy* mean?" I asked.

My family and I are reading pages 68 through 74 of *The Desire of Ages,* where it tells what Jesus was like when He was a little boy.

Dad thought for a moment. "That means that Jesus' mind was always active, thinking and studying important stuff. The book says the child Jesus loved to learn. He listened to His mom as she taught Him about nature, and He enjoyed reading the ancient scrolls at the synagogue."

I lifted my hand. "I'd better get my mind busy too!" I headed for my bedroom and soon returned with several of my favorite books. Sitting down beside the wood stove, I began to thumb through the pages. There were colorful pictures of lions, birds, and even a beaver.

"God made all these things, right?" I asked.

"Yes," Dad nodded. "And trees, flowers, rocks, and rivers. He did all that before He became a little boy here on earth. When He was growing up, He kept His mind busy studying the secrets of nature, learning all He could about the world around Him.

"Then that's what I'm going to do," I announced.

"Wonderful," Dad said. "Your mind will stay filled with beautiful thoughts about God's love and power."

So far, I like being busy.

–Josh

JESUS IN MY HEART . . .

"Wisdom"

15
NOVEMBER

The child grew and became strong; he was filled with wisdom, and the grace of God was upon him.
Luke 2:40, NIV.

And Jesus had 'wisdom beyond His years.'" (*The Desire of Ages,* p. 68). Mom closed the book. "Looks like we found our word for today," she said. *"Wisdom."*

"What does it mean?" I asked.

"Wisdom means that you stop and think before you do something. For instance, you know that the oven in the kitchen can get very hot, so you don't come close to it when I'm baking bread. Also, if it's snowing outside, you put on your warmest coat.

"And this afternoon, before you began playing with your new fire truck—the one with the loud siren—I saw you look to see if your baby sister was sleeping. Then you played a quiet game until she woke up. Very wise of you."

"Just like Jesus," I said proudly.

"Being wise lets you practice what you've learned," Mom added.

Today while I was playing farmer in the yard Mom called, "It's time to come in." I didn't want to. I still had corn to plant. Then I thought, *If I don't go in, Mom will be upset. But if I put my tools away and do what she says, it will make her happy.*

When I hurried in, I noticed that Mom had just made some oatmeal cookies—my favorite. I think I made a wise decision. Don't you?

–Sarah

16
NOVEMBER

JESUS IN MY HEART . . .

"Beautiful Character"

Jesus went through all the towns and villages, teaching in their synagogues, preaching the good news of the kingdom and healing every disease and sickness. Matthew 9:35, NIV.

The book we're reading for worship says that when Jesus was a child, He had a *beautiful character* (*The Desire of Ages,* p. 68). I asked my mom what that meant.

"It means that when He met people, they liked Him right away," she said. "Children enjoyed playing with Him because He was happy and fair. Jesus was fun to be with."

I frowned. "I saw a man on television that was mean and hurt people. He didn't have a beautiful character, did he?"

"No," mother said. "He wasn't like Jesus at all."

This afternoon some new neighbors moved into the house next door. When I saw that they had a girl about my age, I waved and smiled. "Hi," I called. "My name is Josh. Would you like to come over and play for a while?"

I saw the girl ask her mother if it was all right, and after my mom went over and visited with them for a few minutes, I met Angela. We played jungle explorer all afternoon! I let her be the leader. Now she's my friend.

I'll always try to be fair and let Angela choose as many games as I do. I think we'll be friends forever.

You see, I want to share Jesus' beautiful character with others because it makes them happy. Just ask Angela.

–Josh

JESUS IN MY HEART . . .

"Thoughtful"

17 NOVEMBER

From His earliest years He was possessed of one purpose; He lived to bless others. *The Desire of Ages*, p. 70.

"Oh, dear," Aunt Jessica sighed when she hung up the phone.

"What's the matter?" I asked. I was staying at my aunt's house while my parents were on a trip.

"It's your cousin Toby. He's sick again. The doctor said he'll have to stay in the hospital for two nights."

"Will he get well?" I asked.

"Oh, yes," Aunt Jessica answered. "But Toby doesn't like hospitals. He gets lonely and scared."

I thought for a moment, then ran to the den. "What are you doing?" my aunt called.

"I'm going to draw a picture so Toby won't be so sad," I answered as I hurried back with some paper and ink markers. "He likes birds, doesn't he?"

"Yes." Aunt Jessica nodded. "He puts seeds out for the blue jays and juncos each winter."

"Then I'll draw him lots of birds—red ones, yellow ones, and even a few green ones, too. He'll laugh when he sees them, but maybe he won't feel lonely or afraid anymore."

"How thoughtful," my aunt said.

"Yup, *thoughtful,*" I agreed. "That's the word I'm learning about this week. I'll explain just as soon as I finish my pictures."

Being thoughtful like Jesus will help Toby feel better, don't you think?

–Sarah

18
NOVEMBER

Jesus . . . faithfully and cheerfully acted His part in bearing the burdens of the household. ***The Desire of Ages,* p. 72.**

JESUS IN MY HEART . . .

"Joyful"

Look at that!" I called excitedly. "Isn't that tree beautiful?"

Dad drove a little farther along the road as I watched the countryside slip by. "Hey, there are some cows. And a horse! And look at that pretty lake over there. See how the sun shines on it?"

"What are you doing?" Dad asked as we bumped along.

"Can't you tell?"

Dad thought for a moment, then began to chuckle. "You're being *joyful,* right?"

"Yup." I laughed. "Just like Jesus was when He was a boy. This morning you read from our book that Jesus had a nice dis . . . dis . . ."

"Disposition," Dad said as he turned the wheel. "That means He was filled with joy over the little things in life."

"So, that's what I'm doing," I said. "I'm enjoying our ride in the country. When I see something I like, I tell you. OK?"

"Fine with me," Dad laughed. "I've known kids who complain all the time. They tell me what they *don't* like. It's nice to have someone share with me what they enjoy."

"Like that red barn?" I called. "It's as old as Grandpa. And check out that flock of sheep!" I'm discovering that joy is easy to find when you open your eyes and look.

–Josh

JESUS IN MY HEART . . .

"Willing Hands"

19 NOVEMBER

Mom looked at the page in *The Desire of Ages* and spoke slowly. "'[Jesus'] willing hands were ever ready to serve others'" (p. 68).

"If Jesus had willing hands when He was a little boy," I announced, "then that's what I want."

The next morning I got up early and cleaned my room. Then I ran to the kitchen to help Mom set the table for breakfast. I even poured the milk without making a mess!

Next I put our trash in a big plastic bag, swept leaves off the porch, and gave my baby sister her bottle when she began to cry.

All day long my willing hands found something to do. After supper I flopped down on the couch and sighed. My hands, feet, legs, and arms were totally tired.

"You look beat," Dad said, glancing up from his computer. "Hard day?"

"It's just Jesus in my heart," I answered with a sigh. "Sometimes it can wear you out." Then I reminded him of what Mom had read that morning.

"Yes, willing hands can be a blessing to many people," Dad said. "I think you made Mom's day much easier. Good for you!"

I grinned. Even though willing hands can wear you out, helping people is really, really fun. Find out for yourself today.

–Sarah

His life revealed the grace of unselfish courtesy. *The Desire of Ages*, p. 69.

20
NOVEMBER

Jesus carried into His labor cheerfulness. . . . It requires much patience . . . to bring Bible religion into the home life.
***The Desire of Ages,* p. 73.**

JESUS IN MY HEART . . .

"Patient"

"What does that word mean?" I asked as my dad was reading from *The Desire of Ages.*

"*Patience*? That means you refuse to get upset."

I get upset a lot, such as when my older brother slams the door while I'm trying to sleep or when my neighbor yells at my dog Max. Max barks. He thinks he's being a good watch-dog. My neighbor thinks he's just being noisy.

"How can I have patience when I feel so upset?" I asked.

"First, ask Jesus to help you. He had lots of patience practice when He was on earth. Then try to figure out how to fix the problem."

The very next day I went to see my neighbor. "I'm sorry Max barks so much," I said. "From now on I'm going to put him in the garage each evening right after supper. Then you won't have to listen to him when he tries to be a watchdog."

"Thanks," my neighbor said.

As for my brother, Mom says he's having a hard time with life and is going to slam doors for a while, so I may as well get used to it. I guess being patient also means trying to sleep even when someone is having a hard time with life.

–Josh

JESUS IN MY HEART . . .

"Truthful"

21
NOVEMBER

He manifested . . . a truthfulness that would never sacrifice integrity. *The Desire of Ages,* pp. 68, 69.

"I know what *truthfulness* means," I told my mom. "It's telling people what really is, not just what you wish."

Mom blinked. "Maybe you'd better explain that to me."

"Well," I began, "do you remember when Grandma came to visit us last Christmas and she asked me if I'd been a good girl all year?"

"Yes."

"I wanted to tell her that I'd been perfect and not gotten angry and always done what you told me to do. I wanted to say that I'd never yelled at my sister or put flour in her socks."

"You put flour in your sister's socks?"

"But I knew I had to be truthful, so I told her I had been good some of the time and not so good some of the time. Then I asked her if she still loved me even though I must be a big disappointment to her."

Mother's eyelids rose. "What did Grandma say?"

"She said she loved me even more because I was truthful. Neat, huh? And you know what? When I have Jesus in my heart, I can't even tell a lie. My mouth just won't make the words."

Mother smiled. "That's wonderful, sweetie. Now can we talk about the flour?"

H'mmm. I guess it's time to be truthful again!

—Sarah

22
NOVEMBER

His mind was active and penetrating, with a thoughtfulness and wisdom beyond His years. *The Desire of Ages*, p. 68.

JESUS IN MY HEART . . .

"Believe"

"The Bible is just a bunch of silly stories," my friend's big brother Colin said with a laugh. "You don't have to do what it says."

When I told my dad what Colin had said, he shook his head slowly. "It makes Jesus sad to hear someone say unkind things about His holy Book."

"Did Jesus learn the stories in the Bible when He was a kid like me?"

"He sure did." Dad nodded. "He learned the stories of Abraham, Isaac, and Jacob and memorized passages written by Moses, Joshua, and King David. To Jesus, Scripture was a whole lot more than stories. It told how to live a happy life, help people, and learn about God."

Dad put his arm around me. "And as Jesus grew, He trusted what the Bible said. Whenever anyone would try to get Him to change His mind, He recited some of those passages. 'This is what the Word of God says,' He'd tell them."

The next time I saw Colin, I told him about the burning bush and how God helped a whole bunch of people and goats walk through a sea without even getting their feet wet. He was amazed.

I guess the best way to *believe* what the Bible says is to learn its stories and share them. That's what Jesus did.

–Josh

JESUS IN MY HEART . . .

"Unselfish"

23 NOVEMBER

His life revealed the grace of unselfish courtesy. *The Desire of Ages,* p. 69.

"I want to play with your truck," Elizabeth said.

Mom has been reading to me from *The Desire of Ages*. It says Jesus was *unselfish* (p. 69) when He was a little boy, so that's how I want to be.

"OK." I sighed. "But be careful. It's my favorite, and I don't want anything bad to happen to it."

Elizabeth grabbed it from me. "Sure, I'll take good care of your silly old truck."

We played roads for a while, built a tunnel in the sand, and made a house out of rocks. But Elizabeth wasn't exactly being careful. She sat on my truck, filled it with stones, crashed it into a piece of wood, and then went home for supper.

After she'd gone, I ran to my truck. When I brought it into the kitchen, something terrible happened. A wheel fell off. Elizabeth had broken my favorite toy.

"Mom," I cried, "I was unselfish, and look." I showed her the broken wheel. "It's not fair."

Mom put her arm around me. "It isn't fair. But what's more important: your truck or being unselfish?"

"Being unselfish sure can be hard on toys," I moaned. "But people are more important."

"That's exactly what Jesus would say," Mom stated. "Now let's see if we can fix that wheel."

–Sarah

24
NOVEMBER

Let your conversation be always full of grace, . . . so that you may know how to answer everyone. Colossians 4:6, NIV.

JESUS IN MY HEART . . .

"Courteous"

This week I learned a new word from *The Desire of Ages,* the book Dad is reading to me. It said that Jesus was always *courteous*—that means He let other people go first (p. 69).

Since my friend Christy and I are asking Jesus to help us live like He did, I decided to call her and ask her if she'd been courteous yet. But my mom was on the phone.

When she finished, I hurried to the kitchen just as Dad rushed in. He had to talk to his boss about something very important—at least, that's what he told me when I handed him the phone.

As soon as he hung up, my older brother Greg started to dial. "I'll be only a minute," he told me.

An hour later he stopped talking long enough to go to the mall. It was finally my turn.

"Hi, Christy," I said when my friend answered. "Guess what? I've been courteous all evening. How about you?"

As she began to answer I heard her mother say, "Christy, please don't talk long. I've got some calls to make."

"I guess we both have to think about others first tonight." I giggled. Christy laughed. Jesus was right. Being courteous makes people happy.

–Josh

JESUS IN MY HEART . . .

"Growing"

25

NOVEMBER

Throughout His life on earth, Jesus was an earnest and constant worker. *The Desire of Ages,* p. 73.

"Now what do I do?" I asked my mother when she finished reading the chapter in *The Desire of Ages* about when Jesus was little. "I've learned all the words, and I'm asking Jesus to live in my heart."

Mom thought for a moment. "Well, you could begin telling others about Jesus—you know, share what you've learned?"

"But I'm just a kid," I protested. "I'm not a preacher or teacher or businessperson. How am I supposed to tell others?"

"What did Jesus do after He was a child?" Mom wanted to know.

"He . . . He grew up."

"That's right. Maybe that's what you're supposed to do now. Your job is to grow up with Jesus in your heart. And every day you can tell someone about Him, whether you're at school or play or even at work. You can start right now by asking God to teach you how to share Jesus' love."

"Oh," I said with a grin, "I know how to do that!"

Mom and I knelt beside the couch, and I began to pray. I'd learned that Jesus hears every word and answers every prayer. I knew I could ask Him to show me how to share His love as I grew up. Say, why don't you ask Him to show you, too?

–Sarah

26
NOVEMBER

Jesus increased in wisdom and stature, and in favour with God and man. Luke 2:52.

JESUS IN MY HEART . . .

The Boy Jesus

Would you like to read the actual words that Christy and her friend read? I'll put them on the next five pages and you can see what Ellen White said about the boy Jesus as He was growing up. I'll change some of the harder words so it will be easy to read. Have fun!

–Uncle Charles

⁂ ⁂ ⁂

"The childhood and youth of Jesus were spent in a little mountain village. There was no place on earth that would not have been honored by His presence. The palaces of kings would have been glad to have Him as a guest. But He passed by the wealthy homes, the courts of royal families, and the famous schools of learning, to make His home in the small, almost forgotten town of Nazareth. . . .

"In the sunlight of His heavenly Father's smiles, Jesus 'continued to learn more and more and to grow physically. People liked Him, and He pleased God' (Luke 2:52, ICB). . . .

"As a child, Jesus showed a special loveliness of disposition. His willing hands were ever ready to serve others. He showed a patience that nothing could disturb, and a truthfulness that would never change. He stayed true to His beliefs and His life reflected the grace of unselfish courtesy."

—*The Desire of Ages,* pp. 68, 69

JESUS IN MY HEART . . .

Blessing Others

27
NOVEMBER

Here are some more words written by our friend Ellen White about the wonderful boy Jesus. If you want to be like Him, this will help you know what to do. Ask God to be close to you as you read these beautiful sentences.

—Uncle Charles

⁂ ⁂ ⁂

"The child Jesus did not attend the synagogue schools like other children His age. His mother was His first human teacher. From her lips and from the scrolls (books) of the prophets, He learned of heavenly things. The very words which He Himself had spoken to Moses, He was taught at His mother's knee. As He grew from childhood to youth, He did not go to the schools of the great teachers. He didn't need to know what they were teaching. God was His instructor. . . .

"Spread out before Him was the great library of God's created works. He studied the lessons found in the earth and sea and sky. Skipping the unholy ways of the world, He studied the life of plants and animals, and the life of man. From His earliest years He had one goal; He lived to bless others."

—*The Desire of Ages,* p. 70

The Jews were amazed and asked, "How did this man get such learning without having studied?" John 7:15, NIV.

28
NOVEMBER

JESUS IN MY HEART . . .

Studying With God

"Nazareth! Can anything good come from there?" Nathanael asked. John 1:46, NIV.

We've learned that Jesus enjoyed studying about nature and science. "But I can't learn such hard stuff," you may say. Think again. Read these words written by our friend Ellen White and see what happens when you study with God as your teacher!

—Uncle Charles

⁂ ⁂ ⁂

"Every child may learn as Jesus did. As we try to get to know our heavenly Father through His Holy Book, angels will draw near, our minds will become strong, and our characters will be made better and better. We will become more like our Saviour. As we look at the beautiful and wonderful scenes in nature, we will learn to love God.

"Talking with God through prayer makes our minds operate better, and we'll be able to fight Satan as we allow Jesus in our hearts.

"The life of Jesus was a life in harmony with God. While He was a child, He acted and talked like a child; but no trace of sin messed up the image of God inside Him. He faced all the temptations of Nazareth, a very wicked city, . . . but He remained a shining example for us to follow through our childhood, youth, and manhood."

—*The Desire of Ages,* pp. 70, 71

JESUS IN MY HEART . . .

Simple Home

29 NOVEMBER

All should find something to do that will be beneficial to themselves and helpful to others. *The Desire of Ages*, p. 72.

What else was Jesus like as a little boy? Read what our friend Ellen White said.

–Uncle Charles

⁂ ⁂ ⁂

"The parents of Jesus were poor, and had to work hard each day. He knew all about poverty and going without things. In His busy life there were no lazy moments to invite temptation; no wasted hours. . . . He cheerfully did His part in helping His mom and dad.

"He'd been the commander of heaven with angels waiting to fulfill His every word. Now He was a willing servant, a loving, obedient son. He learned how to make furniture and with His own hands worked in the carpenter's shop with Joseph. Wearing simple clothes, He walked the streets of the little town, going to and from His humble work. He didn't use His heavenly powers to make His life easy. . . .

"Jesus didn't use His muscles recklessly, but stayed in good health so He could do His best work. He was not willing to make mistakes, even as He handled His tools. He was perfect as a workman, and He was perfect in character. By His own example, He taught that it is our duty to work hard and do the very best we can."

—*The Desire of Ages*, p. 72

30
NOVEMBER

JESUS IN MY HEART . . .

Our Sharing Saviour

A happy heart makes the face cheerful. Proverbs 15:13, NIV.

Do you want to be like Jesus? Listen to these beautiful words written by our friend Ellen White. Then humbly ask God to help you become just like His Son.

—Uncle Charles

* * *

"So long as He lived among men, our Saviour shared the life of the poor. He knew by experience their cares and hardships, and He comforted and encouraged all humble workers. Those people who fully understand the teachings of Jesus will never ask, 'Is this person rich or is this person poor?'

"Jesus always worked with cheerfulness. . . . He was never so worried about earthly things that He forgot to think about God and worship Him. He shared the gladness of His heart by singing psalms and heavenly songs. Often the citizens of Nazareth heard His voice raised in praise and thanksgiving to God. . . . When His friends complained about being tired of working, Jesus cheered them up with a sweet melody from His lips. His praise seem to chase the evil angels away, and the minds of those listening to Him were carried from earthly cares to their heavenly home. . . .

"Old people, those who were sad, the little creatures in the grove, donkeys and camels, and the children at play all were happier for Jesus' being near."

—*The Desire of Ages,* pp. 73, 74

MY TIME WITH GOD . . .

Making Music

1
DECEMBER

O Lord, our Lord, how majestic is your name in all the earth!
Psalm 8:1, NIV.

God gave each of us at least one talent. Want some good news? We can have more!

My main talent is talking. I *love* to talk. Every chance I get, I tell my friends about how God cares for us and wants us all to be healthy and happy.

My other talent (the one I'm working on) is singing. I figure singing is just like talking but with a few notes thrown in. I'm not very good at it yet.

Mom says I have real potential, which is another way of telling me to go sing in another room.

During my time with God each day, I open my *International Children's Bible* (usually to the Psalms) and sing a few verses. That's right. I read the words, put them to music, and practice my new talent.

Every morning while my dad is watching the news on TV and Mom is getting ready for work, I sing Bible verses. And you know what? Two things are happening. First, I'm learning that God has wonderful lessons waiting just for me in the Bible. And second, my notes are sounding better and better.

Why don't you try it? Maybe someday we could sing a duet!

–David

2
DECEMBER

**She gave birth to her firstborn, a son.
Luke 2:7, NIV.**

MY TIME WITH GOD . . .

Making Gifts

It's hot outside. I mean *hot!* Most people aren't thinking about Christmas. But I am.

All this month, during my time with God, I'm making Christmas presents to give to my friends. They're going to be surprised! We celebrate the birth of Jesus just once a year. In a few weeks it's all over, so I'm getting busy.

For my friend Alexander, I'm drawing a picture of the Bethlehem shepherds out in the fields. They look cold. Alexander doesn't have air-conditioning. Might help.

For my neighbor Mrs. Cho, I'm making a silver star out of tin foil that she can hang above her door. It will remind her of the wise men who came from a faraway land to visit the child Jesus.

And for my dad, I'm making a little manger out of cardboard that he can put on his desk. I work on my gifts a little bit each day.

Jesus wants to be our Friend every month of the year, and He likes it when we take time to remember His birth in Bethlehem.

The gifts I make remind me and my friends of that special time long ago. It's fun to think about Christmas, even when it's hot outside!

–Trisha

MY TIME WITH GOD . . .

Happy Birthday!

3 DECEMBER

Today I asked Mom if I could put my birth certificate in a picture frame and hang it on my bedroom wall. A birth certificate tells what your official name is, when and where you were born, how much you weighed, and who your parents were.

I'm Jason. I was born in California eight years ago and weighed eight pounds, six ounces. I still have the same mom and dad.

Next I made a birth certificate for Jesus. How? I opened my Bible and found these words in the New Testament: "Joseph was the husband of Mary, and Mary was the mother of Jesus" (Matthew 1:16, ICB). "Jesus was born in the town of Bethlehem in Judea during the time when Herod was king" (Matthew 2:1, ICB).

Since I didn't know how much Jesus weighed, I put down eight pounds six ounces, same as me.

Now I have *two* birth certificates on my wall. They remind me that my friend Jesus was once a baby just like I was. That's why He understands my problems and will listen when I need to talk to Him about something important.

During my time with God, I can look at the two birth certificates and remember that Jesus knows what it's like to be a kid.

—Jason

Joseph was the husband of Mary, and Mary was the mother of Jesus. Matthew 1:16, ICB.

4
DECEMBER

Carry each other's burdens. Galatians 6:2, NIV.

MY TIME WITH GOD . . .

Prayer List

Yesterday my sister came home from school mad. She said a friend did something unkind to her. Then my cousin had to go to the hospital for an operation, and my dad went around moaning and groaning because he has to buy new tires for the car. My other sister, Kara, got a D on her math test. Let's just say it wasn't a very good day.

That's when I got an idea. The Bible says God wants to help people solve their problems. Well, with so much stuff going on, I sometimes forget who is having what trouble. So I made a paper heart and put a prayer list on it.

I hung the heart on the refrigerator with magnets and told everyone to write their prayer requests on it. Then each night during my time with God, I kneel and pray for each item on the list.

It works! Now when I talk to my friend Jesus, I know exactly what to say.

My sisters like my prayer list and write on it every day. They're glad I'm praying for them. It lets them know that God and I love them very much.

Why don't you make a prayer list heart too? It's a wonderful way to show your family and friends that you care.

–Jon

MY TIME WITH GOD . . .

Secret Deeds

5
DECEMBER

Your Father, who sees what is done in secret, will reward you. Matthew 6:6, NIV.

One thing I've discovered while reading my Bible is that Jesus did good things even if no one asked Him to. So I decided to start doing my own secret deeds. (A deed is something you do.)

Last Monday I swept the front walk. On Tuesday I emptied all the trash baskets in the whole house. Wednesday I cleaned my room and found my favorite race car, the one I thought I'd lost for good. Thursday night was Adventurer Club, so I didn't have time to do anything special.

On Friday I shined my dad's shoes. He was surprised when he found them all ready for Sabbath.

I did these things without anyone asking me to. Guess what? It was fun! Sure, it was hard work, but Jesus never ran away from hard work. He rolled up His sleeves and got busy helping other people.

Each day during my time with God, I plan what secret deed I'll do next. Then I kneel and thank Jesus for showing me the very best way to live. I may have to work hard, but when I see people smiling and happy because of my secret deeds, it's worth it!

–Tara

6
DECEMBER

MY TIME WITH GOD . . .

Remembering Others

Resist the devil, and he will flee from you. James 4:7, NIV.

Last month my church held some evangelistic meetings and several people decided to get baptized. The preacher asked us to pray for these special people because he said the devil would work hard to make them change their minds.

That's when I started my "Fight the Devil" list. On it I put the names of those at my church who are going to be baptized soon.

Now during my time with God, I ask Jesus to help them fight the devil and not get discouraged and change their minds.

Yesterday several of the people on my "Fight the Devil" list got baptized. We sang some songs and welcomed them into our church. I smiled so hard my lips hurt, because I knew that they had allowed Jesus to help them beat Satan and his evil angels.

Am I going to take those people off my list now? No way! The preacher said we should pray for new members, too. He said Satan still wants them to forget about God. But I know that as long as I'm praying, and they're trying their best to believe what the Bible says, the old devil doesn't stand a chance. And I've got the list to prove it!

–Andrew

MY TIME WITH GOD . . .

Saying No

7
DECEMBER

Those whom I love I rebuke and discipline. Revelation 3:19, NIV.

When I was a little kid, my mom and dad said no a lot! If I reached out to touch the hot stove, they'd say, "No." If I started walking toward the street where cars were rushing by, they'd say, "No."

When I got older I discovered something interesting. My parents weren't saying no because they didn't want me to have any fun. They were saying it so I'd stay safe.

During my time with God last night, I read Exodus 20:2-17. Guess what? God said no too. He said we must not steal, kill, cheat, forget the Sabbath, or worship other gods.

Like my parents, He said no for a good reason.

That's why I made something for my wall. It's a great big "NO" printed in red letters. Now, when Satan tempts me to steal Matt's pencil when he's not looking or forget to keep the Sabbath holy or sneak a peek at Kay's math quiz answers or say unkind things about my teacher, I remember that word. Then with a happy smile on my face, I say, "No."

It works. I feel much better when I refuse to obey Satan. Why don't you join me and start saying a great big "NO" to temptation today. Trust me, you'll be a *lot* happier.

–Natalie

8
DECEMBER

If someone strikes you on one cheek, turn to him the other also. Luke 6:29, NIV.

MY TIME WITH GOD . . .

Making Others Happy

If you knew my older sister Jessica, you'd agree I've got a problem.

She says I'm stupid. She says I get in her way all the time. She says I look like an ugly monster with green ears. Just yesterday she said I'm *droll.* I don't even know what that word means, but I have a feeling it's not very nice.

I checked my Bible to see what Jesus would do with a problem like this. Sure enough, there were several stories about when people said unkind things to Him. But He didn't get mad. He just forgave them and always said nice things back. Being like Jesus isn't going to be easy!

This morning Jessica stuck her head into my room and called, "Looks like a pigpen in here." That wasn't true, because I'd straightened everything up last night.

I grinned at my sister and said, "Good morning, Jessica. Don't forget to take your umbrella to school. Looks like rain."

She stared at me for a long time. Then she did something very unusual. She smiled! And her face didn't even break.

Doing what Jesus says not only makes me happy, but it can also cause my sister Jessica to smile. Unbelievable!

–Hunter

MY TIME WITH GOD . . .

New Again

9
DECEMBER

If anyone is in Christ, he is a new creation. 2 Corinthians 5:17, NIV.

My Sabbath school teacher said Jesus wants us to be "brand-new" inside. She told our class that He wants to take our sad, sinful hearts and give us new, happy hearts.

Can He do that?

Last winter during one of my times with God, I went for a walk in the woods behind my house. The leaves had all fallen off the trees, and there was snow on the ground. The forest looked sad. No birds sang in the branches (except for a few crows), and no butterflies fluttered about. There weren't even any frogs croaking. It seemed like the whole forest had gone to sleep.

Then came spring. Wow! What a change. Green leaves appeared on every tree. Mockingbirds and song sparrows arrived and began singing loudly. Brightly colored butterflies flew from flower to flower, and old bullfrogs called, "Ribbit, ribbit," from the pond.

That's when I realized that God *could* make hearts new again. If He can fill the forest with happy sounds and beautiful flowers, He can certainly put happy, beautiful thoughts in our minds, giving us new, happy hearts.

Each time I kneel to pray, I thank God for the lovely forest behind our house and the new heart He gives me every day.

–David

10
DECEMBER

MY TIME WITH GOD . . .

Answer Jar

He hears the prayer of the righteous. Proverbs 15:29, NIV.

If I ever forget how much Jesus loves me, I just check out my answer jar.

You see, I learned that the children of Israel wrote down everything Jesus did for them while they were wandering around in the desert. Not a bad idea!

So during my time with God, I started my own book, except it's a jar. Each time God answers a prayer, I write it down on a little piece of paper and then I toss it in my answer jar.

Let me read you a few. This one says, "Uncle Daryl found a job." We asked God to help him find a new place to work. He did.

This one says, "Mom feels better today." My mother got very sick, and even the doctor was worried. So we prayed and prayed, asking God to help the doctor figure out what's going on. He did.

And this paper says, "Grandpa got baptized today." My grandpa had some Bible studies with our preacher, and we prayed that he would learn about Jesus and want to love Him. He did.

See what I mean? Anytime I feel discouraged and think God doesn't care about me, I look in my answer jar. Yup. He loves me. The pieces of paper prove it.

–Jason

MY TIME WITH GOD . . .

Paper Route

11
DECEMBER

Speak the truth to each other. Zechariah 8:16, NIV.

I deliver papers on Sabbath afternoon. No, not newspapers! The ones I deliver tell kids like me about Jesus. They've got games, puzzles, and tons of neat stories.

Here's how it works. First I ask everyone in my Sabbath school class to bring their old *Primary Treasures* to church. Then I take the papers around to my friends in my neighborhood. Sometimes kids in my class help. That's the most fun.

I give a paper to Mark, who lives in the trailer park across the street; to Terry, who lives in the big white house on the corner; to Beth Ann, who lives with her grandmother behind the grocery store; and to Edwina, who's in the apartment three doors down from me. Then I visit the Andersons who have eight children. Eight! They need all the *Primary Treasures* they can get.

I want all the kids in my neighborhood to read the stories and study their Bible so they can learn about Jesus and know how to fight Satan.

After I finish my Sabbath paper route, I ask God to bless my friends and help them enjoy the papers as much as I do. Maybe you have some old *Primary Treasures* lying around. Why don't you start your own paper route this very Sabbath?

–Trisha

12
DECEMBER

I have called you by name, and you are mine. Isaiah 43:1, ICB.

MY TIME WITH GOD . . .

The Name Game

The other day I found out what my name means. Dad looked it up in a book. He said that *Dorinda* means "beautiful gift."

OK. OK. Maybe I'm not the most beautiful girl in the world, and no one has ever given me away as a gift. But that's what my name means, and I like it.

I asked my dad what his name meant. He turned a few pages and said, "My name means 'the king who must work hard to pay the rent.'" Yeah, right.

The Bible says that Jesus knows my name. He knows yours, too. That got me wondering. When Jesus hears my name, does He think I'm a beautiful gift or does He get a little sad and say, "Today *Dorinda* means 'mad at mother' or 'selfish with her toys'?"

Each evening during my time with God, I ask Jesus to forgive me for the bad things I've done and to remember me as a beautiful gift.

I made a sign that says "I have called you by name, and you are mine" (Isaiah 43:1, ICB). I wrote *Dorinda* under the verse and put my dad's name there, too. We're both happy God knows all about us, even our names.

–Dorinda

MY TIME WITH GOD . . .

Jesus Forgives Me

13

DECEMBER

Who can forgive sins but God only? Mark 2:7.

The other day I made a big mistake. When my friend Carl wasn't looking, I took his eraser and put it in my desk. It was a really neat eraser with a picture of a horse on it.

All day long I felt terrible. Jesus says we shouldn't take what doesn't belong to us, but I wanted that eraser a lot!

Finally, I couldn't stand it any longer. I told Carl what I had done and asked him to forgive me. He looked at me strangely, took back his eraser, and told me to stay out of his desk.

I felt a little better, but I knew there was one more thing I had to do.

That night, during my time with God, I asked Him to forgive me too. I'd broken one of His laws of love and was really sorry.

Guess what? After that, I felt great! I'd given the eraser back to Carl and asked him to forgive me. Then I'd told my friend Jesus that I had made a mistake. He forgave me too.

I like the verse in the Bible that says "Who can forgive sins but God only?" (Mark 2:7). Even if Carl won't trust me anymore, God will. His forgiveness brought joy back into my heart.

–Tara

14
DECEMBER

MY TIME WITH GOD . . .

The Everybody Club

Whoever wishes, let [him or her] take the free gift of the water of life. Revelation 22:17, NIV.

I like doing stuff with my classmates and friends. That's why I wanted to join the basketball club at school.

"You can't join our group," their leader said. "You're too short."

So I tried the reading club. "Can't join our group," their leader announced. "You read too slowly."

So I decided to check out the swimming club. Big mistake. At my first meeting I almost drowned. Swallowed a mouthful of water and coughed a lot.

Choir club? I don't think so.

Then I heard about the Thunderbirds. That's a bunch of kids who meet each Tuesday afternoon and make lots of noise in their clubhouse. Sounded like fun.

"You can't join the Thunderbirds," their leader stated flatly. "You're from Colorado. We don't like people from Colorado. Only people from Maryland and Pennsylvania and maybe West Virginia can join. Goodbye!"

I felt terrible! So I started my own club. It's called the "Everybody Club," and anyone—I mean *anyone*—can join. Guess what? We have more members than all the other clubs put together!

During my time with God, I thanked Him that anyone who chooses to love and obey Him will go to heaven to live forever. Now *that's* an Everybody Club! Want to join? No problem.

–Jon

MY TIME WITH GOD . . .

Emergency List

My God shall supply all your need. Philippians 4:19.

My neighbor, Mrs. Williams, is very old.

One day when I was visiting her, I saw her looking through her phone book. "Oh, dear," she said. "I can't find the number of the drugstore. I've called it many times before. My old brain forgets so much nowadays."

That's when I had an idea. During my time with God, I took a sheet of paper and drew pretty flowers around the edge. Then I asked my mom to look up the number of Mrs. Williams' drugstore. We wrote it down. Then we found the number for the police station, the fire station, and Mrs. Williams' doctor. Of course we added "9-1-1" to the list, too.

"Wait," I said when we were finished, "we've got one more thing to add." Carefully Mom and I printed these words: "If the lines are busy, pray. God will hear you."

The next day I took the paper to her house and offered to tape it to the wall right beside her kitchen phone. Mrs. Williams clapped her hands with joy. "Now I won't forget the numbers," she said, giving me a hug. "You've made an emergency list for me. Thank you very much."

Then she gave me an apple.

Why don't you make an emergency list for someone you know?

–Natalie

16
DECEMBER

Surely your goodness and love will be with me all my life. Psalm 23:6, ICB.

MY TIME WITH GOD . . .

Good Shepherd

"The Lord is my shepherd" (Psalm 23:1). That's how a beautiful chapter in the Old Testament begins, telling how Jesus is like a good shepherd, taking care of His sheep.

I want to be like Jesus, but I don't have any sheep. I do have a bird named Sunshine.

So I pretend I'm the Good Shepherd and Sunshine is my sheep. Then I read the chapter like this.

"Chris [that's me] is Sunshine's shepherd. The little bird has everything he needs. Chris gives Sunshine rest in a clean cage. He brings him lots of water and gives him food so he can be strong and healthy.

"Sunshine depends on me to take care of him. Without me, he'd get sick or even die."

Psalm 23 says that Jesus takes care of us the same way. He brings the rains to water the crops so we can have food. He helps moms and dads work hard to earn money so we can live in a house and stay warm all winter.

Now when I talk to my little bird and he sings to me, I think about how much Jesus cares for us. As King David said in Psalm 23: "Surely your goodness and love will be with me all my life" (verse 6, ICB).

Thank You, Jesus, for being our Good Shepherd.

–Chris

MY TIME WITH GOD . . .

Helping Hands

17
DECEMBER

Do for other people the same things you want them to do for you. Matthew 7:12, ICB.

Twenty-three plus 12 plus one. I scratched my head and counted my fingers. "That's 38. No, 37? 36? Yes, 36 . . . I think." I'm not too good with numbers.

When I told my dad that I wished someone would help me, he smiled and did something very strange. He opened my *International Children's Bible* to Matthew 7:12 and read, " 'Do for other people the same things you want them to do for you.' "

"So?"

"So if you want someone to help you with your homework, why don't you offer to help another person first?"

That night, during my time with God, I wrote down the names of three kids I knew who were having problems in English. I like English. I'm good with words.

The next afternoon I asked Marty if he wanted me to help him write his poem—the one Mrs. Carson had assigned. "Sure," he replied. "I'm having a lot of trouble with it."

After we figured out a word that rhymes with *turtle,* he said, "Hey, thanks. Can I help you with your homework?"

"How are you with math?" I asked.

"No problem," he laughed. "Everyone knows math!"

Amazing how things sometimes just work out.

–Andrew

18
DECEMBER

MY TIME WITH GOD . . .

Family Prayer Journal

Ask, and it shall be given you. Matthew 7:7.

Have you ever received a gift and then forgotten who gave it to you?

Last week my mom reminded me to thank Aunt Deanne for the dog with the stick in its mouth that sits up on my dresser. "Aunt Deanne?" I gasped. "I thought she gave me the yellow shirt with the bird on it."

"That was Aunt Donna. And Aunt Joyce gave you the blue socks with the bows. Don't you remember?"

See what I mean?

Sometimes we forget the good gifts Jesus gives us too. That's why we have a prayer journal that we check every night during family worship. Inside we write down our prayer requests and any answers we know about.

When we kneel to pray, we read some of the words from our prayer journal. Last night we asked God to help my cousin Jeremy. He's sick with the flu. In a few days we'll probably write "got well" by that request.

Once we prayed for my great-grandfather, but he didn't get well. Beside that request we wrote, "Asleep, waiting for Jesus to come and take him to heaven, where he'll never be sick again."

Somehow Jesus will answer every prayer in your family's prayer journal.

–Hunter

MY TIME WITH GOD . . .

Goodness Garden

19 DECEMBER

A man reaps what he sows. Galatians 6:7, NIV.

My neighbor, Mr. Kerb, grows a garden each summer with lots of sweet corn, red tomatoes, green peppers, and onions.

Last spring he held up a handful of seeds for me to see. "Can't have a harvest without planting," he said. "Same with life. When you put good things in your mind, good things will come out through your actions."

That night I made a little reminder of what my neighbor had said. I got one of Mom's houseplants (she said it was OK), and I drew some signs. One said "Kindness," and one said "Cheerfulness." The other ones had "Prayer" and "Forgiveness" written on them.

I glued my signs to some sticks and stuck them in the pot.

"What's that?" Mom asked.

"My goodness garden," I said. "It's to remind me to plant good things in my mind so good things will come out in my actions."

Mom was impressed. "What a wonderful idea," she said.

When I showed it to Mr. Kerb, he was impressed too. He pointed at the words I'd written and said, "Those will make the best garden ever. Always be sure to share your harvest of good deeds with others."

–David

20
DECEMBER

Then he arose, and rebuked the wind and the raging of the water: and they ceased, and there was a calm. Luke 8:24.

MY TIME WITH GOD . . .

Safe From the Storm

Last week we had a big storm on our farm. The wind howled, lightning flashed, and thunder shook the ground. Then the electricity went off.

I was scared. My sister Angelita was scared. Even our dog Fernando was scared.

"What are you doing down there?" Dad asked when he found us under his bed.

"Hiding from the storm," I explained.

Dad sat down on the rug. "This is a strong house, and we have lots of food to eat and a fireplace to keep us warm. As long as you don't go outside, you're safe."

Suddenly a loud clap of thunder rolled past our house. "And besides," Dad continued, "Jesus is stronger than the storm. He'll take good care of us."

The next day I went out and looked around. Tall trees had come crashing down. The stream by our house had turned into a roaring river, and there was mud everywhere.

Right then and there I bowed my head. "Dear Jesus," I said, "next time I'll try not to be so scared, because I know You're watching over us. Amen."

I sat on a fallen log. With Jesus by my side, I don't have to be afraid, even when the lightning flashes and the thunder rolls.

–Jason

MY TIME WITH GOD . . .

Hard Praying

21
DECEMBER

Whatever you ask for in prayer, believe that you have received it, and it will be yours. Mark 11:24, NIV.

Two weeks ago my mother got very, very sick. Dad took her to the hospital, and the doctors operated on her for six hours.

When Dad came home, he looked worried. He didn't eat any supper, and later I heard a strange noise coming from his bedroom. I stopped and listened. My dad was crying.

Have you ever been so scared that you didn't know what to do? That's how scared I was that night. Quickly I ran to my room and knelt by my bed. "Dear Jesus," I prayed, "help the doctors make Mom better. Help my daddy to be OK too. And help me not to be so scared. Please, Jesus. Please."

I heard the door to my room open, and soon my dad was kneeling beside me. He held me in his arms, and we both cried and prayed. Even though I was still worried and sad, I knew that Jesus was hearing our prayers and, no matter what happened, He'd stay with us.

Sometimes just knowing that Jesus listens to every prayer makes you feel a little better.

Today Mom has to have another operation. I'll keep on praying hard, because I know Jesus wants to help her and my dad and me.

—Trisha

22
DECEMBER

So do not fear, for I am with you. Isaiah 41:10, NIV.

MY TIME WITH GOD . . .

Picture Power

I'm shy. When my teacher asks me to read something in class or work out a problem at the board, my knees shake, and my mouth suddenly doesn't have any spit in it.

When my mom introduces me to someone, I say "Hi" and try to smile, but all I really want to do is run.

Then I read how Jesus talked to five thousand people. Later He walked on water. Wow! That's brave.

I want to be like Jesus. I want to share His love. Most of all, I don't want to be afraid of reading in class.

So during my time with God, I drew two "power pictures." The first shows Jesus talking to a whole bunch of people on a hillside. The other one shows Jesus walking right over some big waves. I took one of the pictures and put it in my desk at school. The other one I put in my Bible.

Today when my teacher asked me to read to the class, I cleared my throat and took a quick look at my power picture. Yup. There was Jesus talking to a crowd.

I walked to the front of the class and read the story. At the end, I even had some spit left!

Thank You, Jesus, for showing me how to be brave.

–Jon

MY TIME WITH GOD . . .

Loving Everyone

23
DECEMBER

A generous man will himself be blessed, for he shares his food with the poor. Proverbs 22:9, NIV.

"We need clothes and food for the poor," the man in church said. "Won't you bring your gifts to the community services center this Tuesday?"

This morning I picked out a warm coat, a pair of gloves, and a sweater. Mom found some canned food and cornbread mix. Then off we went.

When I walked into the center, I saw lots of people sitting in chairs. They smiled. I smiled back. There were black faces and white faces, old men and young women, moms, dads, wiggly children—all waiting for some new clothes and food.

It made me sad. I always have enough food and clothes. Mom and I never go to the center to *get* stuff. We always *leave* things there.

Then I saw a woman putting a new coat on her son. How happy she looked!

I know Jesus loves everyone. But I think He enjoys loving poor people the most because they need Him so much. That's why, during my time with God, I thank Him for allowing me to help Him love others, especially the smiling people waiting at the community service center.

–Tara

24
DECEMBER

If you forgive others for the things they do wrong, then your Father in heaven will also forgive you for the things you do wrong. Matthew 6:14, ICB.

MY TIME WITH GOD . . .

Forgiving My Friend

The other day Harold punched me in the arm. I was mad!

During my time with God, I just wanted to sit and think about how I was going to get even with Harold.

But I decided I'd better read at least one verse in my Bible, since God wasn't mad at anyone and wanted me to spend some time with Him. So I opened it and dropped my finger down on a verse. This wasn't my usual way of reading but, remember, I was mad.

H'mmm. "If you forgive others for the things they do wrong, then your Father in heaven will also forgive you for the things you do wrong" (Matthew 6:14, ICB).

Wait a minute. I needed God to forgive me when I said those unkind things about my cousin and cheated on last week's geography quiz.

If Jesus is willing to forgive me, I should be willing to forgive others. Even Harold.

The next day when my friend came up to me I whispered, "Hey, Harold. I forgive you for punching me in the arm."

He blinked. "Good," he said. Then he punched me in the stomach.

Seems some people don't want to be forgiven. That's their problem. I just want to be like Jesus and do what He asks me to do.

–Andrew

MY TIME WITH GOD . . .

Sharing My Joy

25 DECEMBER

She wrapped him in cloths and placed him in a manger, because there was no room for them in the inn. Luke 2:7, NIV.

Come sit beside me, and I'll tell you why I like Christmas.

Oh, sure, I enjoy getting and giving gifts. That's always fun. But what I like most is thinking about when Jesus came as a little baby in Bethlehem. He must have looked so small in that big manger. I wonder if the animals came over and sniffed Him to see what this strange new thing was. Can you imagine being sniffed by a donkey?

Then I think about Mary and Joseph. I remember when my brother Mike was born. My mom and dad smiled and smiled for about a year. They were so proud of their new little baby. Jesus' mom and dad were proud too.

Then it's fun to remember the shepherds. They probably had never seen a baby who was born in a place where animals lived.

I wonder if little Jesus laughed and blew bubbles, as Mike did when he was just born.

But what I like *most* about Christmas is remembering the gift God gave to us all—His Son, Jesus. That's gotta be the best gift anyone ever got.

So this Christmas I'm going to spend a little time just sitting and thinking about how it was when Jesus was born in a manger.

Why don't you join me?

–Hunter

26
DECEMBER

Each man will be like a shelter from the wind and a refuge from the storm.
Isaiah 32:2, NIV.

WORDS OF LOVE . . .

Stormy Nights

The best place to be
  On a stormy night
Is snug in my bed
  With covers pulled up tight.

Where I sleep to the rhythm
  And patter of rain
As it beats a tattoo
  On the closed windowpane.

Let the stormy wind blow
  Through the treetops tall;
It won't wake me up
  From my slumber at all.

All cuddled up under
  The blankets and spread;
I surely am glad
  To be nestled in bed.

I know God will keep me
  Safe from the storm
Whenever I'm sleeping
  So cozy and warm.

–Dorothy Minner
(my wonderful aunt)

WORDS OF LOVE . . .

Insects

27
DECEMBER

Here's another poem written by my sweet aunt Dorothy. She wrote it for every boy and girl who loves to sit and study the many strange creepy, crawly creatures God has created. Maybe she had *you* in mind!

—Uncle Charles

I love to watch the big black bugs
Go crawling through the grass.
Sometimes I pile sticks in a row
And do not let them pass.

My mother said God made the bugs
And every living thing.
He gave the bees their droning buzz
And made the crickets sing.

The fireflies with tiny lights
Are beautiful to see.
God made all the crawling things;
And God made you and me.

Ants are creatures of little strength, yet they store up their food in the summer. Proverbs 30:25, NIV.

28
DECEMBER

Whoever loves his brother lives in the light, and there is nothing in him to make him stumble. 1 John 2:10, NIV.

WORDS OF LOVE . . .

My Big Brother

Do you have someone in your family you admire a lot? Perhaps it's a sister or brother. Maybe even an uncle or aunt. Well, this poem is for you! All you need to do is change the words "my big brother" to "my aunt Sally" or "my big sister." Have fun!

Who is the best friend that I have?
  My big brother.
Who plays with me and makes me glad?
  My big brother.
When I fall down and hurt my knee
  Who hurries out to comfort me?
And who can climb the tallest tree?
  My big brother.

Who makes me laugh when I am sad?
  My big brother.
Who sits by me when I feel bad?
  My big brother.
When Jesus comes with angels grand
  To take us all to heaven's land
Guess who'll be there to hold my hand?
  My big brother.

—Uncle Charles

Raindrops and Rainbows

Be strong and of a good courage; be not afraid. Joshua 1:9.

Pitter-pat, pitter-pat. Raindrops hit the roof. Will the sun ever shine again? Don't get discouraged. There just might be a surprise waiting for you up there among the dark clouds.

—Uncle Charles

It's raining awfully hard today;
It hasn't stopped at all.
So I can't go outside to play
With my new bat and ball.

I'll have to stay inside instead
And play with games and things;
Or even nap upon my bed
While Mother sweetly sings.

I'm glad it rains sometimes, you know,
For Mother talks to me
Of how it makes the garden grow
And waters every tree.

Sometimes she tells about the flood
That came in Noah's day;
And then we see the rainbow come
When rain has gone away.

—Dorothy Minner

30
DECEMBER

Everything God created is good. 1 Timothy 4:4, NIV.

WORDS OF LOVE . . .

Puppy Power

Perhaps this Christmas you got a new puppy. Congratulations! They can be tons of fun. But puppies are a big responsibility. They depend on you for everything. Are you up to the job? Can you handle it? Here's a poem you can learn that might help you see just how important you are to that newest member of your household . . . and to God.

I have a little puppy;
He likes to play with me.
He'll run around and chase a ball
And scare cats up a tree.

I take good care of puppy;
I feed him every day.
And when he cries I hold him close,
And this is what I say:

"I love you, little puppy.
I always will; you'll see,
'Cause Jesus said that I should love
The same way He loves me."

–Charles Mills

WORDS OF LOVE . . .

Praise the Lord

31
DECEMBER

Praise the Lord, for the Lord is good; sing praise to his name, for that is pleasant. Psalm 135:3, NIV.

We've come to the end of the year. I can't think of a better way to celebrate than to read a wonderful poem written by David, the lowly shepherd boy who became king of Israel. Perhaps you'd like to memorize these beautiful words of love.

Remember, from this moment on, always keep Jesus in your heart.

—Uncle Charles

PRAISE THE LORD!

Praise God in his Temple.
  Praise him in his mighty heaven.
Praise him for his strength.
  Praise him for his greatness.
Praise him with trumpet blasts.
  Praise him with harps and lyres.
Praise him with tambourines and dancing.
  Praise him with stringed instruments and flutes.
Praise him with loud cymbals.
  Praise him with crashing cymbals.
Let everything that breathes praise the Lord.

Praise the Lord!

—Psalm 150, ICB